TURNING THE TIDE OF WAR
50 BATTLES THAT CHANGED THE COURSE OF MODERN HISTORY

First published in Great Britain in 2001 by
Hamlyn, a division of Octopus Publishing Group Ltd
2–4 Heron Quays, London E14 4JP

ISBN 0 600 60318 0

A CIP catalogue record for this book is available
from the British Library

Printed and bound in Italy

10 9 8 7 6 5 4 3 2

Designer: Kenny Grant
Maps: Andrew Thompson
Picture Researcher: Liz Fowler
Senior Production Controller: Louise Hall

hamlyn

TURNING THE TIDE OF WAR
50 BATTLES THAT CHANGED THE COURSE OF MODERN HISTORY

TIM NEWARK

CONTENTS

INTRODUCTION

The decisive battle is the holy grail of military commanders – a battle won in a day that transforms their future, bringing them victory and fame – but combat is usually much messier than this. A victory one day can be reversed the next. Military superiority can be let down by political incompetence. A decisive victory may not bring decisive peace. The steady attrition of guerrilla warfare can overwhelm a powerful foe.

In this book, decisive battles have been chosen for several reasons. Sometimes they are a climactic point in a successful or disastrous campaign; at other times they represent a decisive step forward in the technology of warfare. Often they refer not to a battle in one day, but to an operation over several weeks or months, indicative of the enlarged scale of modern warfare. All of them reflect great moments in history when the sacrifice of countless soldiers has changed the way we view the world.

ESSENCE OF VICTORY

How are battles won and lost? Overwhelming power and precise organization are the most obvious ingredients for decisive victory. Nazi Germany in 1941 knew exactly what it was doing during Operation Barbarossa. It applied its already successful blitzkrieg tactics on a massive scale, helped by Soviet chaos and a lack of willingness to face up to the inevitable threat of invasion. The Soviet Army had also been ravaged by ideology, given Stalin's political determination to rid it of any dissident officers. Both morale and military competence had to be rapidly rebuilt.

Pearl Harbor in 1941 was another brilliant piece of organization, with overwhelming force directed at an unprepared enemy; similarly in France in 1940 and Singapore in 1942. But when the enemy is no longer surprised and counters with its own battle experience and organization, then the tide of war changes significantly. Allied victories at El Alamein, Midway, Stalingrad and Kohima showed how even the most initially impressive military forces can be held and defeated.

GREATEST MILITARY FLAW

Underestimation of the enemy is the greatest of military flaws. Germany and Japan in the Second World War believed they were racially as well as militarily superior to their enemies. They found it hard to accept that their enemies could defeat them and threw away the lives of hundreds of thousands of their soldiers because of their over confidence. During the Battle of Britain, it seemed a foregone conclusion to the German air force that it would triumph over the smaller, inexperienced British RAF. German victories in Poland and elsewhere had affected the Germans' judgement, and when they were confronted by highly determined, well-trained pilots armed with the latest ingenious aviation technology, they were faced with a far more difficult contest.

Imperial arrogance found its graveyards at Gallipoli and Isandlwana, both wake-up calls for the British and their Western imperial colleagues, giving intimations of later bitter colonial conflicts. At Dien Bien Phu, French imperial arrogance was brought crashing down by the Vietnamese.

Sometimes, superior technology can bestow awesome power on the battlefield. At Omdurman and a century later, during Desert Storm, highly advanced weaponry can make a battle seem very one-sided, allowing the victor to impose his will around the world without meaningful opposition. On other occasions, the arrival of superior weaponry can just tip the balance. In Afghanistan, Muslim guerrillas held on to their land despite being faced by superior military technology. With the arrival of hand-held anti-aircraft missiles, given to the guerrillas by the West, Soviet air power was fatally undermined.

FIGHTING SPIRIT

When technology is more even, it is often fighting spirit and belief in a cause that can give the decisive edge. At Valmy, a French revolutionary army simply stared down its less motivated opponents, opening a new era of ideological warfare. At Assaye, sheer old-fashioned aggression won the battle.

Sometimes it is the dominant power that loses faith in its own cause. In Mogadishu, the US Army could see little point in forcing international aid on a country that saw it as an aggressor. Sometimes, victors do not even recognize their own success. During the Tet Offensive, Western journalists persisted in portraying this as a Vietnamese victory, even though the Vietnamese had actually suffered a catastrophic defeat at the hands of the US Army, such was left-wing prejudice among the media at the time.

Some victories represent an inevitable expression of growing international influence. At San Juan Hill, the United States declared itself a global military power. At Geok Tepe, the Russians consolidated their hold on central Asia. At Trafalgar, British naval power reached its zenith.

At other times, victory hangs in the balance and it is a very near-run thing indeed. At Waterloo, Napoleon came near to victory, defeated only by British and allied tenacity. At Cambrai, British tanks proved themselves to be battle-winners, only to have their achievements overturned by newly perfected German stormtrooper tactics. The relentless power of organization and sheer military fighting prowess is evident during D-Day, Inchon, the Six Day War and the capture of Port Stanley. Sheer professionalism in these instances is hard to beat.

Sometimes two sides are too evenly balanced. At the Somme and Ypres, British and German forces ground away at each other, causing tens of thousands of casualties. This attrition reached a breaking point on Germany's Black Day, with the collapse of German morale. Wars of attrition have no winners.

LESSONS OF WAR

There are many lessons to be learned from the conflicts in this book. Perhaps the primary lesson is the need for a country to be strong in defence so as not to encourage any rival to overestimate its ability to win a war against it. It was because Germany and Japan believed they could easily win their conflicts that they embarked on world wars. Appeasement does not work, but only encourages the overconfidence of aggressive foes. A nation must never be afraid to talk about war or its armed forces. Only perceived weakness encourages war. Responsible aggression dissuades it.

In the second half of the 20th century, the United States prevented a third world war by acting strongly and aggressively in its dealings with the Soviet Union and its allies. Mutually assured destruction did prevent a third world war. It can only be hoped that future politicans do not ignore these lessons of history. Learning them all over again will be very costly in lives.

TIM NEWARK

VALMY, 1792

Valmy signified a new age of warfare, one in which ideology would be the fuel of conflict. When the revolutionaries of the untrained French 'citizen army' were ranged against the well-drilled ranks of the Prussians, it was their high morale that proved the decisive factor in the victory that day – although the Battle of Valmy was more of a psychological victory than an outright military one.

The citizen armies raised by the French revolutionary governments fought many battles and wars, something of an irony for a regime born out of idealism and the desire for international fraternity. 'Liberty, Equality, Fraternity or Death,' declared a French soldier at Pontoise in 1794, a slogan which made it clear that anyone who disagreed with the revolution was considered an enemy, pitting France against the rest of Europe. The French revolutionary armies supposedly brought 'freedom from oppression'- but they did so at the point of a bayonet.

In previous eras, wars had usually been fought for political advantage and material gain. This remained true in the 1790s, too, but now there was the additional factor of ideological self-righteousness. It is this conviction that identifies these wars as marking the beginning of 'modern warfare'. Furthermore, successive French revolutionary governments became more and more extreme under the stresses of conflict, so much so that war became a method of maintaining their increasingly desperate grip on power. In this sense, the military and ideological campaigns of Hitler and Stalin can be said to have their roots in the French revolutionary regimes of the 1790s.

'CITIZEN SOLDIERS'

A revolution implies a break with the past, but very often the new government simply makes much more efficient use of the previous regime's power structures. According to Alexis de Tocqueville in his analysis of the French Revolution, 'The only change is that the centralization of power in France has become far more conspicuous now that all the relics of the past have been pruned away.' From the 17th century, France had been steadily transformed into a powerful bureaucratic state run from Paris, and with increased control over its people, the state could put massive armies into the field to enforce its political will. This continued to be the case, in fact even more so, during the rule of the revolutionary governments, except that whereas in the past soldiers had been hired or impressed into service, they were now all 'free men' and had to be persuaded to fight – hence the birth of the 'citizen soldier'.

'I have no pity for the enemies of my country,' wrote a *cannonier* of the French Revolutionary Army in Caen in 1793. 'They have spilled, and continue to spill, the blood of my brothers,

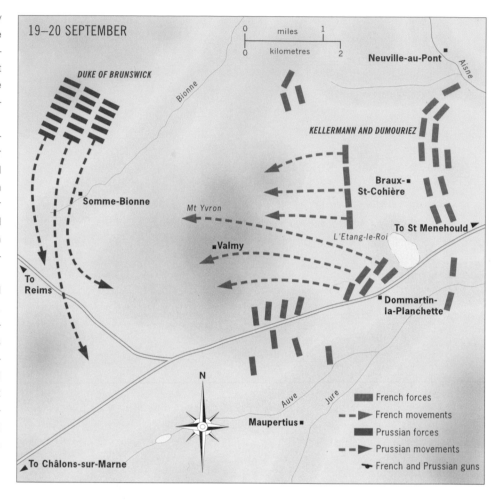

Above: **The opening manoeuvres of the Prussian and French armies around Valmy in September 1792.**

Left: **The beginning of ideological warfare: a French Revolutionary poster of 1793 promises *'Liberté, Egalité, Fraternité ou la Mort'*.**

who all demand vengeance, and those who have played the part of counter-revolutionaries deserve death at angry hands.' Vengeance and fear motivated these politicized soldiers, and they in turn roused other, less politically involved, comrades until a whole nation was roused in anger. All the government had to do was direct these men towards the perceived enemy and the spirit of fury of these 'citizen soldiers' would do the rest. Or at least, that was the idea.

THE ROAD TO VALMY

Suspecting that the upheaval of the revolution had weakened France, some neighbouring countries considered it a good time to come to the aid of the French royal family. In August 1792, Prussia and its German-speaking allies invaded, threatening terrible punishment to the citizens of Paris if they harmed their king. The reaction of the Parisian mob was to storm the palace of the Tuileries and take the royal family prisoner. Fear and anger ruled the streets and, not surprisingly, rabble-rousing politicians believed that enemies within should be the first to die. 'In the towns,' declared Fabre d'Eglantine, 'let the blood of

traitors be the first holocaust [*le premier holocauste*] to Liberty, so that in advancing to meet the common enemy, we leave nothing behind to disquiet us.'

When the city's guardian fortress of Verdun fell to the Prussian-led force, the revolutionaries vented their anger on more than 1,000 prisoners, both political and criminal, who were hacked to death in the event known as the 'September massacres'. The government in Paris might have been expected to gain confidence in the belief that such fervour could be directed at its foreign enemies, but the army of revolutionaries had already proved unstable. In an earlier clash with the Austrians on the border with the Austrian Netherlands (modern-day Belgium), the poorly trained and organized French force had fled. Revolutionary generals had been promoted, only to be put on trial and then executed amid scenes of paranoia that would also afflict totalitarian armies in the 20th century.

However, commitments in other foreign theatres affected the Prussian army and its allies. Austria could not field as many men as it would have liked for the invasion of France, while the German army that advanced into France was only 80,000 men

Below: **The September massacres in Paris – provoked by the threat of Prussia to invade France and punish the revolutionaries – created a climate of fear and anger which helped the revolutionary soldiers face Prussia's professional army at Valmy.**

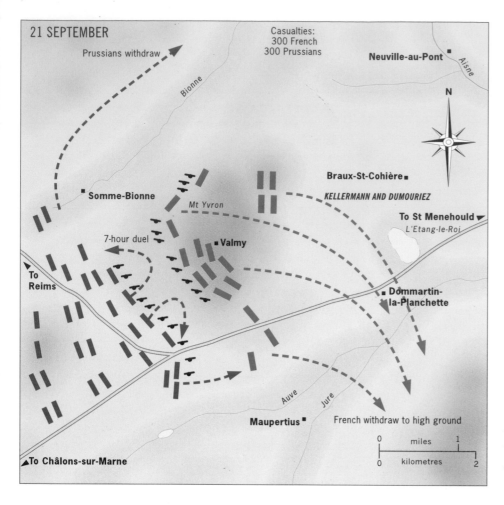

21 SEPTEMBER

Casualties:
300 French
300 Prussians

Prussians withdraw

Bionne

Neuville-au-Pont

Aisne

N

Braux-St-Cohière

KELLERMANN AND DUMOURIEZ

Somme-Bionne

Mt Yvron

To St Menehould

L'Etang-le-Roi

7-hour duel

Valmy

To
Reims

Dommartin-
la-Planchette

Auve

Jure

Maupertius

French withdraw to high ground

To Châlons-sur-Marne

0   miles   1

0   kilometres   2

Yron found themselves in the front line against the Prussians. Despite the artillery fire, Brunswick's force pressed on towards the road, where it came under more cannon fire. An artillery duel followed, but to no decisive effect on the advance. As the fog and gun smoke lifted, Brunswick placed his main army opposite Valmy, but the view that materialized did not please him. The French were well positioned and in no hurry to leave the battlefield. They did not look like the anarchic rabble that he was expecting.

Nevertheless, Brunswick ordered his men to begin the advance. As they did so, Kellermann understood that aggression was perhaps the one quality his soldiers possessed above everything else. He placed his hat, bearing the revolutionary cockade, on his sword and shouted 'Vive la nation!' With that, his men were triggered into wildly roaring 'Vive la nation! Vive la France! Vive notre général!' It was one of those decisive moments when armies ponder whether to fight or flee. The French did not run and so Brunswick lost his nerve and halted the advance. An artillery duel then took place while Brunswick agonized over what to do next. In council with his officers, he decided not to proceed with the battle and, as darkness fell, the French left the battlefield bolstered by the knowledge that they had stared down the great foreign threat.

It was a bizarre 'victory', with little blood actually shed, but the psychological impact of it was enormous. It demonstrated that morale was perhaps the most important aspect of any army, more so even than training or weapons, and the French Revolutionary Army possessed bucketloads of it, giving birth

strong, which was half what its commander, the Duke of Brunswick, had hoped for, and the numbers continued to fall throughout the campaign. Brunswick had considered linking up with other armies on the French frontier, but news emanating from Paris about the bloody anarchy there persuaded him to march his force directly on the French capital.

General Dumouriez took command amid the chaos afflicting the French defences and marched his Army of the North away from the frontier with Belgium and southwards towards Sedan, the Argonne forest giving him a natural barrier between his army and the Prussians. Brunswick, though, outmanoeuvred the French, penetrated the Argonne and forced Dumouriez to take up a position in the southern part of the forest area. Brunswick's caution in following up his advance allowed Dumouriez to receive further reinforcements of more than 25,000 men under Kellermann, to bring the total strength of his army up to 36,000. Having only some 34,000 men directly under his command, Brunswick wanted to link up with the Austrians from the north, but a false report that Dumouriez was withdrawing encouraged Brunswick to try to cut off the French retreat on the road to Châlons and force the French into battle near the village of Valmy.

'VIVE LA NATION!'

Brunswick's advance guard moved towards the French through a thick fog. Out of the gloom came the roar of a cannonade. Kellermann's French reinforcements on the hill of

Above left: **The movements of the Prussian and French troops on the second day of battle at Valmy.**

Left: **French troops – commanded by General Kellerman, wearing revolutionary colours in his hat – face down Prussian soldiers at the Battle of Valmy on 20 September 1792.**

to a new form of ideologically driven warfare. The poet Goethe was with the Prussian army at Valmy and he perceived the importance of events, consoling his cowed comrades thus: 'From here and today there begins a new epoch in the history of the world, and you can say that you were there.' Prussia's Colonel von Massenbach similarly felt that it was a significant moment: 'The French Revolutionaries have come through their baptism of fire... The 20th of September has given the world a new shape. It is the most important day of the century!' Perhaps the Prussians were dignifying their own performance with hyperbole. Napoleon Bonaparte called it merely 'the affair of Valmy', one in which it had been the artillery that had proved its worth. 'In the initial campaigns of the war of the Revolution,' he concluded, 'France always excelled in the artillery.'

What is clear is that after Valmy, France's revolutionaries felt secure enough to proceed with the execution of the royal family and then embark on a series of foreign wars that would see France conquer Belgium, the Netherlands and Switzerland, along with parts of Germany and Italy, and establish a victorious engine of war that Napoleon would subsequently inherit and use to become master of the whole of Europe. Without the French Revolutionary Army, there would have been no Napoleonic Wars. It cannot be said, however, that all the subsequent battles engaged in by the French were victorious. An ideologically driven army is strong in confrontation, but if its opponents do not budge, then its own morale can collapse quickly. For example, at Hongen in March 1793, Dumouriez's army suffered a rout, leaving more than two thousand casualties for only forty injured Austrians.

LAUKHARD, PRUSSIAN MILITARY OBSERVER AT VALMY

Above: **The main confrontation near the mill on the hill of Yron captured in a dramatic painting by J.B. Mauzaisse after a painting by Horace Vernet, 1831.**

FEAR AND ANGER

Fear and anger motivated the early French Revolutionary Army. The threat of foreign invasion or counter-revolution encouraged tens of thousands of men to volunteer for military service in 1791 and 1792. The rallying cry of 1789 was 'Every citizen should be a soldier and every soldier should be a citizen.' A Prussian military observer called Laukhard noted this spirit of dedication: *'The volunteers were not as straight as a die, as were the Prussians, and were not as polished, well trained or skilled in handling a gun or marching in step; nor did they know how to tighten their belts around their tunics as the Prussians did, yet they were devoted to the cause they served in body and soul. Nearly all those I encountered at that time knew for whom and for what they were fighting and declared that they were ready to die for the good of their patrie. The only alternatives they knew were liberty or death.'*
Quoted in *The French Revolutionary Wars 1787–1802* by T.C.W. Blanning (Arnold, 1996).

ASSAYE, 1803

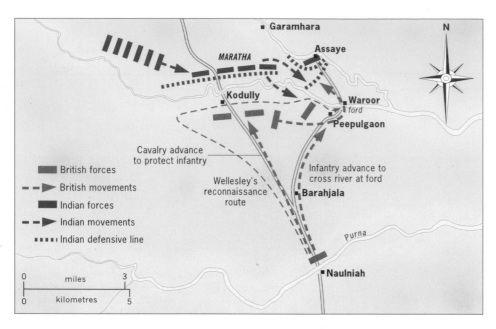

British forces

British movements

Indian forces

Indian movements

Indian defensive line

Garamhara

MARATHA

Assaye

Kodully

Waroor
ford

Peepulgaon

Cavalry advance
to protect infantry

Wellesley's
reconnaissance
route

Infantry advance to
cross river at ford

Barahjala

Purna

N

0   miles   3
0   kilometres   5

Naulniah

Above: The British advance against the Maratha army at Assaye on 23 September 1803.

Right: A Maratha cavalryman. The army of the Marathas was an impressive combination of traditional warriors in armour with lances and swords and European-trained infantry armed with muskets and supported by cannon.

Considered by the Duke of Wellington to be his finest victory, the Battle of Assaye was one in which a small but well-trained British army faced native forces well equipped and well tutored in European combat techniques. Won against overwhelming odds, it demonstrated the indomitable spirit of the colonial powers when faced with militarily sophisticated opponents. Assaye also served as an early showcase for the Duke of Wellington's talents.

European imperialism began in earnest in the 16th century with the conquest of the Americas. European soldiers operating in the New World overcame the native cultures with surprising ease. A number of factors accounted for this, among which were logistical organization and extraordinary bravery, by means of which handfuls of Spanish conquistadors were able to defeat great kingdoms such as that of the Aztecs. A similar pattern was repeated elsewhere in the world, with native cultures being confronted, found to be ill-prepared and far less able to withstand the early modern warfare techniques which confronted them. The Russians conquered Siberia, while in India the trading stations of Portuguese, French and British merchants were turned into the stepping stones of empire.

BRITAIN IN INDIA

Britain's involvement in India during the 18th century had reached a crucial point with the Battle of Plassey in 1757, when Robert Clive defeated the nawab (governor) of Bengal. The nawab's army was ten times the size of Robert Clive's

force of two thousand sepoys (native soldiers trained by the British) and nine hundred Europeans. Despite the overwhelming odds, Clive was victorious and the nawab was executed. This victory secured Britain's possessions in the subcontinent and entitled it to raise massive revenues from the native population, which Britain then used to increase its military presence further.

The influence of the Mughals, the most dominant power in southern Asia up to that point, had been in decline since 1707 with the death of Aurangzeb. The British were clearly in the ascendant, but unlike those in the Americas, where native cultures never really rose to the challenge posed by European military power, the rulers of India understood the nature of the force they were up against. While the British considered themselves as successors to the Mughals, there was an indigenous force in the form of the Maratha confederacy that also claimed the right to rule India. The confederacy was a grouping of various influential clan chiefs under the

Above: **A contemporary engraving shows British troops advancing in the face of Maratha artillery during the Battle of Assaye.**

leadership of a *peshaw* (chief minister); at times, the clans warred with one another, particularly for leadership, but they also combined in various coalitions to resist the British. The result was three Maratha wars fought in 1775–82, 1803–05 and 1817–18.

Recruiting European military advisers, frequently from one of the competing imperial powers, such as the French, the *peshaws* and clan chiefs rapidly transformed their feudal armies and equipped their soldiers with artillery, muskets and Western-style military training. In a very short time, these native armies could rely on twice as many cannons as the British. Major Thorne, a veteran of many battles in the region, complained of 'the changes that have taken place among the

warlike tribes of India through the introduction of European tactics and French discipline, which, combined with their natural courage, often bordering on enthusiastic frenzy, and their numerical superiority, has rendered our conflicts with them sanguinary in the extreme'.

By the late 18th century it was no longer easy for Britain to overawe its opponents in India. And yet, such was their hunger for the wealth to be derived from India that the British took on ever more difficult and challenging campaigns in an effort to subdue the native population. Against such a background, the Battle of Assaye emerges as being typical of a period in which British forces outfought – rather than outgunned – otherwise impressive native armies. It is also interesting to note that the British were commanded by a young Arthur Wellesley, later to become the Duke of Wellington. Assaye demonstrates the strength of British fighting skills in the face of superior numbers; Wellington, when asked forty years later which was his finest moment in battle, answered with one word: 'Assaye.'

WAR WITH THE MARATHAS

The Marathas had replaced the Mughal dynasty in central and northern India, and in 1779 they defeated the British at the Battle of Wadgaon, following Britain's attempt to favour a candidate for *peshwa*. It was only a matter of time before there would be a further clash, and in 1803 it arose. This time the British were determined to intervene more forcefully. Richard Wellesley, governor general of Bengal, sent his younger brother Arthur to offer protection to *Peshwa* Baji Rao II, who had been defeated by the Holkar clan. Other clans then objected to the British intervention. Wellesley penetrated Maratha territory and stumbled across an army at the junction of the Juah and Kaitna rivers. It was an impressive array: some 30,000 cavalry; 10,000 infantry, trained and equipped in the Western style by French soldiers; and 200 pieces of artillery. All Wellesley commanded was 4,500 regulars, mostly sepoys, and half of these were cavalry. Despite this, Wellesley was supremely confident, demonstrating efficiency and organization in abundance.

Later historians have praised Wellesley's logistical abilities above his triumphs in battle, and it is important to consider how the British supported their armies in India, because it frequently proved decisive in campaigns. Throughout history, most armies had supported their troops by taking what they needed from the lands they passed through. Understandably, this alienated local people, who frequently fought back and added to the difficulties of a campaign. The British forces in India, however, adopted a system in which they bought food and supplies from merchants who came to their camps. This not only resulted in less incidental fighting, but also ensured the goodwill of the local population. Intelligence information could also be obtained at these military bazaars, sourced from merchants acting as spies. The relatively wealthy British enjoyed the support of merchants who were not slow to exploit their generosity. Wellesley did not invent this system but, with his excellent eye for detail, he ran it superbly and it gave him an added edge over his Maratha opponents.

Having left his baggage train in the village of Naulniah, which he instructed to be fortified, Wellesley rode out to inspect the position of his enemy at Assaye. Wellesley was well practised in this process of reconnaissance, getting to know the landscape of the forthcoming battle so as to be able to use it to his advantage. Ignoring the suspect knowledge of his guides, he discovered a ford across the Kaitna that he could make use of to speed up the transport of his troops without making them vulnerable. It meant he could also surprise the enemy. Wellesley led the way into the river, but as his troops waded into the water, some Maratha artillery opened up. Fortunately for him, it was half-hearted fire and it ceased when Wellesley formed his men up on the opposite shore.

Wellesley placed his Madras sepoys between two units of regular British troops and began the advance. Maratha cavalry were reported to have crossed the river further west and could have threatened Wellesley's rear, but because his baggage train was well fortified, he did not mind losing communication with it for the duration of the battle. The Marathas had lost the advantage of having their troops protected by the river, but they still possessed superior numbers and a formidable array of cannons. As the two lines of artillery began to duel, Wellesley knew he would lose the encounter if it was prolonged and so he ordered his men forward, with the kilted troops of the 78th Highlanders leading the way.

SHEER AGGRESSION

Sheer aggression was the only way to win this contest; the British fixed their bayonets and charged the well-trained Maratha troops. The two Maratha commanders, Berar and Scindia, lacked the courage of Wellesley and retired from the fighting, but their senior European adviser, Pohlmann, a Hanoverian, remained in command of the Indian troops. The 78th Highlanders halted at 55m (180ft), fired their muskets in a mighty volley, then charged and plunged in with their bayonets.

Below: **Maratha artillery rake the lines of British soldiers at the Battle of Assaye. Wellington considered this one of the hardest-fought battles of his career.**

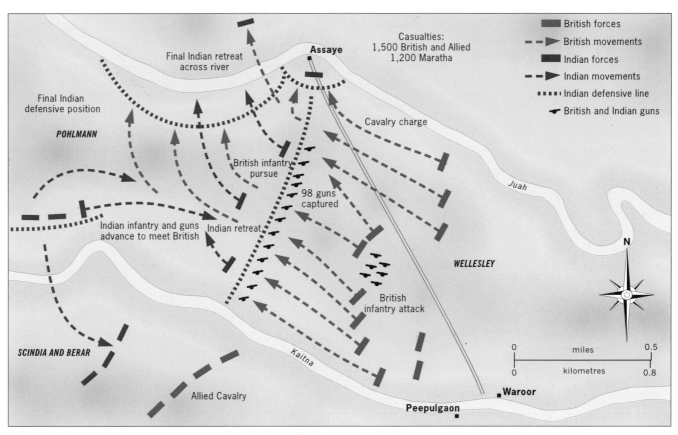

Casualties:
1,500 British and Allied
1,200 Maratha

Final Indian retreat
across river

Assaye

Final Indian
defensive position

POHLMANN

Cavalry charge

British infantry
pursue

98 guns
captured

Indian infantry and guns
advance to meet British

Indian retreat

Juah

WELLESLEY

British
infantry attack

N

SCINDIA AND BERAR

Kaitna

0   miles   0.5

0   0.8
kilometres

Allied Cavalry

■ **Waroor**

Peepulgaon ■

■ British forces
--- ▶ British movements
■ Indian forces
--- ▶ Indian movements
•••• Indian defensive line
↜ British and Indian guns

Above: **A typical sepoy soldier armed with musket and wearing Western-style uniform. These men formed the backbone of Britain's empire-building armies in the late 18th and early 19th centuries.**

Above right: **On 23 September 1803 British troops chased the line of Maratha troops back and broke them, forcing them back into Assaye and then across the Juah river.**

It was this sort of hard, close-quarters fighting that the British favoured and which would frequently send their enemies reeling, in theatres of war from India to Spain.

Having taken a line of Maratha artillery, the 78th Highlanders fired a second volley, which finally broke Pohlmann's troops on the southern flank. The Madras sepoys followed up on this success and also broke the Maratha line. Carried away by their triumph, however, some of the sepoys became disorganized and vulnerable to the nearby Maratha cavalry, but the British cavalry was there to protect their flank and the sepoys regrouped. At the forefront of the action, Wellesley had his horse shot from beneath him. On the northern flank, the 74th Highlanders came under intense fire and had to form a defensive square with ramparts composed of the bodies of their dead comrades. They stood their ground long enough for the British cavalry to gallop past and clear the ground before the village of Assaye.

The entire British line now swung round and pushed Pohlmann's men back to the Juah. Wellesley became caught up in the fighting and a second horse was fatally wounded beneath him. His bravery must have inspired his men; it certainly stood in stark contrast to that of the Maratha leaders, who seemed more concerned with their personal safety. Faced by a renewed British attack, the Marathas decided they had had enough and crossed the river, leaving behind much of their equipment.

Wellesley's victory decisively curbed Maratha power in central India, but his losses had been heavy, with some 1,500 troops dead and wounded – a casualty rate of more than 27 per cent. The Marathas had lost at least 1,200 dead and had abandoned 98 cannons on the battlefield. A further British victory at Argaum ended the war, but the British had many more campaigns to fight in India against tough opponents, and their final conquest of the subcontinent was a very hard-won experience not achieved until the middle of the 19th century.

COLIN CAMPBELL, 78TH HIGHLANDERS

CLOSE-RUN THING
'The General was in the thick of the action the whole time. No one could have shown a better example. I never saw a man so cool and collected...

though I can assure you, till our troops got the order to advance the fate of the day seemed doubtful; and if the numerous cavalry of the enemy had done their duty I hardly think it possible

we could have succeeded.'
Quoted in *Wellington: A Personal History* **by Christopher Hibbert (HarperCollins, 1997)**

TRAFALGAR, 1805

A truly decisive sea battle in which Vice-Admiral Horatio Nelson demonstrated his mastery of naval fire power by breaking the line of French and Spanish ships and ended once and for all Napoleon's ambition to conquer Britain. Nelson's bold action became a much-admired manoeuvre, copied by naval commanders ever after. This sea victory ensured that British naval power would dominate the oceans of the world for the next century.

Seapower had always been important – in that it protected maritime lines of trade and therefore the creation of wealth – but in the 16th century, in the wake of the discovery of the Americas, seapower had assumed a new level of importance for a number of European nations. The Dutch, British, Spanish and French navies fought each other to secure hugely profitable colonies and control of the sea lanes that led to them. This fighting at sea continued for more than two

Above: **The final stage of the Battle of Trafalgar, with the French ship** *Redoutable* **about to surrender to Nelson's flagship** *Victory.* **The devastation of the close fighting is clearly shown by the wrecked** *Redoutable* **on the left.**

hundred years, with none of the major players gaining a clear-cut advantage over the others.

A maritime arms race led to the creation of bigger and faster ships, capable of maintaining more powerful arrays of cannons. By the end of the 18th century, Spain, Portugal and the Netherlands had declined in power, thus their ability to protect their overseas empires had weakened and it left the main contenders for global sea power as Britain and France. If Napoleon was serious about conquering Europe and then the world, he would have to win the war at sea. Trafalgar became the decisive battle on this front.

NELSON AGAINST NAPOLEON

With France dominating the continental landmass, there was little Britain could do to limit its power there, but at sea the Royal Navy was strong and Britain used this to contain French maritime ambitions. During the 1790s, Britain emphasized its naval power by taking a number of French colonies in the West Indies. However, a more ambitious assault on Corsica in 1794 failed and Britain had to retreat from the Mediterranean. A Spanish attempt to join its forces with the French fleet was foiled at the Battle of Cape St Vincent in 1797.

In 1798 a British fleet under Vice-Admiral Horatio Nelson returned to the Mediterranean and defeated the French at the Battle of the Nile. This re-established Britain's control of the region and posed a threat to the French port of Toulon. Furthermore, Nelson's victory helped to encourage the central European powers to join a new coalition against Napoleon. In 1804 Napoleon began preparations for an invasion of Britain. With Spain as his ally, there was the tempting possibility of finally achieving naval dominance over the British in the English Channel through a joint fleet operation under the command of Admiral Pierre Villeneuve. The French broke out of Toulon and into the Atlantic and the West Indies, but were harried by British vessels into turning back and seeking the safety of the port of Cadiz, where they were then blockaded.

With this turn of events, by the summer of 1805 Napoleon had decided against the invasion of Britain and shifted his army from the coast of northern France into central Europe, where he threw the Austrians off balance at Ulm (see Austerlitz, pp.20–23). The French and Spanish fleet at Cadiz was now given a different objective: the re-establishment of French power in the Mediterranean. In October 1805 it set sail for Italy but was intercepted off Cape Trafalgar, near Cadiz, by Nelson's British fleet.

Above: Horatio Nelson (1758–1805), one of Britain's greatest commanders and victor at Trafalgar. The portrait is by Lemuel Abbott, *c.* 1797.

Although diminutive in stature, Vice-Admiral Horatio Nelson was a fighting leader who inspired the dearest devotion of his followers. He was fearless under fire and as a result had been badly wounded twice in battle, impairing the sight in his right eye during the assault on Corsica in 1794 and losing his right arm while engaging a Spanish treasure ship near Tenerife in 1797. He often discussed his own death, settling on either 'a peerage or Westminster Abbey!' before the Battle of the Nile. After the battle, he was delighted to receive a coffin from his captains made out of the timber from a French flagship.

'ENGLAND EXPECTS'

When he received Napoleon's orders to ferry troops to Naples in the Mediterranean, Admiral Pierre Villeneuve knew that Nelson was waiting at sea to engage him in battle. He therefore set sail in the *Bucentaure* and slipped out of Cadiz with a combined force of 33 ships (18 French, 15 Spanish). Nelson commanded 27 ships-of-the-line and was impatient for action. On 21 October, Nelson caught up with Villeneuve, who tried to head back to Cadiz. Nelson formed his ships into two columns and drove them at right angles towards the ragged line of French and Spanish ships.

Nelson's flagship, HMS *Victory*, was first in the column and he directed it towards the twelfth ship in the opposing line, Villeneuve's flagship. He ordered his signaller to hoist up flags conveying a message to the rest of his fleet: 'England expects that every man will do his duty.' Captain Hargood of HMS *Belleisle* gave a practical order to his gunners, one probably typical of that delivered by other British captains: 'Put in two round shot and then a grape, and give her that.' Round cannonball shot was for breaking a ship's hull at a distance and the grapeshot, like a shotgun, was intended for close-quarter fighting to clear the deck of any resistance which might be offered to a boarding party. Nelson ordered one final message to fly from his masthead: 'Engage the enemy more closely.'

As the British columns of ships closed on the French and Spanish line, all hell broke loose. Broadsides erupted from the Spanish and French ships and the British sailors lay down on their decks. They had to accept this first assault, because they were approaching head-on and could not yet fire their guns in unison. Under the withering fire, masts splintered and sails collapsed. Men were blown to pieces and crewmen became impatient. 'Shall we not show our broadside and fire?' asked an officer on the *Belleisle*. 'No,' replied Hargood, 'we are ordered to go through the line, and

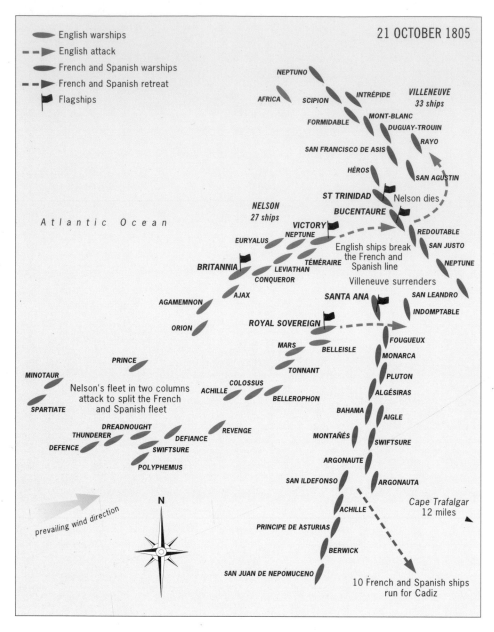

- ⬤ English warships
- --▶ English attack
- ⬤ French and Spanish warships
- --▶ French and Spanish retreat
- ⚑ Flagships

NEPTUNO

AFRICA SCIPION INTRÉPIDE VILLENEUVE
33 ships

FORMIDABLE MONT-BLANC
DUGUAY-TROUIN
SAN FRANCISCO DE ASIS RAYO

HÉROS
SAN AGUSTIN

ST TRINIDAD Nelson dies

NELSON
27 ships BUCENTAURE

Atlantic Ocean

VICTORY REDOUTABLE
NEPTUNE SAN JUSTO

EURYALUS English ships break
the French and NEPTUNE
Spanish line

BRITANNIA TÉMÉRAIRE
LEVIATHAN Villeneuve surrenders
CONQUEROR

AJAX SANTA ANA SAN LEANDRO

AGAMEMNON INDOMTABLE

ORION ROYAL SOVEREIGN

FOUGUEUX

MARS BELLEISLE MONARCA

TONNANT PLUTON

PRINCE ALGÉSIRAS

MINOTAUR COLOSSUS BAHAMA AIGLE
ACHILLE
Nelson's fleet in two columns
SPARTIATE attack to split the French BELLEROPHON
and Spanish fleet MONTAÑÉS SWIFTSURE

DREADNOUGHT ARGONAUTE
THUNDERER DEFIANCE REVENGE
DEFENCE SWIFTSURE SAN ILDEFONSO ARGONAUTA
POLYPHEMUS

Cape Trafalgar
ACHILLE 12 miles

prevailing wind direction PRINCIPE DE ASTURIAS

N BERWICK

SAN JUAN DE NEPOMUCENO 10 French and Spanish ships
run for Cadiz

Above: Nelson and his British ships – in two columns – breaking the line of Spanish and French ships during the Battle of Trafalgar on 21 October 1805.

go through she shall, by God!' The *Victory* suffered particularly badly, being the first to enter the enemy line and duly receiving fire from all quarters. Nelson and his officers, like all good naval officers of the period, coolly paced the decks, giving their men encouragement.

BREAKING THE LINE

Once the British ships had penetrated the enemy line and come close to their foes, they fired their own broadsides to tremendous effect. The first broadside of the *Victory* crashed into the *Bucentaure* and instantly wounded 200 French sailors and destroyed 20 of her guns. British marines added their own musket fire to the ferocious volley. The French had placed snipers in the rigging of their ships, but Nelson had a personal disdain for this, claiming that their gunfire could ignite the sails, although in reality he shared a British naval belief that the commander's job was to capture an enemy ship and not kill its crew.

Having raked the *Bucentaure* with fire, the *Victory* rounded gently and closed with the *Redoutable*. Both ships inflicted heavy fire on one another. The British crew were shocked to see the French suddenly shut their gunports, but Captain Lucas of the *Redoutable* saw this as his opportunity to board Nelson's flagship and he wanted the fighting to be carried out by sailors and marines armed with muskets, grenades and cutlasses. Nelson was particularly vulnerable in this kind of engagement because of his refusal to take cover – and sure enough a French sniper wounded him as he stood on the deck fully exposed. Barely a quarter of an hour into the fighting British sailors had had to carry Nelson below deck.

Lucas thought he had his moment of triumph and was about to send his sailors aboard the *Victory*, when the *Redoutable* was rammed by the *Téméraire*, which crashed into it on the other side. In the meantime, the *Victory* kept firing its cannons into the *Redoutable*, breaking it apart beneath its captain's feet. All three ships were now stuck together and they drifted helplessly. The *Victory* finally broke free and sent a boarding party aboard the French ship. It was sinking fast but would not surrender, Lucas threatened to set it and the *Téméraire* alight if the British did not help him save his ship. Meanwhile, beneath the decks of the *Victory*, Nelson was dying at the moment of his great victory.

The fighting continued for five terrible hours as both sides blasted away, ships becoming disabled as their masts were broken. The *Belleisle* fought the *Fougueux* until both ships were wrecked, the *Belleisle* losing all three of its sails. Captain Hargood was knocked down by a splinter that bruised him from hip to neck, but still he stood on deck and urged his crew on, sharing a bunch of grapes with his captain of marines in the midst of the fighting.

Eventually Nelson's tactics proved their worth and the French and Spanish fleet began to disintegrate. By breaking the line of the enemy with his columns, he had created a local superiority of numbers in the centre of the battle. Villeneuve was compelled to surrender and ten of his ships broke off the battle to head for the safety of Cadiz. The British were masters of the sea, having captured 17 enemy ships and sunk one. Many of their own ships were badly damaged but none of them had been lost to the enemy. The wind rose after the battle and prevented the British from taking many of the enemy ships as prizes, but the dead Nelson could not be denied his victory and he became one of Britain's greatest military heroes.

Trafalgar did not end the naval duel between Britain and France – Napoleon was still as determined as ever to blockade British exports to Europe – but it did define the boundaries of dominance. Napoleon remained master of the land, going on to victory two months later at Austerlitz, while Britain controlled the seas. No other nation could contest this and Britain used its sea power in the 19th century to create and maintain a global empire that became the largest the world had ever seen.

Above: **This painting by Denis Dighton shows Nelson struck down by a French sniper's bullet. British captains routinely walked the decks of their ships, defying enemy fire in order to maintain the morale of their crew.**

FRENCH EYEWITNESS TO THE BATTLE

Far from being a motley assortment of impressed seamen, the majority of Nelson's sailors were professional crewmen who performed well under fire. One French captain at Trafalgar was particularly impressed by how quickly the British sailors recovered from the trauma of battle:

'The act that astonished me the most was when the action was over. It came on to blow a gale of wind, and the English immediately set to work to shorten sail and reef the topsails, with as much regularity and order as if their ships had not been fighting a dreadful battle. We were all in amazement, wondering what the English seamen could be made of. All our seamen were either drunk or disabled, and we, the officers, could not get any work out of them. We never witnessed any such clever manoeuvres before, and I shall never forget them.'

Quoted in *The Oxford Illustrated History of the Royal Navy* edited by J.R. Hill (Oxford University Press, 1995)

AUSTERLITZ, 1805

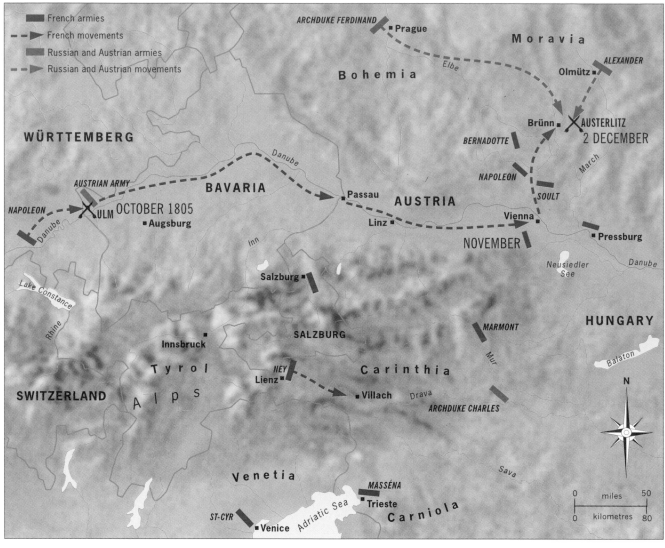

Above: **Napoleon wearing the uniform of the *Grenadiers à Pied* of the Imperial Guard in a portrait by Paul Delaroche. Napoleon's closeness to and concern for his soldiers added to his strength as a charismatic commander.**

Left: **Napoleon's strategic movements in early December, 1805 as he confronted the forces of the Austrian and Russian armies.**

One of Napoleon Bonaparte's finest victories, the Battle of Austerlitz showed him as a master of manoeuvre, with his force outperforming the larger one ranged against it, and splitting it in half. Success left him unassailable in western and central Europe, but, believing he was invincible, he then invaded Russia and precipitated the collapse of his empire. Overconfidence can be a commander's greatest enemy.

Like Julius Caesar, Napoleon was first and foremost a charismatic military leader. His troops believed that if he was at their head, they could not fail – he was a 'man of destiny' up against mere politicians. He was also observed to care closely for his men. 'Our beloved Emperor,' wrote Captain Coignet, 'did everything he could do to procure provisions for us.' Many soldiers took their mood directly from him. 'I passed the Emperor,'

recalled Lieutenant Vossler. 'He seemed somewhat cold and aloof. Perhaps he had been looking forward to a more resounding victory.' In fact he was ill, but the sight clearly disappointed Vossler. Even when things started to go wrong in Russia, French soldiers retained belief in their commander. 'He [Napoleon] passed close to a grenadier who had been wounded in the foot,' observed Heinrich von Brandt, 'and this brave man called out, "Oh, sire! Why were you not at our head yesterday? We would have crushed the Russians."'

DICTATOR OF FRANCE

Napoleon's military reputation was forged in northern Italy in 1796–97, where, leading France's Army of Italy, he achieved a string of victories against larger armies. He combined fierce

battlefield aggression with skilled strategic manoeuvring, which enabled him to defeat the superior numbers of the enemy by attacking them piecemeal. Success on the battlefield was fast becoming the primary achievement of the Revolutionary government in Paris and in 1797 a *coup d'état* ushered in the pro-Bonaparte Directory.

In 1798, France invaded Egypt in an attempt to weaken British control of the sea. The French defeat at the Battle of the Nile ended this hope, but Napoleon further increased his grip on political power in 1799 when he claimed personal recognition for the various military successes by replacing the Directory with a Consulate. The civilian administration was now firmly the servant of the military and Napoleon was at liberty to indulge his own ambitions through conquest.

With Britain Napoleon's sole remaining opponent, an international peace was established at Amiens in March 1802. The existence of a military dictatorship in France was confirmed in May that year when a popular vote confirmed him as First

Consul for life. Peace treaty or not, there seemed to be no end to his ambition and desire for French expansion. He was only finally dissuaded from his plans to invade Britain by the Royal Navy's control of the seas, emphatically confirmed at Trafalgar in 1805 (see Trafalgar pp.16–19). The force with which he intended to invade England was then absorbed into the *Grande Armée*, a body of some 200,000 men with which he proposed to assume his 'rightful' hegemony over the rest of Europe. By this time it often appeared that the military successes of the Revolution meant that war was being pursued by Napoleon as an end in itself. Meanwhile, in May 1804 Napoleon proclaimed a hereditary empire, in part to undermine the plotting of royalists against his regime.

AUSTERLITZ MANOEUVRES

By 1805, Britain's prime minister, Pitt, had assembled the Third Coalition to oppose Napoleon. Having made fresh conquests in both Italy and Germany since 1802, Napoleon now took the

Below: **The French camp, on the night before the battle of Austerlitz, painted by Louis-François Lejeune (1775–1848) in 1808. Napoleon talks to his generals and inspires his men.**

initiative against his enemies in central Europe and in 1805 he wrong-footed them with a series of brilliant military manoeuvres. In October, he surrounded an Austrian army of 30,000 men at Ulm and forced it to surrender. By November, Vienna was under occupation, just two months after the Austrians had sought to move against France. Advancing north from Vienna, he began to concentrate his army of 65,000 men near Brünn.

His enemies were hopelessly fragmented. Archduke Ferdinand, with 18,000 men, was in Prague, while both the emperors of Austria and Russia, with 90,000 men in total, were in Olmütz, and 80,000 more men were prevented from coming through the Alps from Italy by a force of 20,000 Frenchmen under the command of Ney. The allied Austro-Russian force moved first, southwards from Olmütz, hoping to overwhelm Napoleon's right flank and cut his line of communications with Vienna. Situated near the village of Austerlitz, Napoleon deliberately made his army appear vulnerable in order to provoke an attack from the allies.

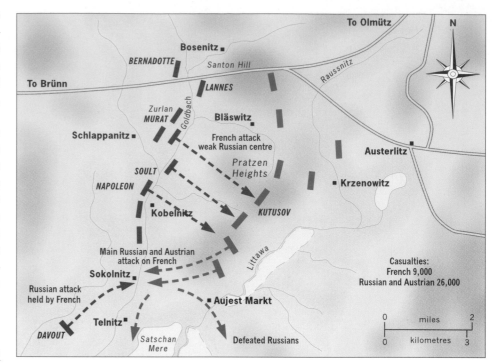

Casualties:
French 9,000
Russian and Austrian 26,000

NAPOLEON'S TRAP

As anticipated, on the morning of 2 December, the Russians and Austrians sent their main assault against the French right wing. The French reeled back and the allies sent more of their men along the line to exploit the momentum, but this was exactly what Napoleon wanted. With his troops initially hidden by winter fog and the smoke of their campfires, he now counter-attacked with Marshal Soult leading a corps against the heights of Pratzen, an act which split the allied army in half. Soult then turned to attack the extended allied left flank. Surprised, the Austrians and Russians fled.

Two more French corps now assaulted the allied right on the Brünn-Olmütz road. The Russians resisted bravely, but in hard fighting the veterans of Napoleon's army proved their worth. This was also the moment when Napoleon's charismatic leadership became a decisive factor, because his soldiers wanted to please him by gaining a victory. Coignet describes the performance at Austerlitz of one of Napoleon's most dedicated cavalry units, the exotic Mamelukes, who were dressed in North African costumes. 'These Mamelukes were marvellous riders,' observed Coignet. 'They could do anything they chose with their horses. With their curved sabres, they would take a man's head off with one blow, and their sharp stirrups tore the loins of the men they encountered. One of them came three different times up to the Emperor bringing a Russian standard. The third time, the Emperor wished to stop him, but he dashed in again, and returned no more.'

Napoleon was more prosaic about the performance of the French cavalry at Austerlitz: 'I could not recommend too highly the instruction of my cuirassiers... This arm, which has rendered me such important services, needs to be well instructed. One could say that instruction does everything. The Russian cavalry did not lack courage [at Austerlitz], and still it has nearly all been massacred, and my Guard has lost nobody.'

Eventually, the Russians were overcome and by nightfall the allied army had collapsed, sustaining some 26,000 casualties

against only 9,000 French losses. 'I have beaten the Austro-Russian army commanded by the two Emperors,' Napoleon wrote to his wife Josephine. 'I am a little weary. I have camped in the open for eight days and as many freezing nights. Tomorrow I shall be able to rest in the castle of Prince Kaunitz, and I should be able to snatch two or three hours' sleep there. The Russian army is not only beaten but destroyed.'

MASTER OF EUROPE

Austerlitz was one of Napoleon's greatest victories and it gave him mastery of central Europe after Emperor Francis of Austria had been forced into unconditional surrender. The czar's forces retreated ignominiously to Russia. Napoleon was at the peak of his success and felt there was nothing he could not achieve. This makes Austerlitz a decisive battle for the rest of his career, because it was from this point onwards that he began to over-reach himself. He believed he could conquer the German states and eastern Europe, and he spent the following decade in pursuit of this ambition. By 1807 he had crushed Prussia; finally, he sought to control Russia and this resulted in the catastrophe of 1812 in which he was forced to retreat from Moscow with a disintegrating army that left him vulnerable.

Raised to dizzying heights by brilliant victories such as Austerlitz, Napoleon made the mistake of many dictators in that he underestimated the strength and endurance of his enemies. 'As with Hitler in 1940,' wrote Alistair Horne, 'the defeated were too humiliated, the victor given too great a sense of superiority for the long-term future to consolidate the victory. If Austerlitz raised Napoleon to the pinnacle of his success, it also turned his head and filled it with the delusion that no force or combination of forces could now stop him conquering the world.' From Austerlitz onwards, Napoleon's days were numbered as the allies grew in strength against him.

Above: **Napoleon's aggressive assault on the centre of the Russian and Austrian position at the Battle of Austerlitz.**

Below: **Artillery soliders of Napoleon's Imperial Guard. Trained as an artillery officer himself, Napoleon was expert in its use on the battlefield.**

Above: **Napoleon victorious at the Battle of Austerlitz, having defeated two emperors. It was the climax of his military career and convinced him that he was unstoppable. Painting by de Mesnier.**

CAPTAIN JEAN-ROCH COIGNET

NIGHT BEFORE AUSTERLITZ

Captain Jean-Roch Coignet is remarkable for two aspects of his life. First, he served as an active soldier throughout Napoleon's campaigns, from 1799 to 1816, a remarkable feat of survival; and secondly, he wrote fascinating memoirs of his times in battle and recorded a particularly moving moment between Napoleon and his soldiers on the eve of Austerlitz:

'That evening the Emperor came out of his tent, and mounting his horse, started off with his escort to visit the outposts. It was twilight, and the horse-grenadiers carried four lighted torches. This was the signal for a charming sight; the whole guard took up handfuls of straw from their bivouacs and set them on fire. Holding a bunch in each hand, the men lighted them one from the other, and all cried out, "Vive l'Empereur!" and tossed

them in the air. The whole corps took it up, and I am sure that two hundred thousand flares were lighted. The bands played and the drums beat to arms. The Russians, from their heights, more than a hundred feet above us, could see seven army corps, and seven lines of fire in front of them.'

From *The Narrative of Captain Coignet: Soldier of the Empire* translated by M. Carey (Chatto & Windus, 1897)

WATERLOO, 1815

The battle that marked the end of the road for Napoleon was a classic demonstration of how a more practical commander, such as Wellington, could defeat a charismatic warlord. By understanding the landscape of war brilliantly and using it both to protect and to conceal his troops, Wellington devised a battle-winning formula that finally toppled the greatest commander of them all.

In 1812, Napoleon's world had started to collapse with the disintegration of his army during the disastrous retreat from Moscow. Prussia reasserted itself and joined forces with Austria and Russia at the Battle of Leipzig in 1813, an encounter that ground him down further. In the Peninsular War in Spain and Portugal from 1808 onwards, the British, commanded by Wellesley, who became the 'Iron' Duke of Wellington as a result, reduced French military power even more. In 1814 the Allies invaded France and occupied Paris; although he was beaten, Napoleon had demonstrated his old genius by manoeuvring brilliantly before his enemies and inflicting several minor defeats on them. Forced to abdicate, Napoleon was exiled to the island of Elba and Louis XVIII was

enthroned. The rest of Europe was relieved; the long struggle with revolutionary and then imperial France appeared to be over. How wrong they were.

NAPOLEON'S RETURN

It did not take long for the people of France to forget the horrors that Napoleon had inflicted on the rest of Europe and they pined for his return. Ex-soldiers recalled only the glory days and not the disasters of his last campaigns. The economic disarray being felt in France was said to require a 'strongman' to sort it all out and Napoleon seized his opportunity. Less than a year after his exile to Elba, Napoleon set sail and landed near Cannes. Accompanied by a thousand of his closest guardsmen, he marched through France towards Paris, gathering support wherever he went.

The rest of Europe was horrified. As Napoleon entered the capital and resumed control of the French government and its army, the Allied powers met at the Congress of Vienna and declared him an outlaw. By 1 June the Allies had raised a formidable array of armies: 95,000 British, Dutch and German

Above: **Scots Greys cavalry charge the French at the battle of Waterloo in this painting by Lady Butler.**

Right: **The opening movements of the Allied, Prussian and French armies around Waterloo in Belgium between 17 and 18 June 1815.**

Above: **The Duke of Wellington, by Goya (1812).**

troops, under the command of the Duke of Wellington, had been assembled in Belgium; 124,000 Prussians under Gebhard von Blücher marched to join Wellington; 210,00 Germans lay along the Rhine frontier; 75,000 Austrians were raised in Italy; and a Russian army of 167,000 slowly advanced westwards. Relying largely on his charisma – the one attribute that never left him – Napoleon managed to raise a force of some 280,000 soldiers, 75,000 of them veterans who needed little urging to join their erstwhile emperor.

Faced by such an overwhelming alliance, Napoleon knew that the only way to defeat these armies was to move quickly and defeat them one by one. It was one of his most brilliant strategies and he was highly skilled at it. Swiftly he advanced north in order to defeat the Prussians and the British separately before they could join forces. On 16 June Napoleon collided with the Prussians at Ligny. His aggression paid off and the Prussians reeled back. In the meantime, Marshal Ney took on a British vanguard at Quatre Bras, a strategically useful crossroads. Napoleon wanted Ney to help him finish off the Prussians, but the British vanguard proved far tougher to deal with than anticipated, giving Wellington time to gather most of his forces at Waterloo.

It has been alleged, by the Napoleonic historian Peter Hofschroer, that Wellington deceived the Prussians into making a stand at Ligny, claiming that he would support them and then not doing so, gave himself further time to assemble his troops. If this is true, it could be said to demonstrate the political astuteness of Wellington, indicating the superb grasp of the realities of war that would later help him at Waterloo. Other historians disagree, saying that Wellington pledged support only if he was not attacked, which he was at Quatre Bras.

Hofschroer does, however, make a valid point when he emphasizes the fact that Waterloo was a battle in which Germans formed the majority of the Allied forces facing Napoleon. Some 25,000 troops from various German states amounted to more than one-third of the Duke of Wellington's army. That said, it was Wellington who commanded the army that gave Napoleon most trouble on the day and it was the toughness of many British regiments, which stood their ground, that made it such a titanic struggle.

CHARISMA VERSUS GOOD SENSE

Having pushed the Prussians back to Wavre, on 18 June Napoleon turned his attention to Wellington at Waterloo. Some of the French generals who had fought the British in Spain were rather anxious about the forthcoming encounter, especially Marshal Soult, but Napoleon rounded on him: 'Because you have been beaten by Wellington you consider him a good general, but I tell you that Wellington is a bad general and the English are bad troops. The whole affair will not be more serious than swallowing one's breakfast.'

Wellington did not underestimate his adversary. Employing the practical methods of war he had learned in Spain and India (see Assaye, pp.12–15), Wellington analysed the landscape of battle and placed the majority of his British regiments on the reverse slope of a low plateau running along the Ohain Road, thus screening them from the enemy and protecting them from any opening artillery bombardments. He used the substantial walled farmhouses of Hougoumont, La Haye-Sainte and Papelotte as fortified positions ahead of his flanks and centre, thus breaking up the cohesion of any enemy advance. Above all, Wellington was being cautious and chose a defensive position in the hope of holding the French long enough for Blücher's Prussians to join him and then together they could overwhelm the French.

Disdaining caution and trusting to his soldiers' passion for him as their leader, Napoleon took the offensive in his old style, although his respected abilities as a battlefield surveyor

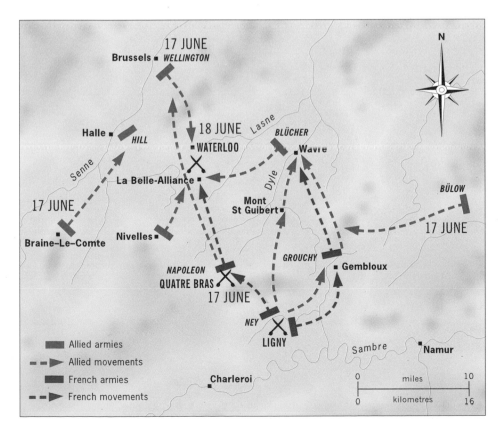

squares and waving their swords at the British, who returned dense volleys of fire. Formed up behind the ridge of the battlefield, many of these British regiments had also managed to escape the worst of the opening barrage of artillery, although French cannons were carried forward during the battle and used to lay down destructive fire in between the cavalry assaults.

'[The French] fired into us with grapeshot,' recalled Morris of the 73rd Highlanders, 'which proved very destructive, making complete lanes through us; and then the horsemen came up to dash in the openings. But before they reached us, we had closed our files, throwing the dead outside, and taking the wounded inside the square; and they were forced again to retire. They did not, however, go further then the pieces of cannon – waiting there to try the effect of some more grapeshot. We saw the match applied, and again it came as thick as hail upon us.' It was brutal fighting, made all the worse by the fact that neither side would give way.

By six o'clock it was clear that Wellington had weathered the storm. His troops had stood firm and it was the French cavalry that gave way. But danger was still present. As Napoleon concentrated on the approaching Prussians, Ney rallied his men and led another brave assault on the British line. This time, they swept over the farmhouse of La Haye-Sainte. Having managed to hold the Prussian advance, Napoleon followed this up with one final blow. He would send in his most loyal and experienced troops – the Old Guard.

Instead of leading them against the weakened Allied centre, Ney took the Old Guard beside the Allied right flank, which was covered by the farmhouse of Hougoumont. Behind the

Left: An infantryman of the 69th Foot – typical of the soldiers who fought for Wellington at Waterloo – loads his Brown Bess musket.

Below: The French advance against Allied lines at Waterloo on 18 June. Napoleon attacked several times, but the Allies held their nerve and their lines failed to break under the onslaught.

appear to have deserted him on the day. Opening with a massive artillery barrage that pummelled the Allied lines, Napoleon sent his infantry formations forward at mid-day. In dense columns, cheering their emperor, such an advance was usually enough to make any faint-hearted foe dissolve, but the British were unmoved. In addition to this, it had rained heavily the previous night and the farmland was muddy, making it hard work for the French soldiers to cross the ground and slowing their impetus. Mud also absorbed cannonballs, stopping them from bouncing dangerously across the ground. Despite this, the French captured Papelotte and by four o'clock the Allied line was pushed back. It was important to keep the pressure on because Napoleon wanted to crush the Allied army before the Prussians arrived, thus Ney took it on himself to order a massive French cavalry attack. Napoleon believed the assault was an hour too early.

STANDING STEADY

As the French cavalry thundered towards the Allied lines, the British formed square formations in which soldiers stood close to their comrades and raised the bayonets on the tips of their muskets so they formed a hedgehog-like defence. Horses do not like charging such obstacles and their charge faltered, reducing the French cavalrymen to circling the

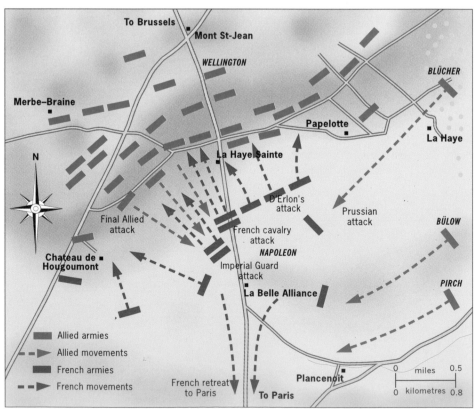

THOMAS MORRIS, 73RD REGIMENT

Above: Prior to Waterloo, British troops held the French advance at the cross-roads of Quatre Bras. Here, British soldiers form the square formation they would later use at Waterloo to defend themselves against French cavalry attacks. Painting by Lady Butler.

FRONT-LINE FIGHTING

Some of the toughest fighting at Waterloo was endured by the British infantry, who formed square formations before the assaults of French artillery and cavalry. Nineteen-year-old Thomas Morris was in a defensive square at Waterloo while he served in the 73rd Regiment and describes his encounter with a French cavalryman:

'The next charge the [French] cavalry made, they deliberately walked their horses up to the bayonet's point; and one of them, leaning over his horse, made a thrust at me with his sword. I could not avoid it, and involuntarily closed my eyes. When I opened them again, my enemy was lying just in front of me, within reach, in the act of thrusting at me. He had been wounded by one of my rear rank men, and whether it was the anguish of the wound, or the chagrin of being defeated, I know not; but he endeavoured to terminate his existence with his own sword: but that being too long for his purpose, he took one of our bayonets, which was lying on the ground, and raising himself up with one hand, he placed the point of the bayonet under his cuirass, and fell on it.'
Quoted from *The Recollections of Sergeant Morris* edited by John Selby (Longman, Green, 1967)

farmhouse were batteries of Allied artillery that furiously bombarded the advancing French columns. Fearless under fire, Wellington coolly rode into the front line to support his troops. His presence was highly valued. 'Wellington came riding up,' remembered a 71st Highlander. 'We formed a square, with him in our centre, to receive cavalry. Shortly the whole army received orders to advance. We moved forwards in two columns, four deep, the French retiring at the same time. We were charged several times in our advance. This was our last effort; nothing could impede us.'

It was gone eight o'clock. The Allies had refused to be intimidated by the Old Guard and the Prussians were pushing their own attack elsewhere on the battlefield. Wellington ordered a general advance. Isolated French units fought desperately to the end, but others had had enough and left the battlefield in a mob. Napoleon's time had run out. He had failed to prevent the British and Prussians linking up and his charisma-based warfare had proved insufficient to defeat a commander like Wellington. Three days later, Napoleon surrendered to the British and was exiled to the remote island of St Helena in the middle of the Atlantic, where he died in 1821.

The Battle of Waterloo was a tremendous victory, bringing an end to the French Revolutionary period and discouraging the re-emergence of any government intent on dominating continental Europe. With Napoleon defeated, military competition from France withered, enabling Britain to prosper and expand its empire around the world. The 19th century would be the 'British century'.

MEXICO CITY, 1847

The culmination of the United States's struggle to dominate the North American continent, the battle for Mexico City was a decisive victory built on dogged determination and American military professionalism. It also took the United States a step nearer to becoming a major power in the world.

After winning its independence in 1782, the United States was determined to control North America. Its clash with Britain in the War of 1812 failed to provide a satisfactory military outcome, serving merely to confirm the boundary with Canada, but it did discourage any further continental interventions by Britain. Far more fruitful was the United States's steady advance westwards, led by traders and pioneers. The major power to contest this territorial expansion was Mexico.

In 1836, the declaration of independence by the Republic of Texas tested the ability of Mexico to maintain a grip on its territories to the southwest of the United States and in California. As the defeat at San Jacinto in April 1836 demonstrated, Mexico was found wanting and it was not long before the United States exploited this weakness further. In 1845, the United States annexed Texas and settlers began to claim land as far south as the Rio Grande. An army of 3,500 US regular troops under General Zachary Taylor was sent by President Polk to uphold these claims. Polk also wanted to acquire California and New Mexico (the modern-day states of California, Nevada, Utah, Arizona, and parts of New Mexico, Colorado and Wyoming). However, his financial offer was rejected and Mexican troops crossed the Rio Grande to clash with Taylor's army. It was the excuse Polk needed and in 1846 the United States declared war on Mexico.

A STRING OF VICTORIES

Some 60,000 American volunteers joined Taylor's army in Texas, but the Mexicans were confident and possessed an

Below: **US troops storm Mexican positions during the battle of Cerro Gordo in which Scott's Americans outmanoeuvred Santa Anna's army, opening the road to Mexico City.**

Above: **General Winfield Scott commanded the US troops that captured Mexico City and ended the war with Mexico.**

Above right: **The course of the Mexican–American War from 1846–48. While US forces invaded California, General Scott took an army to the Mexican capital.**

army four times bigger. Despite the numbers, the Americans gained the upper hand in northern Mexico with a succession of victories, helped by their superior use of light artillery. These culminated in the two-day Battle of Buena Vista in February 1847 in which Taylor defeated Santa Anna (the victor at the Battle of the Alamo). Shortly prior to that, a second US army, under Colonel Stephen Kearny, had marched westwards and claimed California for the United States in January 1847.

Although they had experienced a string of defeats, the Mexicans refused to surrender and President Polk ordered his army to march on Mexico City. Because the landward approach was 800km (500 miles) across difficult country, a third army of 9,000 under General Winfield Scott was delivered by landing craft across the Gulf of Mexico to Vera Cruz. Mexican naval power was negligible and the approach therefore went uncontested, with Vera Cruz falling in March 1847. Scott's force next had to face Santa Anna and an army of 13,000 men at Cerro Gordo, but the Mexicans were encircled and defeated. The road to Mexico City was open and the Mexicans requested an armistice. Presuming the Americans were now overstretched, the Mexicans used this time to reposition their troops and on 8 September they resumed fighting.

HALLS OF MONTEZUMA

Alongside the command skills of Taylor and Scott, the US army in Mexico was aided considerably by a talented collection of officers who had been trained at the US Military Academy, West Point. They included Robert E. Lee, Ulysses S. Grant, Thomas J. Jackson and George B. McClellan, junior officers who would later become commanders in the American Civil War on opposing sides. The experience gained in the Mexican War certainly helped them in their future careers. Ulysses S. Grant rode with Scott in the final approach to Mexico City and left a concise account of the battle for the Mexican capital.

The bulk of Santa Anna's army was inside Mexico City when the armistice broke down, but he also had a significant number of troops installed in a nearby mill at Molino del Rey and the fortress of Chapultepec. Grant claims that Scott thought guns were manufactured in the mill, but it was actually a store for grain. Aqueducts supplying Mexico City ran from these two points as well, making them crucially important to Santa Anna. The great stone arches of the aqueducts were incorporated into the city's defences, with earthworks thrown up between them to protect the artillery.

General Scott's subordinate General Worth led the assault on Molino del Rey. Advancing during the night, the US forces were in place by daybreak on 8 September. Although within range of

artillery fire from Chapultepec, the US assault was successful and the Mexicans were chased out of the mill. 'Had this victory been followed up promptly,' complains Grant, 'no doubt Americans and Mexicans would have gone over the defences of Chapultepec so near together that the place would have fallen into our hands without further loss. The defenders of the works could not have fired upon us without endangering their own men.' Grant perhaps was a little too critical, for the losses taken by the Americans in that day's fighting had been quite considerable – more than 750 casualties, reducing Scott's army to less than 7,500. It would be another five days before the fortress on the hill was attacked.

Scott brought up his artillery and let them bombard Chapultepec for a day. On the morning of 13 September, two columns, each with 250 volunteers, took scaling ladders and attacked the Mexican-held fortress. It was another bitter struggle. US Marines were among the first troops to scale the walls of the fortress, an action that later featured in the famous Marine Hymn, inspiring the verse line 'From the Halls of Montezuma to the Shores of Tripoli.' So brave were the US Marines involved in the fighting that 13 of their 23 officers received brevets. Major Twiggs, overall commander of the storming parties, was seen to carry his favourite double-barrelled hunting rifle into action, but he did not survive the combat. The Mexicans were no less brave and the defenders included one hundred young cadets of the Military Academy, which was based in the castle. Eventually the fortress was taken and Scott's army directed its attention to Mexico City. US military organization and preparations had proved superior to that of the Mexicans.

ARCH BY ARCH

Advancing arch by arch along the aqueduct that led to the capital city, the Americans encountered some resistance in the form of Mexican artillery fire. Grant led a small unit in an effort to outflank Mexican troops on the city road by occupying the belfry of a church. 'This took us over several ditches,' he recalled, 'breast deep in water and grown up with water plants. These ditches, however, were not over eight or ten feet [2.5–3m] in width. The howitzer was taken to pieces and carried by the men to its destination. When I knocked for admission a priest came to the door, who, while extremely polite, declined to admit us. With the little Spanish then at my command, I explained to him that he might save property by opening the door, and certainly would save himself from becoming a prisoner, for a time at least; and besides, I intended to go in whether he consented or not. He began to see his duty in the same light that I did, and opened the door.' The gun was assembled and placed in the belfry, where it sent shot among the Mexicans on the road. It was a crucial action, further reducing the resolve of the defenders.

By the night of 13 September, Americans troops were encamped in houses outside the city walls. They began to cut passageways through the houses towards the walls in anticipation of having to storm the city. But during the night, Santa Anna and his army withdrew. His last act was to release all the occupants of the prisons, hoping they might cause the Americans some trouble. Politicians from Mexico City now approached Scott, asking him to respect the rights of their citizens.

The next morning, US troops formed a column and proceeded. 'On entering the city the troops were fired upon by the released convicts,' reported Grant, 'and possibly by deserters and hostile citizens. The streets were deserted, and the place presented the appearance of a "city of the dead", except for this firing by unseen persons from house-tops, windows, and around corners.' The US soldiers quickly suppressed the guerrilla activity and General Scott took up residence in the president's palace, a complex of buildings nicknamed the 'Halls of Montezuma'. The war was virtually over and peace negotiations began.

Victory against Mexico gave the United States complete dominance of North America. It had no rivals on the continent and from this point on became a global power. An internal empire of states was completed by the acquisition of territories on the Pacific Coast and the securing of its southern boundary with Mexico. Some Americans wanted President Polk to annex Mexico, but this was not deemed necessary. The USA had already gained 1,300,000 sq km (500,000 sq miles) of extra territory, including the regions of California, Nevada, Utah, Arizona, New Mexico, and parts of Colorado and Wyoming. In return, the US government gave the Mexicans $15 million.

This remarkable conquest, however, had not been achieved without a high cost: some $100 million of campaign expenses and the death of more than 13,000 US troops, mostly from disease. Some voices were raised in criticism. Ralph Waldo Emerson declared: 'The United States will conquer Mexico, but it will be as the man who swallows the arsenic which brings him down. Mexico will poison us.' Some historians have claimed that the tensions unleashed in the southern states over the issue of extending slave ownership into the new territories led to the American Civil War.

Left: **Two soldiers of the 5th US Infantry during the Mexican–American War, one of the earliest conflicts to be captured on film. They wear the wide non-regulation clothing typically worn by volunteers during this campaign.**

Below: **The final series of combats in the US assault on Mexico City.**

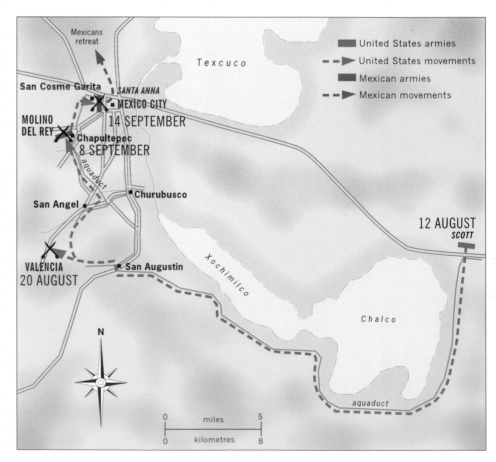

Above: Escalante's painting of the Battle of Molino del Rey, one of a series of combats fought during Scott's approach to Mexico City.

LIEUTENANT NAPOLEON J.T. DANA

FANCY JACKETS

The US army that marched into Mexico was not wholly prepared for the rigours of campaigning. Many volunteers had swollen its ranks and uniforms varied considerably, if they were worn at all. In summer 1846, Lieutenant Napoleon J.T. Dana wrote to his wife while advancing on Monterey, offering an account of his appearance:

'We wear all kinds of uniforms here, each one to his taste, some shirtsleeves, some white, some blue, some fancy jackets and all colours of cottonelle pants, some straw and some Quaker hats, and that is just the way, too, that our fellows went into battle... I have on my old straw hat, those blue-checked pants, made by your dear hands, which are torn in both legs and pretty well worn out, and that loose coat you made, which you recollect washed white. I don't think there is much danger of a ranchero shooting me for an officer of high rank. My trimmings don't show much. Both pairs of those check pants I have worn pretty well out.'

Quoted in *Mexican–American War 1846–48* by Ron Field (Brassey's, 1997)

GETTYSBURG, 1863

The Confederate cause in the American Civil War was never better led than by General Robert E Lee, but at Gettysburg he misjudged his enemy and suffered a crucial defeat. His determination to break the centre of the Union line of defence culminated in a brave but doomed frontal assault. From this point onwards, the Confederacy was on the defensive.

Robert E. Lee, the leading general of the Confederacy, had learned the lessons of Napoleon very well. Lee understood the art of manoeuvre and the impact of strategical and tactical aggression. It was precisely what the South needed. In a prolonged war with the North, which consisted of more industrialized and prosperous states, the more agrarian South could not expect to win. The North could call on a population of 22 million, while the states of the South had just 5.5 million whites and 3.5 million slaves. A more cautionary voice would have recommended a defensive campaign, but Lee and the president of the Confederacy, Jefferson Davis, both of whom had been trained at West Point, knew that in similar circumstances Napoleon would have taken the offensive. Early victories could give the South political leverage far beyond its actual strength. It might also attract important support abroad, such as from Britain.

In June 1862, Lee forced Union troops away from the Confederate capital of Richmond by sending a cavalry force to threaten Washington, D.C. In September 1862, Lee crossed the River Potomac and invaded the North. His movements were frustrated by a Union Army led by George B. McClellan and Lee became trapped behind Antietam Creek. Despite this, Lee fought such an aggressive battle that he inflicted more casualties on his opponents and withdrew undefeated. In May 1863, Lee was outnumbered and outflanked at Chancellorsville, but he rejected a defensive battle in favour of attacking one flank after the other, thereby winning a brilliant victory. By now, Lee's troops believed he was a genius and felt they could not fail; perhaps Lee even thought that himself. In summer 1863, Lee swept through the Cumberland Valley in order to strike Washington, D.C., from the north. However, his troops stumbled on Union soldiers at Gettysburg and Lee rapidly had to plan a battle.

BATTLE BY ACCIDENT

At this time, as armies advanced through enemy territory, they would send out parties of troops to search for food and supplies. A.P. Hill, one of Lee's divisional commanders, heard that there was a good supply of shoes at the town of Gettysburg and sent his men off to gather them. As the Confederate soldiers wandered into the town on 1 July they were confronted with two brigades of Union cavalry, who were on reconnaissance. Although heavily outnumbered, the Union forces were armed with repeating breech-loading carbines and this superior fire power kept the Confederates at bay. The news that a fight was developing at Gettysburg duly reached Lee, who decided to deploy his troops and bring the North to battle.

With more and more Confederate troops flooding into Gettysburg, the Union brigades fell back and took control of the high ground overlooking the town. It was a defensive move and it encouraged Lee to think he had the advantage: that if he just kept up the pressure of his attack, then the Union forces would cave in. He was thinking in Napoleonic terms, but infantry fire power and artillery had evolved considerably during the intervening 50 years. Repeating rifles and more devastating artillery power meant that the tactical advantage had shifted from the

Above: **General Robert E. Lee was the greatest of the Confederate generals, but let earlier success encourage a Napoleonic attitude on the battlefield which led to disaster in the face of improved fire power.**

Left: **The manoeuvring and major battles of the Union and Confederate armies during 1862–63, which culminated in the three-day conflict at Gettysburg.**

Map

Union army
Union movements
Confederate army
Confederate movements

Pennsylvania
N
Carlisle
Chambersburg
LEE
MEADE · GETTYSBURG
1–3 JULY 1863
Hagerstown
West Virginia
Martinsburg
ANTIETAM CREEK
17 SEPTEMBER 1862
Frederick
Harpers Ferry
Baltimore
Maryland
Front Royal
LEE
Washington
McCLENNAN
BURNSIDE AND HOOKER
Appalachian Mountains
Shenandoah
Potomac
CHANCELLORVILLE
1–6 MAY 1863
LEE
FREDERICKSBURG
13 DECEMBER 1862
Chesapeake Bay
Virginia
27 JUNE 1862
GAINES MILL
Richmond
West Point
McCLENNAN
MALVERN MILL
1 JULY 1862
Harrison's Landing
Williamsburg
Petersburg
Yorktown
Fort Monroe

0   miles   50
0   kilometres   80

Above: **This painting by Thure de Thrulstrup shows the Union line along Cemetery Ridge withstanding the Confederate assaults. A Union artillery carriage rushes forward to support the line of infantry.**

offensive to the defensive. Troops who launched a daring charge could be annihilated before they reached the opposing line in sufficient numbers to break through. Lee did not fully appreciate this, even after the lengthening casualty lists of the first years of the war, and continued to believe in the efficacy of charismatic leadership.

By the second day of the battle, Major General George Meade had deployed his Union troops effectively along the high ground, which ran from Culp's Hill on his right flank, along Cemetery Ridge in the centre, to Little Round Top on his left. The Union army would not be drawn into an attack and every hour Lee let pass, more and more Union troops arrived to reinforce the defensive position. Lee had lost any advantage of impetus he might have possessed on the first day and was compelled to organize his troops opposite the Union positions, but on lower ground. Deciding he could wait no longer, Lee launched an assault in the late afternoon.

LITTLE ROUND TOP

Lee aimed to envelop the Union left flank, sending Longstreet's I Corps against the weakly defended Little Round Top with the

aim of then turning in on the centre. A mighty artillery barrage began the greatest combat ever fought on American soil. A diversionary Confederate assault went up against Culp's Hill. The convex Union line of defence meant that it was easier to reinforce each of Meade's flanks, whereas communications were stretched along the concave Confederate lines. Longstreet's troops surged up the wooded slopes towards Little Round Top, where Colonel Joshua L. Chamberlain commanded the 20th Maine on the extreme edge of the Union left flank. Line after line of Alabama troops launched themselves at the men from Maine, but the Union troops stood firm.

A year before Gettysburg, Chamberlain had been Professor of Rhetoric and Modern Languages at Bowdoin College, where he had succeeded the husband of the author of Uncle Tom's Cabin. He was a passionate supporter of the movement for the abolition of slavery and this fervour fired his defence at Little Round Top. For over an hour Chamberlain and his men resisted repeated Confederate assaults, but with more than one-third of his men casualties and ammunition running low, he had to face what looked like the final attack that would overwhelm them. Digging deep into his courage, he ordered 'Bayonet!' His men knew exactly what was required and fixed bayonets to their guns. Yelling fiercely, 200 survivors of the firefight threw themselves down the hill and charged the Confederate forces. Having exhausted themselves with countless uphill assaults, the Alabama troops broke; some surrendered, while others fell back. Little Round Top was saved and the Union left flank was secure. Elsewhere, Confederate attacks were also beaten back. Lee had failed in his main objective.

PICKETT'S CHARGE

By the third day of the battle neither side was willing to give way. Meade would not be triggered into going on the offensive and this compelled Lee to once more consider the decisive assault that would leave his opponent reeling. This time, he decided to break the Union army in half by launching a massive attack at its centre. It was a Napoleonic gesture - but in an age of modern fire power. Lee assembled some 15,000 troops for this major thrust, and although Major General

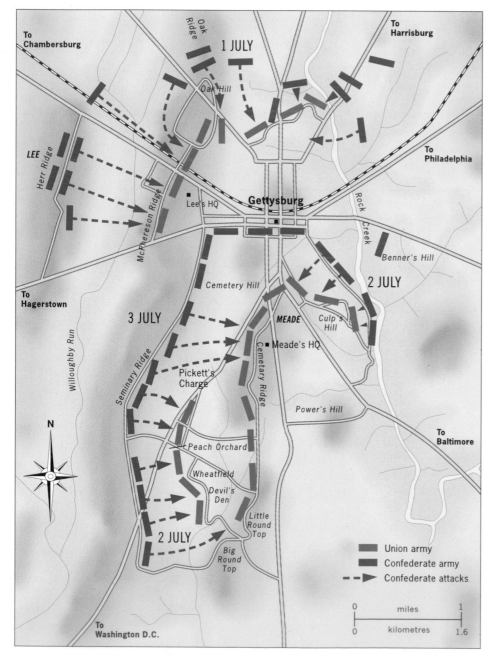

Union army

Confederate army

- - -> Confederate attacks

0   miles   1
0   kilometres   1.6

George E. Pickett was only one of three divisional commanders leading the soldiers, his name would forever be associated with the attack. Announcing their intentions with a two-hour artillery bombardment of Cemetery Ridge, Meade responded by shifting extra troops from both his flanks to reinforce the centre of his position.

The main Confederate attack began in mid-afternoon as thousands of Lee's soldiers advanced through the wheatfields towards the Union lines in front of Cemetery Ridge. 'Now the enemy's guns have quieted down and our heads are poking up above the breastwork all along the line,' recalled Steven Allen Osborn, a Union soldier in Meade's army. 'Then the cry is raised "There they come!" It was a grand, but awful sight to see those three lines sweeping forward to almost certain death. First there is the report of one lone [Union] cannon up to our right, quickly followed by the most awful, unearthly roar of letting go of some 60 guns along our line. To the right of us their line kept advancing but opposite us we could see they were staggered and were giving ground but rallied and came on.'

Meade had removed his artillery out the way of the Confederate bombardment, but now rushed them forwards so that they could rake the advancing Confederates with deadly volleys. Lee's troops showed incredible bravery, pressing on through the withering storm of fire. Confederate Brigadier General Lewis A. Armistead thrust his sword into his hat, held it high, and shouted: 'Come on boys! Give them the cold steel! Who will follow me?' In an earlier age, a determined charge with bayonets might have cleared the Union lines, but now as the surviving Confederates approached within range of Union muskets and rifles, they were ravaged by yet more fire power.

Armistead walked on with his hat held high and reached the stone wall that formed part of the Union defences, but around him there were only a few hundred men out of the 15,000 that had begun the advance. It was a slaughter and Armistead himself was shot dead as he stood among the Union cannons. Meade immediately counter-attacked and swept away the few troops that had penetrated his line. Those lucky to be alive returned to Lee and he could do nothing but withdraw.

'Pickett's Charge' has been called the 'high water mark' of the Confederacy because it represented the supreme bravery and daring of its troops and its commanders, but no army could withstand such a shock as this and Lee's reputation suffered a severe blow. He had brought the Confederacy to the edge of destruction and was forced to fight a war of defensive manoeuvre ever afterwards, no longer able to challenge the North with bold advances. The days of the Confederacy were numbered, although the actual surrender was delayed until 1865. Gettysburg also represented the end of the Napoleonic approach to war and announced the beginning of modern, industrialized warfare, with an escalation in fire power and consequently a need for strong, entrenched defensive positions.

Gettysburg was a particularly bloody battle: Union casualties for the three days amounted to 3,155 killed, 14,529 wounded and 5,365 missing; Confederate losses were 3,903 killed, 18,735 wounded and 5,425 missing. In wars of previous eras the bodies of the dead were usually left on the battlefield to be looted and then thrown into mass graves, but sacrifice on this scale for the unity of a nation and in the service of political ideals was deemed worthy of far greater respect. President Abraham Lincoln visited the battlefield four months later and linked the fighting there with the political liberty of the nation. 'From these honored dead,' Lincoln declared in his Gettysburg Address, 'we take increased devotion to that cause for which they gave the last full measure of devotion; that we here highly resolve that these dead shall not have died in vain.' The battlefield was preserved as a National Park and the dead were buried in a cemetery. It marked the beginning of an age in which the lives of a nation's soldiers would be more highly valued.

Left: **A photograph by Alexander Gardner of a dead Confederate sharpshooter at Little Round Top, July 1863.**

Far left: **The three days of fighting at Gettysburg. Pickett's Charge (middle) was the tragic and deciding combat of the battle.**

Above: **Confederate General Armistead, with his hat on his sword point, leads the final charge against Federal cannons.**

Above right: **Major General George Meade, commander of the Union Army at Gettysburg, used his defensive positions brilliantly to draw on the attacks of the Confederate Army until it was exhausted.**

WALTER HARRISON, CONFEDERATE OFFICER WHO WITNESSED 'PICKETT'S CHARGE'

CHEERFUL BUT ANXIOUS
'The Confederates were cheerful, but anxious at the delay. They were restless to be "up and at 'em"; eager to have what they knew was inevitably before them commenced and ended... The enemy had the exact range of our line of battle, and just overshooting the artillery opposed to them, as usual, their shot and shell told with effect upon the infantry, exposed as they were without cover of any sort. Here was a situation more trying than the quiet inactivity of the morning. Many of the men, and several valuable officers were killed or disabled long before a movement was ordered: but the line remained steadily fixed. Our artillery continued to pour in a telling response for about two hours when the enemy's batteries slackened their fire. Then the order for the infantry charge was given, and the men sprung to their feet with a shout of delight.'
Quoted from *Pickett's Men* by Walter Harrison (New York, 1870)

SEDAN, 1870

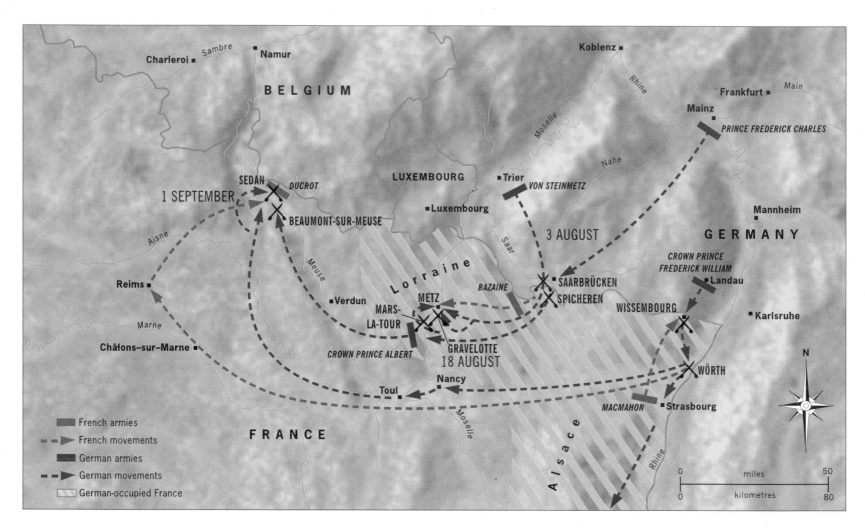

In its swift and efficient defeat of France, Prussia demonstrated that its army was Europe's new, invincible power. Artillery pounded the city of Sedan and dashing French cavalry charges failed to have any effect on the superiority of such fire power. It was the end of a flamboyant era, but overconfidence among the victors would subsequently encourage Germany to embark on two disastrous world wars.

Germany's march to these world wars began with Prussia's wars of aggression in the 1860s and 1870s. Otto von Bismarck, foreign minister of Prussia from 1862 onwards, aspired to unite the loose confederation of German states under the leadership of Prussia, and it was a series of wars which helped him to achieve this end. In 1864, Prussia and Austria fought Denmark to secure control over Schleswig and Holstein. Bismarck then oversaw the growth of the Prussian Army so it could match that of Austria, which also laid claim to leadership of the German states. In 1866 this rivalry broke down into war and Prussia

rapidly defeated Austria at the Battle of Königgrätz, making Prussia the undisputed leader of the north German states. Bismarck knew that the south German states, no longer in the shadow of Austria, would have to be brought in line through another war, and Emperor Napoleon III of France gave him the opportunity he needed.

THE FRANCO-PRUSSIAN WAR

Napoleon III was alarmed by the events between the German states. A diplomatic argument then developed over a Prussian-backed Hohenzollern claim to the Spanish throne. France opposed this, and Bismarck irked Napoleon into declaring war in July 1870. Napoleon III was confident in his decision because his last major international test in 1859 against Austria had ended in triumph. It was a grave error.

French military organization could not match that of Prussia, and whereas the Prussians mobilized rapidly by using trains to

Above: **The Prussian invasion of France was swift, culminating in the French army being surrounded and defeated at Sedan.**

transport troops, the French were slow and incompetent in their preparations for war. The south German states joined with Prussia against France, and three German armies under the command of General von Moltke and his efficient general staff clashed with the French along the Rhine frontier.

The French were outnumbered – some 224,000 troops to 380,000 Germans – and outmanoeuvred by the Prussian general staff, who had learned the lessons Napoleon had inflicted on them more than half a century earlier. This trust in a war of movement bore tremendous fruits in the clash with France, but it became integral to German military thinking in the next century: in France in 1870, the Prussian method proved too successful, too quickly, and an overconfidence in it led to the disastrous stalemate of the First World War and dramatic setbacks in the Second World War.

After a rapid series of defeats, Napoleon III relinquished control of the army to his generals. The results were little better and culminated on 18 August with the Battle of Gravelotte-St Privat, where despite hard fighting by the French, Moltke remained in control of the battlefield and bottled up a French army at Metz.

General MacMahon, one of Napoleon III's victorious generals of 1859, rushed to relieve these battered forces by leading a 120,000-strong army into northern France. Clashes with the German forces along the River Meuse forced him to take a defensive position in a bend of the river at Sedan.

Then further German forces suddenly enveloped him, creating a catastrophic situation. Napoleon III, who was travelling with the army, had the wounded MacMahon replaced by Ducrot. The French had their backs against the Belgian

Below: **French cavalry attack German infantry during the Franco-Prussian War, but are overwhelmed by German fire power, a pattern that was repeated at Sedan.**

frontier with Moltke's 200,000 troops pressing in from the south, west and north.

CAVALRY AGAINST GUNS

The fighting at Sedan began at 04.00 hours on 1 September. It was a battle in which artillery played a predominant role, with the German artillery especially relentless. Arranged in a semi-circle on the heights above Sedan, they subjected the town to a terrible day-long bombardment. Émile Zola, the novelist, was present at the battle and felt the French suffered from an inferiority in artillery: '[German] percussion shells almost all went off at enormous distances, whereas the French ones with fuses had a much shorter range and most often exploded in the air before reaching the target. And no other resources were left but to make oneself as small as possible in the furrow where one was cowering... All round Sedan the eight hundred pieces of German equipment, a girdle of bronze, were firing at once, blasting the fields with a continuous thunder and this converging fire, all the surrounding height aiming at the centre, would burn and pulverise the town within two hours.'

It was a desperate situation, and by noon the French had to call on their cavalry to break out of the encirclement. Four times the French cavalry charged the German lines. 'Would the cavalry charge again?' wondered Ducrot. 'As often as you like,' replied Gallifet, commander of the cavalry, 'so long as there's one of us left.' It was a gallant effort, admired even by the Germans, but modern fire power treated such daring mercilessly.

William Russell, the famous war correspondent of *The Times*, was present at the battle, watching it from the positions of the Prussian general staff, who were also accompanied by their king, Wilhelm I, and Bismarck, the architect of the war. He described the impact German infantry guns had on one of the French cavalry charges: 'The leading regiment of [French] cavalry moved out of the hollow at a walk, quickly changed to a trot. They were mounted upon white and grey horses, and presented a very gay appearance in the sun. They were going to charge. As they reached the top, the trot was quickened to a gallop, and in two to three seconds they seemed to sweep down upon the infantry, as if to annihilate them.'

Above: **Red-trousered French Zouave soldiers clash with Prussian infantry near Sedan.**

Above: **The Prussian infantry advancing during the Battle of Sedan.**

'brother,' wrote Napoleon III. 'Not having been able to die in the midst of my troops, I can only hand over my sword into the hands of Your Majesty. I am Your Majesty's good brother – Napoleon.' It was an empty attempt at friendship. Sedan was a humiliating and crushing defeat for the French and one which would have long-lasting effects for Europe into the 20th century.

In just one day the French had endured some seventeen thousand casualties, and more than one hundred thousand soldiers were taken prisoner. German losses were just nine thousand. The capture of Napoleon III meant the immediate collapse of the French Empire when he signed his surrender on 2 September. Revolution followed in Paris as a new republic was proclaimed. The German forces then went on to besiege the capital and fighting continued into 1871 until a peace treaty was finally signed in May.

The terms were tough for France, which ceded the regions of Alsace and Lorraine, both important industrial areas. The rest of the German states were thoroughly impressed by Prussia's leadership and Bismarck won what he had intended when, in 1871 at Versailles, a united Germany was proclaimed with Wilhelm I becoming its emperor. This was the beginning of the Second Reich. It was also the beginning of Germany's period of overconfidence in its own military abilities. France, however, would never forget this humiliation and fought bitterly the next time German armies returned.

In an earlier age, such an impressive charge would have unnerved the infantry before them, but the advantage now lay with the infantry, armed with powerful breech-loading rifles. 'It was not until the front had reached within a couple of hundred yards of the [German] infantry,' recalled Russell, 'that there came out the whiff and roll of a volley, which was kept up like the rattling of a catherine-wheel. The result was almost incredible. The leading squadron was dissolved into a heap of white and grey horses, amidst which men were seen trying to disengage themselves, while others held up their hands as if to avert the charge of the squadron behind them... The ground presented in one moment a most singular appearance. It was as though someone had strewn a carpet with fragments of white paper, with here and there dots of brighter colour.'

HUMILIATION

By 17.00 hours, the town of Sedan was filled with panicking civilians and desperate soldiers, all of them clogging the tiny streets in an effort to escape. Napoleon III, ill but rouged to make himself look healthy as he rode his horse among his soldiers, realized that holding out against the Germans would only lead to further slaughter. He ordered that a white flag be raised and sent a chivalric but humbling message to Wilhelm I. 'Monsieur, my dear

Above: **Napoleon III (left) and Bismarck, who contrived the war against France, after the former had surrendered his army at Sedan. Painting by Wilhelm Camphausen.**

WILLIAM RUSSELL, WAR CORRESPONDENT FOR THE TIMES

DEBRIS OF EMPIRE

'What debris a ruined empire leaves after it! It was almost impossible to ride through the streets for fear of treading on bayonets or sabres. Heaps of shakos, piles of musketry, all sorts of military equipments, knapsacks and belts, and thousands of imperial eagles torn off infantry caps or belts, were lying piled up here and there... One man I felt a most intense desire to be executed on the spot... He was literally staggering under the weight of an enormous bag on his shoulders, on his way towards the [German] frontier; and I afterwards learned that it was filled with watches and purses he had taken from the dead and dying, and with gold lace and silver cut off the uniforms of those who had fallen.'

Quoted from *William Russell: Special Correspondent of The Times* edited by Roger Hudson (The Folio Society, 1995)

ISANDLWANA, 1879

Isandlwana was one of the greatest blows struck against the forces of 19th-century imperialism; events there reminded the colonial powers not to underestimate the capabilities of indigenous opposition. Initially cowed by British fire power, the Zulu warriors then advanced rapidly towards the British line and overwhelmed it in a savage wave of hand-to-hand fighting.

By the late 19th century the Western way of warfare seemed unmatchable. European empires held sway over most of the globe from Africa to Asia, and even the European settler republic of the United States had become the dominant power in North America after a succession of colonial wars. Artillery, rifles, machine guns and sound logistics were used by Europeans anywhere in the world to subdue native resisters, who frequently only had access to weaponry from a different age. Two battles in the 1870s, however, shook this sense of confidence to its roots.

Above: **C.E. Fripp's painting of British soldiers fighting a desperate last stand against the Zulus at the Battle of Isandlwana in 1879. The annihilation of British soldiers shook the empire to its roots.**

Left: Lieutenant General Lord Chelmsford, the British commander at Isandlwana.

Right: The Zulu advance on the British position at Isandlwana. It took the traditional Zulu battle formation of the 'horns of the beasts'.

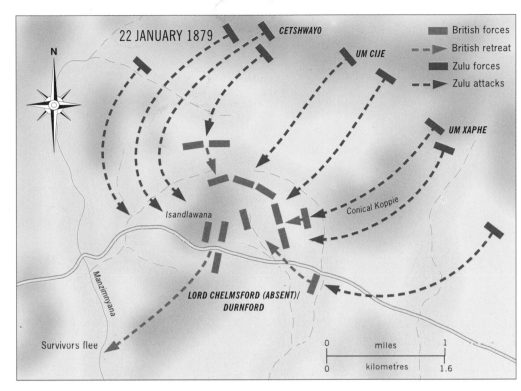

In June 1876, at the Battle of Little Bighorn, Lieutenant Colonel George A. Custer and a couple of hundred officers and men of the 7th US Cavalry were wiped out during an attack on a Sioux encampment. Custer had been advised to take machine guns before he set off, but he refused, believing in the superiority of his rifle-armed men. But the Native Americans were also armed with good rifles and they easily overwhelmed the poorly prepared American force. Three years later, an even bigger disaster awaited British soldiers, the troops who had forged an empire, in southern Africa when they were faced with native warriors armed just with spears.

LITTLE REASON FOR FEAR

The history of southern Africa shows that the arrival of Europeans and the seizure of territory by force was only new in respect of the identity of those who were responsible for the annexations; prior to the activities of the British and Dutch, many of the local peoples had suffered a similar fate at the hands of the Zulus, an aggressive people who had conquered neighbouring tribes and formed a powerful kingdom in the region. In the Transvaal, Boer settlers disputed ownership of the land with the Zulu king Cetshwayo. At first, Britain supported the claims of the Zulus, but when the British Empire assumed control of the Transvaal, it was

thought politic to defend the rights of settlers and prove the British dominated the region by challenging the most powerful native group. In December 1878, an ultimatum was presented to Cetshwayo, one which the British knew he could not accept. The next month, a British army advanced into Zululand.

Lord Chelmsford, commander of British forces in southern Africa, led some five thousand British soldiers and eight thousand native auxiliaries into Zululand on 11 January 1879. His men were supplied with the latest weapons and he had little reason to fear an enemy armed only with spears and outdated rifles. British Martini-Henry rifles could fire up to 12 shots a minute, while Gatling machine guns, rockets and artillery were even more destructive. Cetshwayo had a larger force of forty thousand warriors, but to stand any chance against a modern army it would have to close as quickly as possible with the British firing line.

Chelmsford's plan was to capture Cetshwayo's capital at Ulundi in a large pincer movement, but to do this he divided his army into three columns, weakening its overall strength. On 20 January, Chelmsford set up camp with his centre column at Isandlwana, at the base of a distinctive-looking mountain called a *nek*, after its resemblance to a saddle. Scouts told him that Zulus were gathering nearby and he decided to confront them

the effect of their rifle and artillery fire was terrifying to the Zulus. A British gunner describes the effect their explosive shells had on the Zulus, recalling that they, 'looked round wondering where the bullets [artillery shrapnel] came from, which they could not understand, the shrapnel bursting fifty yards [45m] from them and the bullets flying about their ears, it is no wonder they were startled, for to see a volley sent into their very midst and not knowing where it came from was enough to startle the bravest of them.' The effect of the British rifles was no less daunting, for although the Zulus had rifles of their own, they were far less experienced in using them and often aimed too high to make an impact.

At Isandlwana, the Zulus sheltered in the hollows at the edge of the flat grassland around the mountain. They quickly learned that when the British artillerymen stood back from their cannons to fire, they should lie low to avoid the incoming shells. While they hid from the worst of the gunfire, they made a low sound like the humming of a swarm of angry bees. Eventually, the local commanders of each group of Zulus in the centre became tired of their warriors lying down and taunted them to stand up and fight. They began to advance at a walking pace, but at a distance of about 120m (400ft) from the British line they shouted their battle cry of 'uSuthu!' and charged. The sight was terrifying. British soldiers fell back towards the camp in a panic, with the Zulus outpacing them and breaking up their formations. Confusion overtook everyone and Zulus soon surrounded every soldier, sometimes so many that not all the warriors could reach their victims.

Soldiers fought blindly and bravely, lashing out at everyone close to them. The desperate nature of the fighting was recorded by a Zulu warrior, uMhoti of the uKhandempemvu: 'I then attacked a soldier whose bayonet pierced my shield and while he was trying to extract it, I stabbed him in the shoulder. He dropped his rifle and seized me round the neck and threw me on the ground under him. My eyes felt as if they were bursting, and I was almost choked when I succeeded in grasping the spear which was still sticking in his shoulder and forced it into his vitals and he rolled over, lifeless. My body was covered with sweat and quivering terribly with the choking I had received from this brave man.'

Both sides inflicted heavy casualties. Eventually, the overwhelming numbers of Zulus secured the victory and those Britons who had survived in the camp tried to flee along the path to the river at the rear of Isandlwana. There they were brought down by Zulus who had encircled the mountain and cut off the escape route. No one was spared, even if they pleaded for mercy. More than 1,200 white soldiers and their native allies were slaughtered, with the Zulus suffering at least a thousand dead, with many more badly wounded.

Lord Chelmsford returned to his camp at nightfall, but only daylight revealed the true horror of the defeat. The British Empire, at its zenith in the popular imagination, had been militarily humiliated. The rout was avenged by the end of the year with the defeat of the Zulus, but it was a foretaste of further, challenging colonial struggles in southern Africa.

before dawn two days later. It was a fatal decision. Leaving half his men in the camp – a mere 1,700, including 700 infantry of the 24th Regiment – he advanced to battle with the other half. A far larger force of twenty thousand Zulus now moved around Chelmsford's flank and lay hidden in the undulating countryside about 8km (5 miles) from Isandlwana.

ZULU ATTACK

The Zulus launched attacks in a crescent formation, called 'the horns of the beasts', in which flanking attacks would crush the enemy. As long as the enemy, in this case the British, held the perimeter of their position they would be safe, because

Above: **A desperate attempt to save the Queen's colours after the British defeat at Isandlwana.**

Right: Advance of Zulu warriors at Isandlwana. This print by R. Caton Woodville conveys vividly a sense of the speed with which the Zulus attacked the British lines.

LIEUTENANT EDWARD HUTTON

FACING THE ZULUS

'The dark masses of men, in open order and under admirable discipline, followed each other in quick succession, running at a steady pace through the long grass. Having moved steadily round so as exactly to face our front, the larger portion of the Zulus broke into three lines, in knots and groups of from five to ten men, and advanced towards us... A knot of five or six would rise and dart through the long grass, dodging from side to side with heads down, rifles and shields kept low and out of sight. They would then suddenly sink into the long grass, and nothing but puffs of curling smoke would show their whereabouts.'
Quoted in *The Anatomy of the Zulu Army* by Ian Knight (Greenhill Books, 1995)

GEOK TEPE, 1881

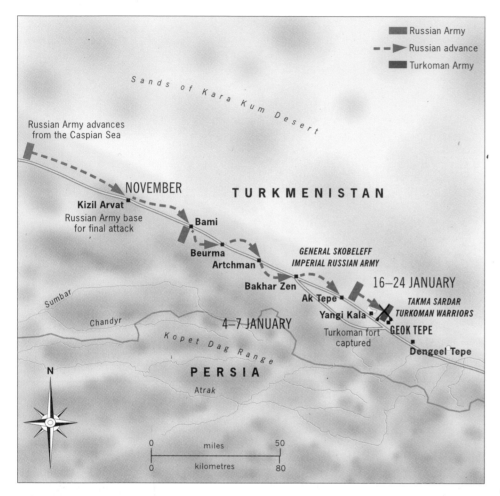

Russian Army
Russian advance
Turkoman Army

Sands of Kara Kum Desert

Russian Army advances
from the Caspian Sea

NOVEMBER

TURKMENISTAN

Kizil Arvat
Russian Army base
for final attack

Bami

Beurma
Artchman

**GENERAL SKOBELEFF
IMPERIAL RUSSIAN ARMY**

Bakhar Zen

16–24 JANUARY

Ak Tepe

**TAKMA SARDAR
TURKOMAN WARRIORS**

Yangi Kala

4–7 JANUARY

Turkoman fort
captured

GEOK TEPE

Sumbar

Chandyr

Kopet Dag Range

PERSIA

Dengeel Tepe

Atrak

N

miles	50
kilometres	80

0 ... 0

Above: **The systematic advance of the Russian army through Central Asia towards Geok Tepe in late 1880 and early 1881.**

The culmination of Russia's conquest of central Asia, the capture of Geok Tepe showed the Russian's mastery of modern warfare and their determination to break a defiant but inferior military power. The decisive victory brought Russia's borders closer to the British Empire in India and threatened to lead to further Russian dominance in Asia.

'Do not publish this,' said General Skobeleff with a smile, 'or I shall be called a barbarian by the Peace Society. But I hold it as a principle that in Asia the duration of peace is in direct proportion to the slaughter you inflict upon the enemy. The harder you hit them, the longer they will be quiet afterwards. We killed nearly 20,000 Turkmen at Geok Tepe. The survivors will not soon forget the lesson.' Skobeleff spoke these words at St Petersburg in 1882 and the savage sentiments therein still resound in central Asia more than a century later.

For centuries, Russia had suffered from the raiding campaigns of Mongols and Turks, but in the 16th century it began to reverse this process. Adopting western European weapons and strategic organization, the Russians took the first steps towards creating an empire by defeating the Tatar khanates of Kazan and Astrakhan and invading Siberia to set up trading strongholds.

The Russian Army grew in strength over the next two centuries until it reached the point in the middle of the 19th century when the government felt confident enough to challenge the Turkic states of central Asia, those which sat upon the ancient Silk Route to China. Russia wished to expand its commercial opportunities by selling manufactured goods to these people, and Russian merchants therefore had to be respected, having frequently been threatened in the past with enslavement. In addition, the Russians had recently suffered the humiliation of the Crimean War and they wished to re-establish their military prestige, especially by making the British feel uncomfortable in India.

In the 1860s, Russian expeditionary forces entered Uzbekistan and captured the key trading cities of Tashkent and Samarkand. In the 1870s the Russians turned their attention to Khiva, capital of the Turkomans, lying to the south of the Aral Sea on the border between Uzbekistan and Turkmenistan. By the end of these campaigns, the empire had been expanded by 210,000 sq km (80,000 sq miles) and the Russian frontier had advanced 500km (300 miles) southwards. The Turkomans had not been wholly beaten, however, and merely retreated into the wilderness. It was then that the Russians found themselves in trouble.

THE BLACK DESERT

Kara Kum means 'black desert', and for hundreds of kilometres its shifting dunes of sand and fossil shells, alternating with barren tracts of cracked clay, stretch across central Asia. This was once a seabed, but the sun long ago evaporated the water and turned it into dead land. It was to this desert that the Turkomans retreated. Two Russian armies went after them, in 1878 and 1879. Heatstroke, bad water and fever thinned their ranks. Even their camels died.

The first expedition gave up and returned. The second expedition, despite the death of its general, carried on to Geok Tepe, the mud-built fortress capital of the Turkomans. The Russians bombarded the fort and slaughtered men, women and children, but when they came to storm it, the maddened tribesmen repulsed them. As the Russians retreated, the Turkomans picked off the stragglers. It was a disastrous defeat for an imperial army that had all but conquered the Turkomans years earlier in 1873. Across the Northwest Frontier in India, the British wondered if the Russian threat was really all that great.

General Skobeleff liked a challenge. His contemporaries considered him a rising star. 'Though he has lived but thirty-five years,' an American attaché to the Russian Army wrote, 'his stupendous military genius is such that... history will speak of him as one of the great soldiers of this century, side by side with Napoleon, Wellington, Grant and Moltke.' A product of the Russian staff college, Skobeleff had observed the Prussians in action and was a veteran of the campaigns of the 1870s in Central Asia, being made governor of Uzbekistan. He was determined to avenge the defeat of 1879 and set about it with tenacious precision.

Skobeleff's first major step was to construct a railway track across the desert so as to maintain his communication and supply line. A telegraph was then erected alongside it. Once his supplies had been delivered across the Caspian Sea by steamboats, Skobeleff was ready, and his troops descended on central Asia in April 1880. Through negotiation, he removed some of the Turkic tribesmen who had allied themselves with the Turkomans at Geok Tepe and they supplied him with thousands of camels. Leading just a thousand men armed with a handful of artillery, machine guns and rockets, Skobeleff attempted a rapid strike against Geok Tepe. The

Below: **A Turkoman stands inside the ruins of the ramparts around Geok Tepe, stormed by the Russians in 1881.**

assault failed, but it demonstrated his determination and convinced him that the only way he could take the city was with a full-scale siege. He now called for twelve thousand men and one hundred guns to reinforce his army.

The Turkomans themselves were not lacking in daring, and their commander, Takma Sardar, personally led a raid against a detachment of Cossacks and transport horses. All of the horses were captured, including Skobeleff's personal charger. Takma Sardar was wounded in the raid and it prompted Skobeleff to write to his officers, 'An enemy whose leader can throw himself upon his adversary's bayonet deserves serious attention, and all commanders must bear this in mind and take all military precautions on all occasions... so as not to be caught unawares.' The Turkomans appealed to the British in India for help, but were ignored. Instead, they had to rely on themselves and some thirty thousand warriors who were raised from the surrounding Turkic tribes to help them.

FINAL ASSAULT

In November 1880, Skobeleff began his general advance with eight thousand soldiers. All the towns of the Tekke Turkoman peoples en route to Geok Tepe were stormed. Raids and counter-raids harassed both sides. Once within sight of the capital, Skobeleff halted his army and scouted the area closely. He deduced that the nearby fort of Yangi Kala supplied the city's water and assaulted this first, capturing it quickly.

At daybreak on 4 January 1881, the Russians pushed out from Yangi Kala to within 730m (800yds) of Geok Tepe, where they laid the first parallel siege trench. A battle then took place during which the Turkomans made a series of desperate onslaughts on the Russian line. In one spot on the Russian left flank, they left more than three hundred bodies. By 7 January, the first parallel trench was strengthened and the second had been begun 365m (400yds) away from the main ramparts.

At dusk on 9 January, a large body of Turkomans burst out from the town, overwhelmed a Russian force and took the second parallel. Skobeleff sent out reserves from Yangi Kala and the Turkoman attack faltered; the Russians had recaptured their trench and artillery, but only at the cost of many dead. However, a simultaneous attack on the Russian camp by Turkoman horsemen was driven off. Skobeleff then ordered the digging of a third parallel trench, and a bombardment of the ramparts on the east side of the city began.

On 16 January, twelve thousand Turkoman warriors made a final sortie from the town and a terrific fight took place, but the Russians were prepared for it and their artillery plus bayonet charges forced the Turkomans back into the town with heavy losses. Skobeleff now ordered his miners to go to work digging tunnels beneath the ramparts. The Turkomans prepared for the inevitable assault.

On the night of 23 January, Russian volunteers carried dynamite into the tunnel dug beneath the town's eastern rampart. The next morning, Skobeleff ordered the main assault. At 07.00 hours, Colonel Gaidaroff began the attack against the southern ramparts with 36 cannons firing in concert against the mud walls. At the same time, the mine, containing two tons of explosives, was ignited under the eastern rampart and a column of earth and smoke rose up into the air. Several hundred defenders were killed immediately. Many of the Turkomans thought it was an earthquake and began to panic, but others bravely stood their ground as the Russians surged into the breaches and fought with bayonet against sabre.

At 13.30 hours, Gaidaroff broke over the southern rampart and entered the town. Soon all three Russian columns were in the town and advancing through the narrow lanes. The last stand of the Turkomans took place around the sacred hill of Geok Tepe, from which the town took its name. Takma Sardar had tried to rally his own men after the mine explosion, but even he had to admit defeat and fled into the desert as the last of his warriors were mown down by Russian artillery. General Skobeleff then entered the city at the head of his dragoons and cossacks.

Left: Central Asian warriors hold the head of a captured Russian. The wars between the Turkic tribes and the Russians in the 19th century were ruthless in the extreme and neither side could expect mercy if captured.

Above: General Skobeleff, commander of the Russian expeditionary force that confronted the Turkomans in 1881 at their capital, Geok Tepe.

Above: **Turkoman warriors armed with antique muskets and a variety of archaic equipment, including mail armour and shields. Although lacking the more modern weaponry of the Russian Army, warriors such as these gave the Russians a very difficult time when the latter invaded their land.**

RUSSIAN INVASION OF INDIA

Despite his devastating victory over the Turkomans, General Skobeleff would not be seduced into grander schemes. The English journalist Charles Marvin tried to goad him into a sensational claim regarding India, but Skobeleff remained practical:

'I do not think it would be feasible. I do not understand military men in England writing in the Army and Navy Gazette, *which I take in and read, of a Russian invasion of India. I should not like to be commander of such an expedition. The difficulties would be enormous. To subjugate Akhal we had only 5,000 men, and needed 20,000 camels. To get that transport we had to send to Orenburg, to Khiva, to Bokhara, and to Mangishlak for animals. The trouble was enormous. To invade India we should need 150,000 troops; 60,000 to enter India with, and 90,000 to guard the communications. If 5,000 men needed 20,000 camels, what would 150,000 need! And where would we get the transport?'*
Quoted in *The Russian Advance towards India* **by Charles Marvin (London, 1882)**

The Turkomans had lost six thousand five hundred people in the defence of their city and eight thousand during the pursuit by the Russian cavalry. The total Russian losses were just over a thousand. Despite this disparity in numbers, Skobeleff's losses during this campaign were greater than those in all previous campaigns in the conquest of central Asia since 1853. That said, it was a decisive victory and the Turkomans never again achieved independence until after the collapse of the Soviet Union more than a century later. From that time on, central Asia remained part of the Russian Empire and the Communists subsequently kept it that way, despite several bloody revolts in the 1920s.

SAN JUAN HILL, 1898

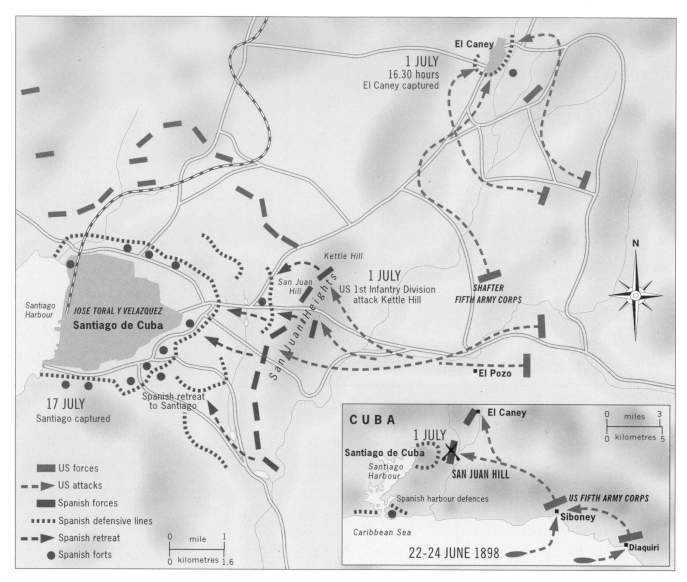

El Caney

1 JULY
16.30 hours
El Caney captured

Kettle Hill

San Juan
Hill

1 JULY
US 1st Infantry Division
attack Kettle Hill

San Juan Heights

SHAFTER
FIFTH ARMY CORPS

N

Santiago
Harbour

JOSE TORAL Y VELAZQUEZ
Santiago de Cuba

El Pozo

17 JULY
Santiago captured

Spanish retreat
to Santiago

US forces
US attacks
Spanish forces
Spanish defensive lines
Spanish retreat
Spanish forts

0   mile   1
0   kilometres   1.6

CUBA

1 JULY

El Caney

Santiago de Cuba

SAN JUAN HILL

Santiago
Harbour

Spanish harbour defences

Caribbean Sea

22–24 JUNE 1898

US FIFTH ARMY CORPS

Siboney

Diaquiri

0   miles   3
0   kilometres   5

Above: Theodore
Roosevelt as Colonel of
the 1st US Volunteer
Cavalry, known as the
'Rough Riders'.
Roosevelt was keen on a
war against Spain and
gained greatly from his
involvement in the
battle of San Juan Hill.

Above left: The US
advance on San Juan
Heights forced the
Spanish to retreat to the
Cuban capital, which
they then besieged.

The United States began its climb to global power status with the demolition, in Cuba, of a remnant of Spain's once mighty New World empire. With more enthusiasm than military skill, American soldiers scrambled to the top of a hill in the face of Spanish rifle fire. Riding a horse in the midst of the action, Theodore Roosevelt utilized the victory to become president of the United States.

The Spanish–American War and the subsequent insurrection in the Philippines, which lasted until 1902, led to the United States absorbing Spain's former possessions as its own and helping to make it an imperial power of substance. It also saw the US Army transformed from blue-clad troopers, more used to fighting on the American frontier, to khaki-clad

soldiers fighting a tropical war of attrition not dissimilar to those fought later in the Second World War and Vietnam. Events in Cuba also elevated a politician, in the person of Theodore Roosevelt, who made no secret of his imperial ambitions for his country, whether it was building the Panama Canal or intervening as a peace-keeper in the Russo-Japanese War.

In December 1897, the US battleship *Maine* was sent to Cuba, ostensibly to protect the rights of American citizens. When at anchor in the port of Havana, the *Maine* exploded and 266 people were killed. Sabotage was claimed and the incident provided the excuse the United States needed to continue its aggressive stance, urging Spain to renounce its sovereignty over Cuba. In April 1898, Spain declared war on

the United States, and the US Congress announced that hostilities had begun. In June 1898, the US Fifth Army Corps, numbering some seventeen thousand men under the command of Major General William Shafter, set sail from Tampa, Florida, and landed on the southern coast of Cuba, some 27km (17 miles) east of Santiago.

TARGET SANTIAGO

General Shafter's target was Santiago, where the Spanish fleet was moored in the bay. The US Navy wanted to attack, but first the land force had to clear the Spanish out of their coastal batteries. The main Spanish line of defence outside Santiago lay on a series of ridges, known as San Juan, and in the village of El Caney. Shafter wanted to attack El Caney first and cut Santiago's water supply. However, poor terrain prevented the attack going ahead on time and Major General Kent led his troops forward to assault San Juan's heights.

Theodore Roosevelt was an ambitious young politician who had raised his own unit of volunteer cavalry known as the Rough Riders. Unfortunately, in the confusion of embarkation, most of their horses had to be left behind and the unit had to advance mainly on foot. On 1 July 1898, the Rough Riders joined dismounted elements of the US Cavalry to begin the attack on the first objective at San Juan, which was Kettle Hill. The advance took place in extremely hot weather, so much so that Shafter was overcome and could not take command.

THE CROWDED HOUR

Confusion reigned on the battlefield and eventually Lieutenant Colonel Roosevelt took control, leading his men forward. Regular troops followed his lead and the attack began. They 'had no glittering bayonets,' wrote Richard Harding Davis, the correspondent for *The Times*, 'they were not massed in regular array. There were a few men in advance, bunched together, and

creeping up a steep, sunny hill, the tops of which roared and flashed with flame.' It was not the dashing cavalry charge Roosevelt had hoped for, but his men bravely clambered up the hill in the face of gunfire from the Spanish defenders.

In the meantime, the 1st Infantry Division climbed up the steeper slopes of San Juan Hill under effective covering fire from Gatling guns. The Spanish numbered only 4,500 against 6,600 Americans, but they were armed with the superior Mauser Model 1893, a bolt-action rifle that fired a smokeless cartridge in a five-shot magazine. It proved far better than the American Krag rifle, a fact that put an end to the latter's service in the US Army. The courage of the Americans under fire, however, unnerved the Spanish and both hills were taken, with the Spanish retreating towards Santiago.

El Caney was finally taken, too, and with it the outer defences of Santiago completely collapsed. The Americans had lost 205 killed and 1,177 wounded at San Juan Hill, but the results were dramatic. The Spanish now feared their fleet would be captured by the land advance and they sailed it out of the safety of the harbour, only to encounter the waiting US fleet, which sank every vessel without a single American craft lost. It was a calamity and it ended Spain's presence in the Caribbean. American attention now shifted to the pacification of the Philippines, potentially a much more prolonged campaign.

Roosevelt called his presence at San Juan his 'crowded hour'. The attack had been far from brilliantly executed, but Roosevelt had shown bravery under fire, leading the assault exposed on horseback while his comrades advanced on foot. The celebrity he gained from this exploit helped him considerably in his political ambitions, securing him the vice presidency. With the assassination of President McKinley in 1901, he became president and led a vigorous campaign to build up the United States's international strength.

Below: **A US infantryman of the type who fought during the war against Spain, armed with a Krag-Jorgensen rifle. The painting is by Frederic Remington.**

CAPTAIN WILLIAM 'BUCKY' O'NEIL, 1ST US VOLUNTEER CAVALRY

DEATH OF A ROUGH RIDER
In the attack on San Juan Hill, Theodore Roosevelt's Rough Riders lost 15 killed and 73 wounded. Among them was Captain William 'Bucky' O'Neill, a former sheriff and mayor from Arizona:
'The most serious loss that I and the regiment could have suffered befell just

before we charged. Bucky O'Neill was strolling up and down in front of his men, smoking a cigarette... He had a theory that an officer ought never to take cover... As O'Neill moved to and fro, his men begged him to lie down, and one of his sergeants said, "Captain, a bullet is sure to hit you." O'Neill took his cigarette

out of his mouth, and blowing a cloud of smoke, laughed and said, "Sergeant, the Spanish bullet isn't made that will kill me." A little later... as he turned on his heel a bullet struck him in the mouth and came out at the back of his head.'
Quoted from *The Rough Riders* by Theodore Roosevelt (New York, 1899)

OMDURMAN, 1898

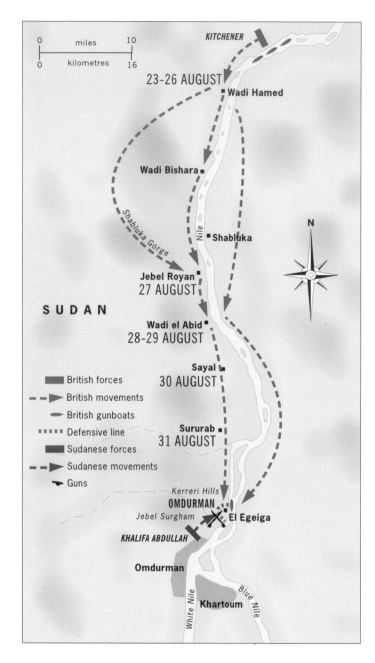

miles
0 — 10
kilometres
0 — 16

KITCHENER

23-26 AUGUST

■ Wadi Hamed

Wadi Bishara ■

Shabluka Gorge

Nile

■ Shabluka

N

Jebel Royan ■
27 AUGUST

S U D A N

Wadi el Abid ■
28-29 AUGUST

Sayal ■
30 AUGUST

■ British forces
- - -► British movements
◗ British gunboats
▪▪▪▪ Defensive line
■ Sudanese forces
- - -► Sudanese movements
⬻ Guns

Sururab ■
31 AUGUST

Kerreri Hills
OMDURMAN
Jebel Surgham ✕ ■ El Egeiga
KHALIFA ABDULLAH

Omdurman

White Nile
Blue Nile
Khartoum

The overwhelmingly decisive defeat of superior numbers of sword- and spear-wielding Sudanese rebels by British and Egyptian soldiers armed with machine guns marked a ferocious point in the evolution of military technology. It heralded a frightening new age of industrialized warfare.

The Battle of Omdurman offered a devastating demonstration of the power of Western weapons. Machine guns and rifles killed and wounded more than twenty thousand desert tribesmen, while British casualties were five hundred. The lure of such fire

power was irresistible and Western colonial powers used the machine gun and repeating rifle to maintain their vast empires in the late 19th and early 20th centuries. It was a brief reign of casualty-free supremacy, though, because during the First World War these same guns would be used to inflict the full horror of industrialized warfare against Western troops themselves.

By 1898, the British Empire was almost at its zenith. Since the defeat of Napoleon in 1815, it had swollen to include all of India, huge swathes of Africa, and numerous other territories around the world. Economically, the British Empire was past its heyday, with the United States and Germany both competing strongly against it, but it could still call upon enormous financial and logistical resources in order to send military forces anywhere in the world to protect its interests.

In addition to the earlier motivations of trade and enrichment, many of the British people had become attracted to the idea that empire was the means to spread their idea of civilization around the globe. Traders and soldiers had been followed by missionaries and civil servants. The British Empire was felt to be an agent of good in the world, taking pride in the abolition of slavery and the establishment of firm principles of law and order in previously anarchic countries. But in the opinion of others it remained a ruthless weapon for imposing British will on any peoples reluctant to welcome such 'benefits'. When Major General Kitchener sailed out to the Sudan to avenge the death of General Gordon, killed at Khartoum, he wished to turn the skull of the man responsible into an inkwell.

AVENGE GORDON

General Charles Gordon was a classic British imperial figure. Intensely religious and a fierce opponent of slavery, he was also a brilliant soldier who had led the Ever Victorious Army, made up of Chinese peasants, during the Taiping Rebellion (possibly the bloodiest war of the 19th century) in China, until he was appalled by the Chinese killing of prisoners who had fallen into his hands. In 1884, he was sent to Khartoum to supervise the evacuation of Egyptian forces from the Sudan following a ferociously successful uprising by the religiously inspired Mahdi Mohammed Ahmed of Dongola.

Mahdist forces besieged Gordon in Khartoum. Although he held out for almost a year, a relief force failed to save him, and the general, along with his garrison, was massacred. British public opinion was outraged and when the British government decided to reconquer the Sudan in the 1890s, the ghost of 'Gordon of Khartoum' loomed over the expedition. In practical terms, the British government was alarmed by the increase of

Left: **The advance of the Anglo-Egyptian force along the Nile into the Sudan where they confronted the rebels at Omdurman.**

Below: **A Sudanese warrior of the type who fought against the British and Egyptians at the battle of Omdurman.**

Above: **Although inaccurate in its representation of the British wearing red (by this time they wore khaki uniforms), this contemporary poster of the battle of Omdurman does give an impression of the tremendous fire-power delivered by the Anglo-Egyptian Army.**

French and Italian colonial interest in the region and wished to maintain an Anglo-Egyptian influence over the Nile Valley.

Major General Horatio Kitchener was put in charge of the campaign and this time he prepared the Anglo-Egyptian advance brilliantly, fully aware that only a decade earlier an entire army of ten thousand Egyptian troops under British command had been wiped out at El Obeid by Mahdist tribesmen. Moving along the River Nile with a flotilla of gunboats, Kitchener had a railway track constructed beside the river to bring up supplies. Among his artillery, he included 20 machine guns. His army – consisting half of British regular soldiers and half of British-trained Egyptian troops – proved more than

capable of dealing with the Sudanese tribesmen led by Khalifa Abdullah and Osman Digna and it defeated them in a string of conflicts over a period of two years. The Sudanese rebels now decided to concentrate their forces at Omdurman, near the Nile and just north of Khartoum.

FIRE POWER UNLEASHED

On the morning of 2 September 1898, Kitchener's army, some twenty-six thousand strong, faced forty thousand tribesmen led by Khalifa Abdullah. The previous day, British cavalry had clashed with the Sudanese, and Kitchener's troops spent the night in a fortified camp called a *zariba*, surrounded by fences of

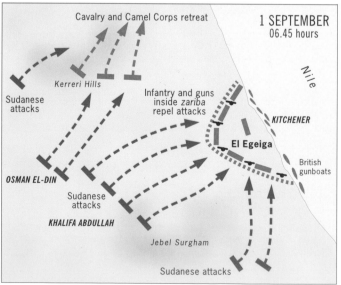

Cavalry and Camel Corps retreat

1 SEPTEMBER
06.45 hours

Kerreri Hills

Sudanese
attacks

Infantry and guns
inside *zariba*
repel attacks

Nile

KITCHENER

El Egeiga

OSMAN EL-DIN

British
gunboats

Sudanese
attacks

KHALIFA ABDULLAH

Jebel Surgham

Sudanese attacks

Above: An illustration by R. Caton Woodville of the charge of the 21st Lancers, one of the last great cavalry charges delivered by the British Army. Winston Churchill rode as one of the cavalrymen.

Left: The early-morning Sudanese assault on the British position.

Right: The Anglo-Egyptian counter-attack.

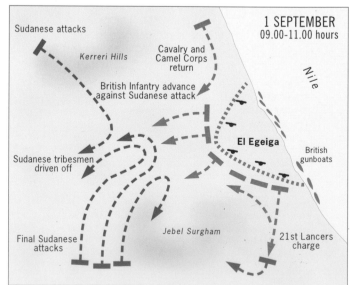

Sudanese attacks

1 SEPTEMBER
09.00–11.00 hours

Kerreri Hills

Cavalry and
Camel Corps
return

British Infantry advance
against Sudanese attack

Nile

Sudanese tribesmen
driven off

El Egeiga

British
gunboats

Final Sudanese
attacks

Jebel Surgham

21st Lancers
charge

thorn bushes. Trumpeters woke the troops at 4.30am because Kitchener expected an attack at daybreak. His cavalry rode out of the *zariba* and saw the cloud of dust that indicated the advance of Khalifa Abdullah's warriors. Winston Churchill was a young cavalryman serving in the 21st Lancers and he described the enemy's approach: 'They are advancing fast, cheering for God, his Prophet and his Holy Khalifa... they think they are going to win.' Khalifa Abdullah rode on a donkey in the middle of his army. His troops were mainly armed with swords and spears, but they did possess some rifles, which they used, albeit to little effect.

When the tribesmen came within 2,600m (8,400ft) of the British lines, Kitchener's artillery opened up, joined by the gunboats on the nearby river. They fired shells which exploded above the enemy, sending shrapnel among the warriors. 'Some burst in the air, others in their faces,' recalled Churchill. 'The white flags toppled over... yet they rose again, as other men pressed forward to die for Allah's sacred cause... It was a terrible sight, for as yet they had not hurt us at all, and it seemed an unfair advantage.'

As the warriors ran through the 1,800m- (2,000yd-) mark, volleys of British fire opened up from Lee-Metford magazine rifles. The Egyptians then joined in with their older Martini-Henry rifles, and the Maxim machine guns began their own growling fire. The best British soldiers were firing 12 rounds a minute and their guns became overheated, having to be replaced by reserve rifles. Bravely and recklessly, the Sudanese tribesmen carried on in the face of this withering fire, leaping over their dead comrades, but none of them reached the *zariba*, falling several hundred metres away. Only 60 Anglo-Egyptian casualties could be counted, as opposed to the thousands of dead and wounded tribesmen that lay before them.

BRITAIN'S LAST CAVALRY CHARGE

Kitchener moved his troops out of their *zariba* and advanced towards Omdurman. It was a gamble and a reserve force of the Khalifa's warriors duly launched two more assaults against the Anglo-Egyptian line, but both were repulsed by rifle and machine gun fire. At the same time, Kitchener launched the British Army's last regimental cavalry charge. Having achieved a victory with his technologically advanced infantry, he used his cavalry to obtain an old-fashioned end to the conflict.

The 21st Lancers urged their horses into action and raced across the desert. Little did they know, however, that the handful of tribesmen visible before them were supported by two thousand warriors hidden in a dried riverbed. When these troops leapt into view, the sensible option for the cavalry would have been to dismount and use their carbines, but the impetus of the cavalry for a charge was too great. 'Everyone expected that we were going to make a charge,' remembered Churchill. 'That was the one idea that had been in all our minds since we started from Cairo. Of course there would be a charge...' Cavalry glamour overrode military sense and the 21st Lancers charged on, their officers carrying pistols or swords, while the rest of the men held bamboo lances.

The charge took 30 seconds and the British horsemen plunged down into the ditch, where they were instantly surrounded by angry tribesmen who slashed at them with swords and spears. The impact of the charging horses knocked some warriors backwards, but others cut at the legs of the horses, trying to dismount the soldiers. Those cavalrymen who fell were immediately cut to pieces. It was a savage encounter and one-quarter of the men who entered the ditch were killed or wounded – the biggest British loss of life on the battlefield. The survivors emerged out of the ditch and rallied as the Sudanese withdrew, happy to have drawn some enemy blood. It was a brave performance, but it actually achieved very little. The battle had already been decided elsewhere by infantry fire power.

A final charge by the Sudanese cavalry drew admiration for its boldness, but its effort was also pointless. The battle was won and Kitchener marched into Omdurman. The Mahdi's tomb, a sacred shrine to the Sudanese, was wrecked by artillery fire and the holy man's body thrown into the Nile. His head was retained, but when Queen Victoria heard of Kitchener's plans for it, he was advised to bury it. British soldiers visited the steps in Khartoum where Gordon had been murdered and some suggested they inscribe on a stone step the single word 'Avenged', but they thought better of it.

Above: Major General Lord Kitchener of Khartoum, portrayed as commander of the Egyptian Army. He led the expedition sent to quell Sudanese rebels in the 1890s.

PRIVATE WADE RIX, 21ST LANCERS

LANCE AGAINST SWORD

Private Wade Rix was a troop commander in the 21st Lancers involved in the cavalry charge at Omdurman. He remembers the brutal fighting that erupted when the cavalry plunged into the dried riverbed to be surrounded by angry Sudanese warriors:

'As my horse leapt into the deep depression my lance entered the left eye of a white robed figure who had raised his double-edge sword to strike. The enormous impact and the weight of the man's body shattered the lance and I cast the broken pieces from me. I quickly drew my sword just in time as another man pointed his flintlock, I struck him down and blood splattered his white robe. Then it was parry and thrust as I spurred my horse on through the melée. Luck was with us, the horse bravely scrambled up the opposite bank of the stream bed and we were through without a scratch.'

Quoted in *The Last Charge* by Terry Brighton (Crowood Press, 1998)

TSUSHIMA, 1905

我驅逐艦速鳥朝霧冒大風雪
於旅順擊沈敵艦之圖
午時明治三十七大年
二月廿四日午前三時

Japan's dramatic defeat of the Imperial Russian Navy signified the birth of a new military power in Asia. Modern Japanese battleships were too quick and too well armed for the old-fashioned Russian vessels. It was a dire warning to the Western empires that their power might be waning.

Just as victory over France in 1870 had given Prussia supreme self-confidence in its own military system, so Japan's triumph against Russia gave it the confidence to embark on major campaigns against the Western powers in the early 20th century. Up to that point, Japan had been testing its ability as a would-be power and had suffered setbacks.

Japan was initially successful in 1895 in its war with China over Korea, but Russia had intervened to grab possessions won by the Japanese and there was little the latter could do about it. By 1902, however, Britain was as concerned as Japan about Russia's presence in Manchuria, and Japan achieved a diplomatic success by signing an alliance in which Britain pledged not to support any similar Western intervention. This left Japan free to deal with the Russian presence in Manchuria. The two agreed a joint protectorate of Korea, but in 1900, with the outbreak of the Boxer Rebellion in China, Russia moved large numbers of troops into Manchuria. 'If Manchuria becomes the property of Russia,' declared Japan's foreign minister in 1901, 'Korea itself cannot remain independent. It is a matter of life and death for Japan.'

RUSSO-JAPANESE WAR

Tension between the two nations came to a head in February 1904, when Japan attacked Port Arthur, the key naval base in Manchuria for the Russian fleet. Like Pearl Harbor several decades later, it was a surprise attack launched before any declaration of war. Russian ships were severely damaged by Japanese torpedo boats and the port was blockaded.

Japanese troops landed in northern Korea and marched to the River Yalu to provide support for the naval actions. The Russian troops were dependent on the Trans-Siberian Railway to bring reinforcements, but this would take time and Russian commanders unwisely urged an instant reaction to the invasion. Outnumbered, but perhaps trusting to their sense of superiority as a Western army, a Russian force confronted the

Above: **This Japanese print shows an old-fashioned Russian battleship being destroyed by a more modern and faster Japanese torpedo boat.**

Japanese and was completely routed at the Battle of Yalu. The Japanese pressed on further into Manchuria.

With the arrival of more Japanese soldiers, Port Arthur was put under siege. At first, the Japanese tried to storm it but suffered tremendous losses. Russian artillery and machine guns set behind trenches and barbed wire meant the fighting was reduced to a succession of suicidal attacks by the Japanese, all of which failed to break into the port. They did, however, provide a foretaste of the terrible effects of desperate charges against entrenched positions, well defended with machine guns. Eventually, after almost a year, a Japanese human wave did overwhelm a vital outpost and Port Arthur was compelled to surrender in January 1905.

Elsewhere in Manchuria, the Japanese and Russian armies clashed in bloody but indecisive battles. Tens of thousands of casualties were endured by both sides in a prequel to the fighting on the Western Front in the First World War. Even after a Japanese victory at the Battle of Mukden in March 1905, the Russian land forces refused to withdraw from Manchuria and a costly stalemate seemed set to last indefinitely.

DECISIVE SEA BATTLE

In October 1904, Russia's Baltic Fleet set sail from its home ports under the command of Admiral Rozhdestvenski. It would take over six months for it to reach Manchuria and join the war against Japan. Bizarrely, while it was still sailing through the North Sea, rumours spread of an attack by Japanese torpedo boats and the Russian ironclads responded

Above right: **The strategic positions and movements of the Russians and Japanese in Manchuria in 1904–5.**

Right: **Admiral Rozhdestvenski, commander of the Russian Baltic Fleet at the battle of Tsushima.**

Far right: **The foredeck of the Japanese battleship *Mikasa*, the largest warship in the Japanese fleet and Admiral Togo's flagship.**

by firing upon British fishing boats near Dogger Bank, killing at least seven fishermen. Britain was outraged and sent its own battleships to shadow the Russian fleet as it passed through the Bay of Biscay.

Dividing to pass through the Suez Canal and around the Cape of Good Hope, the Russian fleet reunited in the Indian Ocean and sailed on to French Indochina, where it made one more stop to prepare for battle. Sailing next for the Russian port of Vladivostok in Siberia, the Baltic Fleet approached the Tsushima Strait, between Korea and Japan. On paper, Rozhdestvenski's fleet appeared impressive, consisting of eight battleships, eight cruisers, nine destroyers and several smaller ships, but these craft were dated in their design and manned by poor-quality crew.

In contrast, just as modernizing Japan had taken the Prussian Army as its model for land forces, so its navy had been deeply influenced by the British fleet. Its ships were built to the latest British designs and featured increased armour protection of the guns, but with little extra weight added which would have affected manoeuvrability and speed. The Japanese fleet had four battleships, eight cruisers, twenty-one destroyers and sixty torpedo boats, the latter having already proved themselves in the clashes around Port Arthur. Vice-Admiral Togo's crewmen were also highly motivated and well trained.

During the afternoon of 27 May, as the Russian fleet sailed in line-ahead formation with Rozhdestvenski's flagship *Suvorov* at its head, Togo made the most of the superior speed of his ships. In a manoeuvre reminiscent of Nelson, he crossed the head of the Russian fleet and subjected it to devastating raking fire. Having crossed the 'T', he then turned his ships to sail along their flank and subject them to even more fire. The

Above: **The Russian battleship *Oslabia* of the Baltic fleet.**

Below: **Smaller and speedier Japanese boats sink a Russian battleship at Tsushima.**

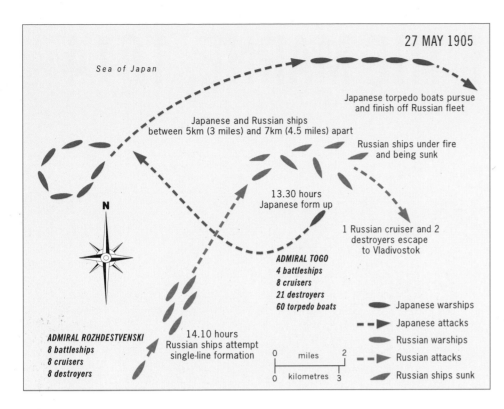

27 MAY 1905

Sea of Japan

Japanese torpedo boats pursue
and finish off Russian fleet

Japanese and Russian ships
between 5km (3 miles) and 7km (4.5 miles) apart

Russian ships under fire
and being sunk

13.30 hours
Japanese form up

1 Russian cruiser and 2
destroyers escape
to Vladivostok

N

ADMIRAL TOGO
4 battleships
8 cruisers
21 destroyers
60 torpedo boats

14.10 hours
Russian ships attempt
single-line formation

ADMIRAL ROZHDESTVENSKI
8 battleships
8 cruisers
8 destroyers

Japanese warships
Japanese attacks
Russian warships
Russian attacks
Russian ships sunk

miles 2
kilometres 3

Above: **The superior speed of the Japanese ships allowed them to cross in front of the Russian fleet to deliver devastating fire power.**

Russians were outclassed in both speed and accuracy of fire. Japanese shells rained down on their poorly armoured ships and within two hours two Russian battleships and one cruiser had been destroyed.

The battle continued until nightfall, by which time Admiral Rozhdestvenski had been wounded and three Russian battleships, including his own flagship, had been sunk. The battered Baltic Fleet now tried to withdraw, but Togo sent his smaller torpedo boats to finish off the badly damaged Russian craft, dropping mines in front of them as they tried to escape. Only one Russian cruiser and two destroyers managed to make it to Vladivostok. The rest of the fleet was either sunk or captured, with some ten thousand sailors dead or wounded. In stark contrast, the Japanese had barely lost a thousand crew and only three torpedo boats.

LESSONS LEARNED AND UNLEARNED

Tsushima brought the Russo-Japanese War to a hasty end. In September 1905 at the Treaty of Portsmouth, Russia agreed to withdraw from Port Arthur and Manchuria. Korea fell within Japan's sphere of influence and Japan also maintained a tight control over Manchuria, although it would not be until 1931 that it formally became part of Japan's overseas empire. The war, however, had an impact way beyond those immediate concerns, because it shaped the world of the early 20th century. Russia's defeat further undermined the government of the czar and a revolution followed in the same year. While that revolution failed to topple the czarist regime, it was not to be long before another swept it away completely and led to the establishment of the Soviet regime.

Japan's success meant it now viewed itself as an equal to other great powers and demanded the right to establish its own empire. The militarization of Japanese politics followed, culminating in Japan's aggressive stance in the 1930s, which led to war in the Pacific region. The defeat of Russia also encouraged other Asian nationalist factions to believe that Western imperialism could be fought and defeated. The illusion of Western military invincibility, established over two hundred years, had been shattered and this would bear fruit in both the Second World War and the period afterwards when most colonies in Asia were relinquished. The road to the war in Vietnam could be said to have some connection to events at Tsushima.

Militarily, the Russo-Japanese War revealed the dreadful devastation that could be caused by modern entrenched warfare, with neither side gaining a clear advantage despite the huge losses of men. British and German observers had seen this at first hand, but the conclusion they drew from it was that any future war needed to be won in the first few months. They believed that Russian incompetence and Japanese lack of experience had led to the stalemate, mistakes that would not be repeated by other Western armies, which would use rapid mobilization and initial manoeuvre to outwit their opponents before they could be dragged into trench warfare. In other words, such a catastrophe would not be repeated in Europe. How wrong they were.

FATHER OF A DEAD JAPANESE SOLDIER

IMPERIAL SACRIFICE

As Japan built itself into a modern state, so it used the state religion to establish a strong loyalty to the nation, one that had not existed in pre-modern Japan. Soldiers had fought for their region rather than the nation, but by 1900 this view was changing, and in order to reinforce the importance of sacrifice to the nation, the Japanese government established shrines for its war dead, the most notable being the Yasukuni Shrine in Tokyo. As the numbers of dead grew in the war against Russia, these shrines became central to the Japanese notion of dying for the emperor. One father visiting his son's memorial was recorded making the following pledge:

'I married very young and for a long time had no children. My wife finally bore a son and died. My son grew up fine and healthy. Then he joined the emperor's forces and died a manly death in southern Kyushi in a great battle. When I heard that he had died for the emperor, I cried with joy, because for my warrior son there could be no finer death.'
Quoted in *The Undefeated* by Robert Harvey (Macmillan, 1994)

FIRST BATTLE OF THE MARNE, 1914

Germany's confident advance through Belgium into France was brought to a halt by the bold and aggressive defence offered by French soldiers, some of them delivered to the battlefield in taxis from Paris. The 'Miracle of the Marne' was the beginning of the stalemate on the Western Front and the subsequent horrors of trench warfare.

By the beginning of the 20th century, the German Army was the model for all other armies to follow. It had proved its brilliance in previous campaigns against Austria and France (see Sedan, pp.36-39), and its institutions were studied by many rivals. Even Britain, which believed it had little to learn from anyone else, made a nod towards Germany by adopting its spiked *pickelhaube* helmet for some regiments.

The German Army's strength lay in its organization, from a general staff of talented commanders down to individual units full of highly trained and motivated soldiers. Preparation was a key dynamic and years were spent preparing for campaigns, with generals playing war games to assess options and under-taking reconnaissance trips to study possible battlefields. All the latest technology was embraced, including trains to deliver soldiers to the front and factories to produce the most powerful weapons then available. Germany was a nation prepared for war.

Germany's greatest weakness was its strength. Ever since the experience of Prussia and the other German states in the 1860s and 1870s, it believed that a European war was not only winnable, but could be won at little cost to the rest of society. It had little regard for the armies of Russia or France and it doubted if Britain would really want to be involved in a war on the Continent. Such was Germany's supreme confidence when it entered the First World War. When faced with the prospect of war on both Western and Eastern fronts, Germany chose to move swiftly against France in order to secure the frontiers of its industrial Rhineland region before turning east to concentrate on the potentially bigger problem of Russia. This thinking was repeated during the Second World War.

Above: **German troops advancing across a field in Champagne towards French positions on the river Marne.**

Right: First Battle of the Marne, 1914. The German opening offensive through Belgium, which was finally halted at the river Marne.

Below: British forces take up positions near Laferte during the First Battle of the Marne.

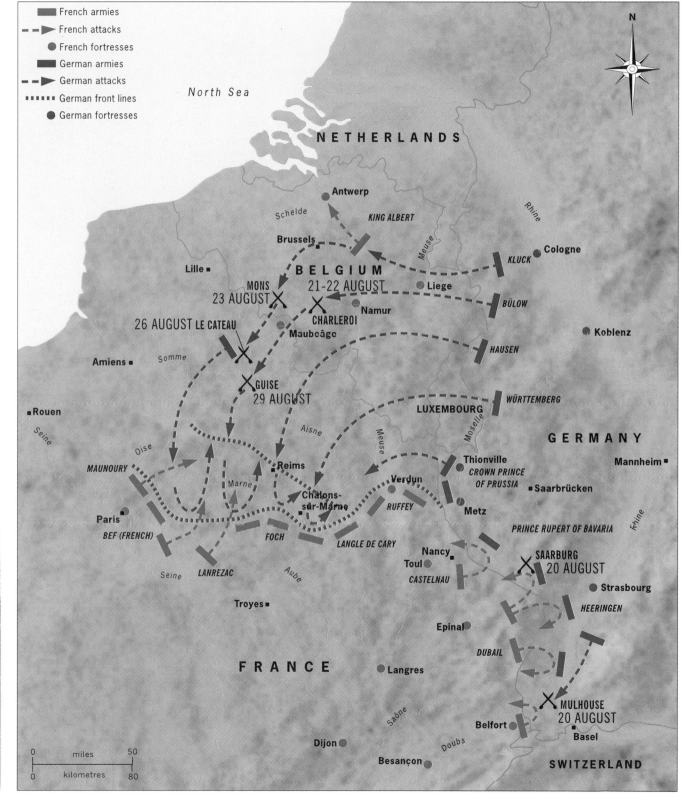

French armies
French attacks
French fortresses
German armies
German attacks
German front lines
German fortresses

North Sea

NETHERLANDS

Antwerp

Schelde

KING ALBERT

Brussels

Rhine

Meuse

KLUCK   Cologne

Lille

BELGIUM
21–22 AUGUST

Liege

MONS
23 AUGUST

CHARLEROI

Namur

BÜLOW

26 AUGUST LE CATEAU

Maubeuge

Koblenz

Somme

HAUSEN

Amiens

GUISE
29 AUGUST

Rouen

Aisne

LUXEMBOURG

WÜRTTEMBERG

Seine

Oise

Moselle

GERMANY

MAUNOURY

Marne

Reims

Meuse

Thionville

Mannheim

CROWN PRINCE
OF PRUSSIA

Verdun

Chalons-
sur-Marne

Saarbrücken

Paris

BEF (FRENCH)

FOCH

RUFFEY

Metz

LANGLE DE CARY

PRINCE RUPERT OF BAVARIA

Seine

LANREZAC

Aube

Nancy

Rhine

SAARBURG
20 AUGUST

Toul

CASTELNAU

Troyes

Strasbourg

HEERINGEN

Epinal

DUBAIL

FRANCE

Langres

MULHOUSE
20 AUGUST

Saône

Belfort

Dijon

Doubs

Basel

Besançon

SWITZERLAND

N

0   miles   50
0   kilometres   80

ATTACK, ATTACK

Because modern fire power was so effective, it was believed by many that a quick offensive was the only way to win a war. The Germans believed this wholeheartedly and their chief of the general staff, Alfred von Schlieffen, devised a plan in which German forces, using trains to reach the front, would advance rapidly through Belgium, thus avoiding France's defensive lines, and attack Paris from the north, thereby encircling French forces in northeastern France. Such swift movement would replicate the success of the Franco-Prussian War. When Schlieffen died, further continuity with 1870–71 was provided when his position was taken by Helmuth von Moltke, nephew of the Moltke who had won those victories.

Not everyone was convinced by such boldness, and Ian Hamilton, a leading general in the British Army, had come away from Manchuria (see Tsushima, pp.54–57) with a different view of modern warfare: 'Several of the commanders were led into disaster during the big manoeuvres entirely because of their blind adherence to the principle of attack at all hazards, for so afraid were they of being thrown on the defensive by even a little hesitation or delay, they did not ever seem to pause to make a thorough reconnaissance or give their cavalry time to bring them in reports.'

When war came, it took barely 24 hours for a German division to enter Luxembourg on 1 August 1914. Twelve days later, seven German armies had crossed the Rhine and were plunging through Belgium towards the French frontier. The Belgians fought fiercely, but were eventually overwhelmed by superior German fire power. France believed this assault was a diversion and stuck to its own plan of invading Alsace and Lorraine, the territory taken from it in the earlier Franco-Prussian War. Moltke had anticipated this and strengthened his own forces on the Rhine. This weakened his sweep through Belgium, but he was proved right to have done it when he soundly blocked the French advance with a devastating counter-attack. By the time the French realized this was a holding force, it was too late. The Germans were fast descending on France's northern frontier.

Meanwhile, Germany's invasion of Belgium had violated its treaty with Britain and a small British Expeditionary Force (BEF) was sent to help the Belgians. With minor support from the French, the British achieved little and joined the general retreat before the German armies. Believing the British threat had been eliminated, the Germans abandoned the Schlieffen Plan and concentrated on rolling up the French forces to their southeast. This exposed the German right flank to attack from a French army in Paris and Moltke now lost control of the situation, for he was unaware of the French force in Paris and uncertain how far south his troops had advanced. In addition, the much faster than expected mobilization of the Russians undermined his plan to concentrate on this front in isolation (see Brusilov Offensive, pp.66–69).

'MIRACLE OF THE MARNE'

General Gallieni, commander of the French forces in Paris, argued strongly that this was the time to attack the Germans. He won over both his commander in chief, General Joseph Joffre, and the British commander, Field Marshal John French. The result was the First Battle of the Marne, which began on 5 September 1914. The Germans, commanded by General von Kluck, halted and turned to face the French assault. Gallieni rushed forward further reinforcements from Paris in 600 taxicabs. A gap had opened up between the furthest German army and the one behind it, and the BEF marched into the void. The Germans faced their first crisis of the war. In fear of being enveloped by the French to their north and the British in the centre, the Germans retreated either side of the River Marne.

'Now, as the battle is joined on which the safety of our country depends,' Joffre told his men on the morning of 6 September, 'everyone must be reminded that this is no longer the time for looking back. Every effort must be made to attack and throw back the enemy. A unit which finds it impossible to advance must, regardless of cost, hold its ground and be killed on the spot rather than fall back. In the present circumstances, no failures will be tolerated.' And the cost for the French was high: some 80,000 casualties in the First Battle of the Marne. The Germans never published their casualty list, but 15,000 prisoners were taken. The British sustained 1,700 casualties.

For the first time, German soldiers were exposed to the full fire power of both the British and the French. Germany's aggressive strategy was successful when opposed by weaker troops, but when it was confronted by an equally resolute and powerful force, it found itself caught in a destructive slogging match (the search for an alternative lay at the heart of military developments from 1916 on). This nightmare was to haunt the German Army through both world wars and eventually proved its downfall, but only after the sacrifice of hundreds of thousands of soldiers.

The Germans retreated to the River Aisne, where they dug

Below: French stretcher-bearers carry away the wounded from the Battle of the Marne.

Above: French cavalry cross the Marne in pursuit of the Germans on a pontoon bridge built in less than three hours.

G.7102

LIEUTENANT JOHANNES NIEMANN, SAXON REGIMENT

BATTLEFIELD FOOTBALL

By Christmas 1914 a stalemate existed on the Western Front, but the full horror of what lay ahead was yet to impinge on the morale of the soldiers on both sides. As they sat in their trenches, feelings of seasonal goodwill took over and an unofficial truce was made in which both sides emerged from their positions to shake hands and exchange souvenirs. Lieutenant Johannes Niemann, in a Saxon regiment, described the two sides playing an impromptu football match: *'Suddenly a Tommy came with a football, kicking already and making fun, and then began a football match. We marked the goals with our caps. Teams were quickly established for a match on the frozen mud, and the Fritzes beat the Tommies 3-2.'*

Quoted in *Christmas Truce* by Malcolm Brown and Shirley Seaton (Macmillan, 1994)

---

trenches and set up defensive positions. As the Allies advanced towards them, the future of warfare on the Western Front became clear. 'With a sinking heart I realised that our extended line made an excellent target,' recalled Corporal John Lucy of the Royal Irish Rifles as they crossed the Aisne. 'The Germans were waiting for us, holding fire. As we cleared the crest, a murderous hail of missiles raked us from an invisible enemy. The line staggered under this ferocious smash of machine-gun, rifle- and shell-fire, and I would say that fully half of our men fell over forward on their faces, either killed or wounded. Some turned over onto their backs, and others churned about convulsively. With hot throats the remainder of us went on, as there is no halt in the attack without an order.'

The Allies failed to push the Germans beyond the Aisne but the Schlieffen Plan was over. The German advance had been halted. Moltke was seen weeping at a staff dinner and was compelled to send out a junior officer called Hentsch to communicate with his generals. It was Hentsch who oversaw the German withdrawal. Moltke was then relieved of his command on 14 September and replaced by Erich von Falkenhayn.

The French hailed the battle as the 'Miracle of the Marne', but sadly they were unable to maintain the impetus to exploit further the German withdrawal. Defensive lines were drawn and the trench warfare of the Western Front took form. A breakthrough was sought elsewhere and military attention shifted northwards to Flanders (see Ypres, pp.74–77).

GALLIPOLI, 1915

Left: Anzac troops landing at Gallipoli in April 1915. Because ship commanders were wary of reefs, the landings had to take place during the day, rather than under cover of night, making the troops vulnerable to Turkish fire.

Below: An Australian soldier in a trench using a periscope to snipe at the enemy.

An opportunity to open up a new front in southeastern Europe was squandered by the British underestimating their Turkish adversaries. Allied troops stormed ashore, only to be met by stiff resistance from enemy soldiers well positioned in the harsh landscape. The agony of Gallipoli discouraged further attempts at amphibious offensives.

With Allied and German armies entrenched opposite each other from the North Sea all the way to Switzerland, there seemed little opportunity of a breakthrough in western Europe in 1915. The more imaginative military war-planners considered opening a new front, and the First Lord of the Admiralty, Winston Churchill, joined with others to suggest employing the Royal Navy in an amphibious assault on Germany's weakest ally, Ottoman Turkey.

By forcing its way through the Dardanelles, the Royal Navy could sail into the Sea of Marmara and capture Constantinople (now Istanbul). Turkey having been eliminated from the war with this one stroke, Russia would then be free to transfer troops from its southern border to reinforce its armies fighting the Germans. Neutral nations such as Romania, Bulgaria and Greece might also be encouraged to join the war against Austria, thus shifting the balance of numbers against the Central Powers.

In retrospect, Churchill has been much criticized for his support of this plan because it turned out so badly. The failures, however, were not strategic but tactical, although the British were guilty of one major fault – they badly underestimated the fighting skills of the Turks.

STRUCK BY MINES

At first, the plan went very well. Sixteen British and French battleships sailed towards the Dardanelles on 19 February. For a month, the Allies bombarded the Turkish batteries on either side of the entrance to the strait and advanced into the Dardanelles with minesweepers leading the way. The Turkish threat had not, however, been eliminated and on 18 March mines sank three battleships and disabled three others. It was a disaster that completely changed the nature of the campaign. The Allied fleet withdrew and it was decided that an expeditionary force would have to land on the Gallipoli Peninsula to secure the safe passage of the navy through the strait.

The troops were brought from Egypt and consisted of British, French, Australians and New Zealanders, the latter two known as the Anzacs. Under the command of General Ian Hamilton, the force amounted to 78,000 men. It has become a cliché to condemn British generals of this period as being out of touch, implying that their incompetence contributed to the death of many of their soldiers, but in most instances this is untrue. Hamilton was a highly regarded soldier who had experience of warfare in South Africa and Manchuria. He knew the nature of modern warfare and that to undertake and execute an opposed amphibious landing was a great challenge.

Unfortunately, it took a month to equip and transport Hamilton's soldiers and the Turks used this opportunity to prepare their defensive positions. Commanded by a German, General Liman von Sanders, the Turks numbered sixty thousand and were well equipped with artillery and machine guns.

HITTING THE BEACHES

Hamilton was aware he was taking risks, because his soldiers were untrained in amphibious attacks and knew little of the land they were attempting to seize. Two main assaults were planned for 25 April: one at Cape Helles on the tip of the peninsula, the other at Ari Burnu, on the west side of the peninsula. Two other attacks were intended as diversions.

There was a sense of confidence, even levity, among the troops who sailed towards Gallipoli, as recorded by Captain Talbot, who landed with the 1st Battalion of the Lancashire Fusiliers: 'I can tell you the sight of the peninsula being shelled by the fleet was grand with the sun rising above it all. We kicked off right outside the supporting ships and went in fairly fast until we were right under the cannon's mouth. The noise of the 10in [guns] were deafening. We never got a shot fired at us till the oars were tossed and then they started in earnest. The first bullet that struck the water brought up loud cheers from our men... I don't think the men realised how hot the fire was, they were still laughing and joking till the end.' The confidence the soldiers had in their navy was misplaced. Not only did their big guns fail to silence Turkish resistance, but the navy had warned the army about the presence of strong currents and reefs. The result was that the British troops had to land at the five beaches at Cape Helles in daylight, making themselves sitting targets for Turkish gunners, who inflicted a deadly fire on three of the landings. Despite this, and submerged barbed wire that entangled them as they waded ashore, the brave soldiers pressed on, with the 1st Lancashire Fusiliers winning six Victoria Crosses by the end of the day. Coming off the beach, elements of the 29th Division captured a hill called Achi Baba. If they had followed through,

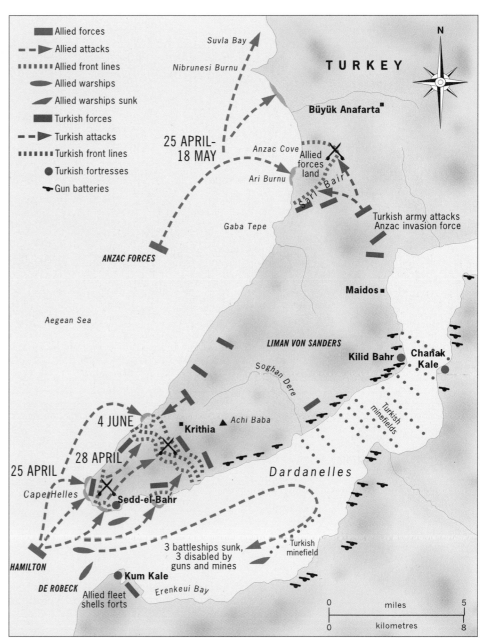

Above: **The Allied landings on Gallipoli peninsula during the attempt to secure passage through the Dardanelles.**

they might have overturned the Turkish lines, but lacking firm orders from commanders out at sea, they paused for tea – sufficient time to allow the Turks to reoccupy the high ground and surround the beach-heads with trenches. Any initial advantage had been lost and, ironically, the troops faced the same grinding attrition they would have endured on the Western Front.

Further north, on the west side of the peninsula, the Anzacs missed their original landing place, and assembled at a place which became known as Anzac Cove. This spared them the

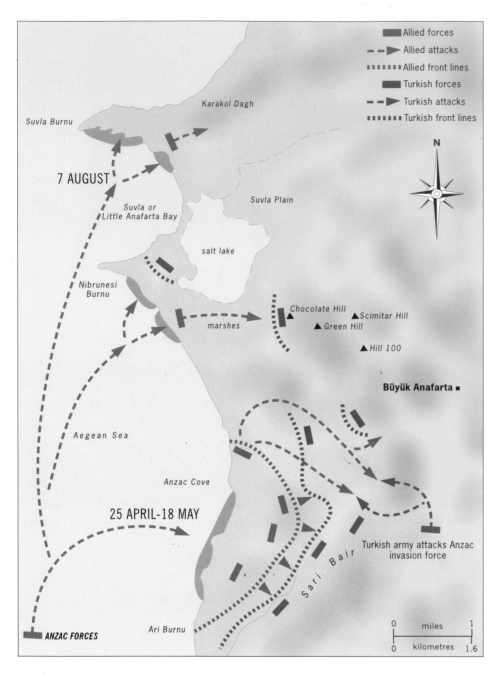

Map labels

Karakol Dagh

Suvla Burnu

7 AUGUST

Suvla or
Little Anafarta Bay

Suvla Plain

salt lake

Nibrunesi
Burnu

Chocolate Hill ▲ Scimitar Hill
marshes ▲ Green Hill

▲ Hill 100

Büyük Anafarta ■

Aegean Sea

Anzac Cove

25 APRIL–18 MAY

Turkish army attacks Anzac
invasion force

Sari Bair

Ari Burnu

ANZAC FORCES

Legend

▬▬	Allied forces
▬ ▬ ▶	Allied attacks
▪▪▪▪▪	Allied front lines
▬▬	Turkish forces
▬ ▬ ▶	Turkish attacks
▪▪▪▪▪	Turkish front lines

N

0   miles   1

0   kilometres   1.6

---

stronger coastal defences at Gaba Tepe and they advanced quickly up the slopes of the beaches, heading for the high ground of Sari Bair. Unfortunately for them, the Turkish defenders in the area were commanded by a highly efficient officer called Mustafa Kemal. He would later be known as Kemal Atatürk and would lead a brilliant campaign to become founding president of the Republic of Turkey. By chance, Kemal was mobilizing his troops for an anti-landing exercise and occupied the whole of the high ground before the Anzacs could reach it. He then launched a bitter counter-attack that forced them back on to the beach, inflicting some five thousand casualties.

The situation was desperate and Hamilton received the following message about the Anzacs: '[they] are thoroughly demoralised by shrapnel fire to which they have been subjected all day after exhaustion and gallant work in the morning... If troops are subjected to shell fire again tomorrow morning there is likely to be a fiasco, as I have no fresh troops with which to replace those in the firing line.' Hamilton's response was uncompromising: 'there is nothing for it but to dig yourselves right in and stick it out... You have got through the difficult business, now you have only to dig, dig, dig, until you are safe.' On this point, Hamilton was wrong: there was much more difficult business to come. The Allies could make no headway out of their beach-heads and, in addition to the obvious dangers posed by the Turks, had to endure three months of blazing hot sand and raging dysentery.

SUVLA BAY

Hamilton was blunt about his failure: 'I might represent the battle as a victory, as the enemy's advanced positions were driven in, but actually the result has been a failure, as the main object remains unachieved. The fortifications and their machine-guns were too scientific and too strongly held to be rushed, although I had every available man in today. Our troops have done all that flesh and blood can do against semi-permanent works and they are not able to carry them.' But the British government would not give in. Some 22,000 more shells were sent to Gallipoli and in August three further British divisions arrived.

Above left: **The major landings of the Anzac troops at Gallipoli. Despite good landings the Anzac troops could not break the Turkish defensive lines further inland.**

LIEUTENANT JOHN HARDING, LONDON REGIMENT

AWFUL DISCOVERY

Many of the new troops landing at Gallipoli in August 1915 were bewildered by the strange terrain. It didn't help that they had to advance at night. John Harding, a lieutenant in the London Regiment, recalls the confusion:
'We were told that we were going to do a night attack. We set off in the dark and marched in column halting at frequent intervals... We seemed to go about a 100 yards at a time and then halt –my recollection is that it was a very, very slow process. We were being guided, so we had no idea where we were going. We went on, I don't know how long and then we were told to halt and lie down. So I, with my platoon, lay down in a little dip in the ground amongst the hills, and there was an awful stench and we'd no idea where it came from. However we got to sleep, but when we woke up in the morning at daylight we saw that we'd been lying alongside four or five dead Turks. Well then we were told to go back to the beach.'
Quoted in *Defeat at Gallipoli* by Nigel Steel and Peter Hart (Macmillan, 1994)

Top: **British troops advance at Gallipoli.**

Above: **This painting by Ellis Silas depicts Australian troops at Gallipoli.**

A major breakout was conceived and the high ground of Sari Bair above 'Anzac Cove' was targeted in order to split the defences of the peninsula. Under cover of night on 6-7 August, without naval support, the new divisions landed at Suvla Bay to the north of the Anzacs. These troops were unused to the conditions of the peninsula, however, and it was left to the Anzacs to make the main assault on Sari Bair. The ground above the cove is rough terrain, comprising a succession of ridges and hollows. In the darkness, the Anzacs lost their way and encountered heavy hand-to-hand fighting with the Turks. The new troops were luckier, meeting little resistance to their landing at Suvla, but once again their initial successes outstripped their orders and as they waited, the Turks recaptured the high ground with reinforcements. Kemal launched a series of counter-attacks which threw the Allies back on to the beaches with losses of thirty thousand men.

Hamilton was eventually relieved of his command in October and a new general recommended the evacuation of all Allied troops from the peninsula. Back home in London, Hamilton and Churchill became the scapegoats for what was termed a scandalous waste of effort. In reality, given greater resources and better preparation, the opposed amphibious assault could have worked, and similar assaults in later wars would work, but Gallipoli could only ever be a sideshow to the main event on the Western Front and failed within the terms set for it. The evacuation of troops from Gallipoli was carried out efficiently with little further loss of life, but it would be a long time before another amphibious campaign would again be suggested by a British commander.

THE BRUSILOV OFFENSIVE, 1916

Russia's dramatic defeat of German forces during the Brusilov Offensive demonstrated how a fast-moving offensive ought to be fought. Meticulously planned and well executed, the Russian advance overwhelmed the Germans. Sadly, the brilliance of its beginning was not matched by decisiveness at its ending and the victory failed to change the final outcome of the war on the Eastern Front.

Russia had suffered a humiliating defeat against the Japanese in 1904–05 (see Tsushima, pp.54–7), which had provoked a revolution and culminated in the czar being forced to accept a constitutional government. Booming industrialization followed and the Russian government hastily equipped its forces with the latest weaponry. In 1907, Russia entered into an alliance with France and Britain (the Triple Entente). Russia could call on an estimated manpower of 25 million and its size greatly concerned both Germany and Austria-Hungary, its main rivals in central Europe. However, Russian communications were poor and Germany believed Russia's mobilization would be so slow that there would be sufficient time to defeat France in the west, before Germany's forces would need to turn to deal with the situation in the east.

When war broke out in eastern Europe in 1914, Russia surprised everyone by mobilizing much faster than expected.

Right: **The Russian offensive in Poland in 1916. Initially successful, it failed to break German resolve.**

Above: **German soldiers and a machine gun crew hold an improvised position on the Eastern Front of Poland at the beginning of the war.**

Right: **Russian soldiers man a trench in Poland. After the initial movement of the war, the Eastern Front became a series of trench systems just as in the west, with both sides searching for a breakthrough.**

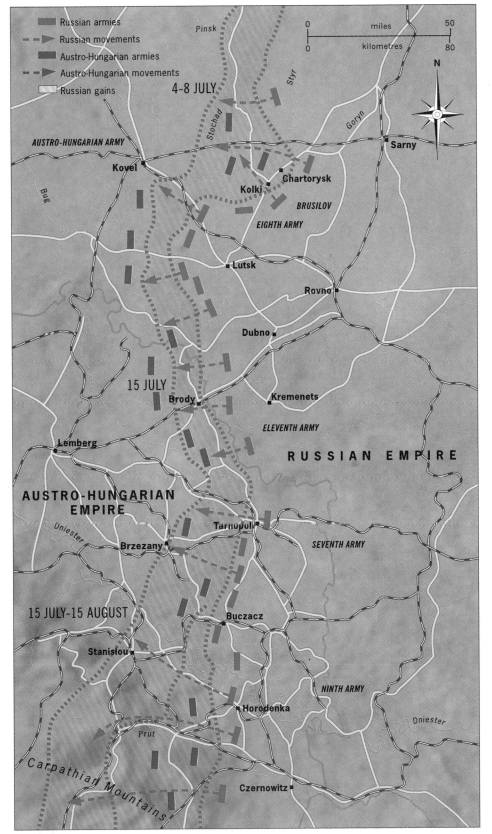

Russian armies invaded East Prussia and Galicia, having the immediate effect of panicking Moltke into shifting troops from the west and thus blunting his attack there (see the First Battle of the Marne, pp.58–61). The Germans struck back, however, and gained a victory at the Battle of Tannenberg. Hindenburg and Ludendorff were now in charge of the fighting on the Eastern Front and the Russians suffered a series of defeats in Poland.

The Russians were more successful against the Austro-Hungarians, but by 1915 all sides had become bogged down in trench warfare, with the Russian Army having lost more than a million men. Germany and Austria-Hungary continued their offensives and by the end of the year, Russian armies were in retreat from Galicia and Poland. The Russian Army was in crisis and the czar stepped in to take command of the military. Munitions production was stepped up and by the beginning of 1916 the Russian Army was in better shape. The German assault at Verdun was putting enormous pressure on the French and Russia decided to help its ally by launching an offensive north of Lake Naroch in March 1916. The attack failed, with heavy losses, and attention now turned to one of the more competent of Russia's commanders, General Alexei Brusilov.

METICULOUSLY PLANNED

Brusilov was an aristocratic cavalry officer who had been put in charge of the Eighth Army. His imagination, combined with attention to detail, made his command one of the more successful elements of the Russian forces in 1915. Placed in overall command of the Russian armies on the southwestern frontier in 1916, he decided against the traditional Russian attrition tactics of swamping the enemy with human waves and chose instead to use surprise and tactical efficiency. He reassured his superiors by suggesting an attack along the entire Austro-Hungarian front line, but in his organization he meticulously planned four simultaneous attacks by four armies under his command (the Seventh, Eighth, Ninth and Eleventh armies).

Brusilov had taken note of developments on the Western Front and employed reconnaissance aircraft to provide him with information. He then dug assault trenches towards the Austro-Hungarian positions. Surprise was all important and his plans were successfully concealed from the enemy. The Austro-Hungarians failed to disturb his preparations, believing their own trench lines were invulnerable. Brusilov's forces of 1,700 guns and 600,000 men barely outnumbered the enemy's 500,000, and this fact also reassured the Austro-Hungarians that the Russians were not planning an attack, because when they did, they tended to swamp the area with soldiers.

Brusilov began his offensive on 4 June 1916 with accurate

artillery bombardments, based on the information obtained by his aircraft. This was then followed through by the attacks of the four Russian armies, which stretched the Austro-Hungarian reserves. Brusilov's own Eighth Army made a dramatic assault south of the Pripet Marshes at Lutsk, destroying the Austro-

Hungarian Fourth Army and capturing the town in only two days. Further south, the Eleventh Army overwhelmed the Austro-Hungarian First and Second armies and broke through the enemy line at Sopanov. South of this was the Ninth Army, which captured the Austro-Hungarian salient at Okna and took eleven thousand prisoners.

An Austro-Hungarian relief force, the Seventh Army, was forced to retreat before Russia's Ninth Army, eventually splitting into two as its transport system fell apart, with the loss of some one hundred thousand men. By the middle of June, the Austro-Hungarian forces in Galicia had virtually collapsed and the Russian high command was awestruck by Brusilov's success. In all, Brusilov's soldiers captured some two hundred thousand prisoners and over seven hundred guns. They had advanced over 80km (50 miles), but he lacked the reinforcements to pursue the enemy further and Brusilov had to call a halt to the offensive. His own losses amounted to fifty thousand men.

DEFEAT OUT OF VICTORY

Panic gripped the German and Austro-Hungarian commands. The Germans could spare no extra troops because of the offensive on the Somme and the Austro-Hungarians were committed to their campaign in Italy. Fortunately for them, the excitement of Brusilov's success meant the Russian high command now interfered on a daily basis, making Brusilov's life more difficult and complex by demanding even greater victories. An Austro-German counter-attack on 20 June led by Marwitz failed to dent the Russian line and a further forty thousand men were lost.

Brusilov finally received a further 12 divisions and used these to resume his offensive on 23 June. The Russian Ninth and Eleventh armies pushed the Austro-Hungarians back further, but although the Germans withdrew as well, they did so in good order. Falkenhayn gathered German reinforcements from the Western Front and the Austro-Hungarians called off their Trentino Offensive. Using superior lines of communication, especially their railways, by the middle of July the Germans and Austro-Hungarians had begun to change the balance of power. The Germans seized upon the weaker northern flank of the Russian advance and pressed home their counter-attacks. In the south, Russian troops got as far as the Carpathian Mountains but were let down by poor supply lines. In the north, the Germans managed to stop the Russian advance and by September Brusilov's victorious offensive had ground to a halt.

The fallout from Brusilov's brilliant battle was manifold. For the Germans, it had dented their manpower on the Western Front and Falkenhayn was forced to resign as supreme German commander. For Austria-Hungary the repercussions were even worse, for its army had virtually collapsed as an autonomous power and its troops had been swallowed up into the German war machine. The Austro-Hungarian Empire would not survive the peace process following the war. Romania had been encouraged to join the war on the side of the Allies, but its participation proved unimportant.

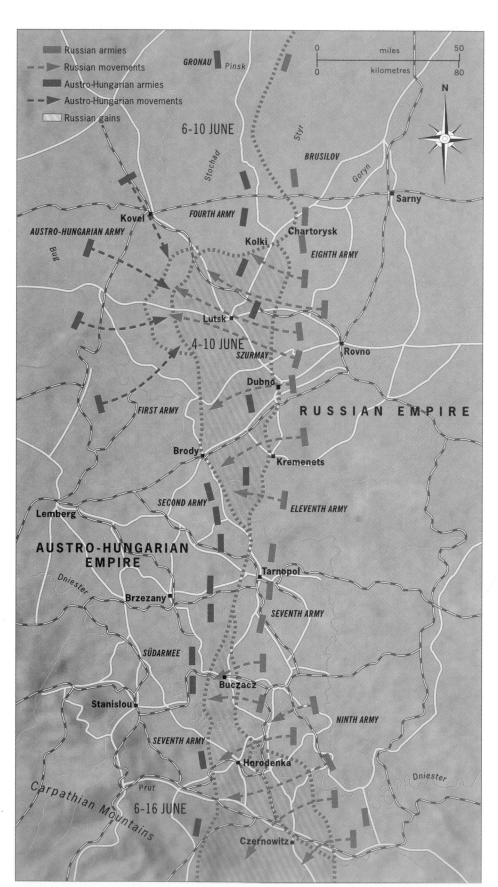

Below: **The final stages of the Brusilov Offensive.**

For Russia, the end result, somewhat surprisingly perhaps, was catastrophic. Although a great victory that had impressed its allies, the Brusilov Offensive had sapped the Russian Army of its finest soldiers; by the end of the offensive its casualties numbered about five hundred thousand, almost equal to those of its enemies. In addition, Russia could not maintain the supplies of food and weapons needed to keep its army going. It was, in effect, a brilliant final flare of dynamism that showed what might have been possible if Russia had possessed a more efficient military system.

The Russian people were fed up with war by this time and by February 1917 revolutionary pressures had built up to the extent where the Russian Army had become virtually paralysed. Soldiers refused to obey their officers and disappeared from the front. The Germans assisted this process by sending Lenin and other exiled revolutionaries back into Russia. By November 1917, the Bolsheviks were in power and they declared an armistice on 16 December 1917. The czar was then executed and the communist regime began its hold on power. And what of Brusilov – the most brilliant of Russia's wartime commanders? Although he joined the Red Army as a general in 1920, and helped to establish the Soviet army, he managed to avoid becoming involved in the deadly struggle of the civil war that was to follow.

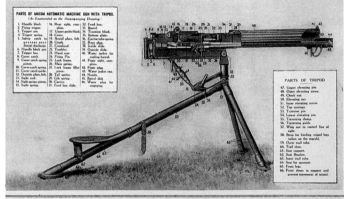

Above: **Boy soldiers in the Russian Army during the latter stages of the First World War, when repeated costly offensives had depleted the manpower reserves.**

Above right: **A Maxim machine gun. The First World War was dominated by machine guns which made it difficult to assault entrenched positions.**

GENERAL DENIKEN

REVOLUTIONARY ARMY

With the failure of the Brusilov Offensive to secure an end to the war on the Eastern Front, the Russian Army became prey to talk of revolution and soldiers began to drift away from it. Russian general Deniken described the situation he saw in early 1917:

'The parapet is crumbling away. No one troubles to repair it; no one feels inclined to do so, and there are not enough men in the company. There is a large number of deserters; more than fifty have been allowed to go. Old soldiers have been demobilised, others have gone on leave with the arbitrary permission of the [revolutionary] Committee. Others, again, have been elected members of numerous committees, or gone away as delegates. Finally, by threats and violence, the soldiers have so terrorised the regimental surgeons that the latter have been issuing medical certificates even to the thoroughly fit.'

Quoted in *The Eastern Front 1914–18* by Alan Clark (BPC, 1971)

SOMME, 1916

Symbolic of the carnage of the Western Front, the catastrophe of the Battle of the Somme forced tactical changes among British commanders. Artillery and machine guns were so dominant that it made it difficult for infantry to press home any meaningful advances. The Somme was a turning point in the conduct of the First World War, with many commanders applying the lessons learned from the awful mistakes made there.

The first day of the Battle of the Somme produced the greatest losses in a single day ever sustained by the British Army in its history – some 60,000 casualties, of whom 19,000 were dead. When the dreadful news reached the British home front, it compounded the revulsion growing among the British people at the unprecedented sacrifices being made in the war. The worthiness of the cause was not seriously doubted at the time – the issues for which the war was being fought were readily understood and were supported by the majority of the population – but in Britain in the years after the war, the losses on the Somme came to epitomize a tragedy which it was felt should never be allowed to happen again. Public interest was responsible for the raising of war memorials throughout the country; the glamour of war was gone for good and would never return.

Myths have also grown up around the first day of the Somme: images of khaki-clad men advancing shoulder to shoulder across no man's land to their certain deaths is matched in the popular imagination with the conviction that the old-fashioned generals who led them there were culpable. In actual fact, very few unit records of the day recall soldiers moving in such a suicidal manner; most of them advanced sensibly in open order, making the most use of cover. Also, the generals themselves had warned the politicians early on that a European war on this scale – so unlike anything else fought over the previous century – would be very costly indeed in lives. There were no illusions about this, only a lack of experience in how to fight such a war.

Above: **A massive mine explosion signals the beginning of the British assault at the Somme. Although locally devastating, such explosions also served as warnings of attack.**

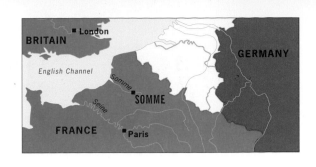

What did cause enormous casualties on the first day of the battle was the failure of British artillery to prepare the battlefield. This was noted by the generals, and new assault tactics were developed which transformed the fighting in the second half of the war. The first half of the war on the Western Front had been largely improvised while generals and soldiers struggled to come to terms with modern industrialized warfare, but by 1917 and 1918 a more professional army was emerging and victory was its prize. The Somme was therefore a turning point in the Allies' understanding of how the war should be fought.

Below: **The British advance of 1 July 1916 and the subsequent German counter-attack.**

Map

ALLENBY THIRD ARMY

Gommecourt

Achiet-le-Petit

British attacks all repulsed

Bapaume

1 JULY 07.30 hours

Ancre

Grandcourt

BELOW SECOND ARMY

Thiepval

Poziéres

Bazentin-le-Petit

Morval

Longueval

12 JULY

Mametz Wood

Combles

Fricourt Wood

Montauban

Albert

Mametz

Mariecourt

14 JULY

N

RAWLINSON FOURTH ARMY

FAYOLLE SIXTH ARMY

1 JULY

Cléry-sur-Somme

Frise

Somme

Herbécourt

0 miles 2

0 kilometres 3

Allied forces
Allied attacks
Allied gains
German forces
German attacks
German front line

THAT TERRIBLE DAY

The Battle of the Somme was fought to relieve pressure on the French, whose sacrifices in the first two years of the war had given the Allies the vital breathing space they needed to halt the German advance. A major assault on Verdun, which began in February 1916, pushed the French to their limit and drained them of manpower. A British push to the north would help to divert German troops from Verdun. General Haig, commander of the British, hoped for significant French assistance with this diversionary attack, but such were the demands of Verdun that the Somme became a largely British and Commonwealth offensive, with the French element contributing one army out of the four participating.

The beginning of the battle on 1 July was preceded by a massive artillery bombardment in which 1.7 million rounds were fired at the German lines. The British Fourth Army was stretched between Gommecourt in the north and Maricourt in the south, with the River Somme running along its southern flank. In the hour before the attack, some 224,221 shells rained down on the Germans positioned on the high ground to the east that was the Allies' target. The barrage was intended to wipe out any German resistance, allowing the British infantry to advance over the cratered land and claim the enemy trenches. This expectation was seriously flawed.

Most of the artillery shells did not possess the explosive power to penetrate the concrete shelters in which the Germans hid. The shells simply churned up the earth, deadening the impact of any other shells and failing even to cut the barbed wire in front of the trenches. Pilots who flew over the battlefield saw only the devastated landscape and gave false assurances that the bombardment had achieved its aim, while down on the ground reconnaissance reports that the wire had not been cut were ignored by senior officers. Counter-battery bombardments had failed to silence the German artillery, which was now fully alerted to an attack. Haig knew little of this and yet has borne the brunt of the criticism levelled since.

NEW RECRUITS

Most of the British soldiers at the Somme were new recruits and had had little time to be trained in tactics more complicated than climbing over the parapet and advancing on the enemy. This they did with great bravery, but as they advanced across no man's land, the Germans emerged out of their shelters and fired their machine guns at them. It was a bloodbath, with British losses reaching 30,000 in the first hour of the attack.

Even the use of mines was not wholly successful. Tunnels had been dug beneath the German line and filled with high

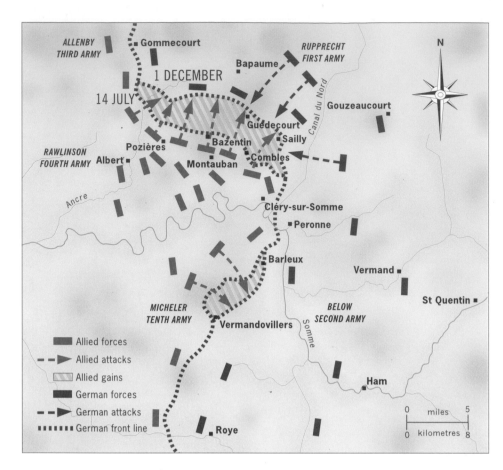

The later stages of the Battle of the Somme in the second half of 1916, revealing few gains for much blood spilled.

the enemy line, bringing to bear a barrage five times more powerful than that on the first day of the Somme on a 5,500-m (6,000-yd) front. The results were instant, completely wrecking the German second line and allowing the infantry rapidly to break the line between Bazentin-le-Petit and Longueval. Unfortunately, however, Rawlinson could not bring cavalry forward to exploit the gap and the advance bogged down.

Elsewhere, bitter fighting saw the Allies take other German positions, but at tremendous cost: the Australians and New Zealanders who captured Pozières sustained 23,000 casualties. The Germans were ordered to counter-attack whenever they lost a position and this cost them dearly as well. 'Among the living lay the dead,' recalled Lieutenant Ernst Junger. 'As we dug ourselves in we found them in layers stacked one on top of the other. One company after another had been shoved into the drum-fire and steadily annihilated.' The weather added to the misery, with heavy rain transforming the battlefield into a sea of mud. Too many small-scale assaults failed to break the stalemate and stem the lengthening casualty lists, with politicians consequently pressuring Haig to act decisively.

It was now that Haig turned to new technology, shipped to France under the guise of 'water tanks' – from which the tank was to derive its name. Haig was immediately impressed by the new armoured, tracked, gun platforms and he wanted them ready more quickly than could be the case. Manufacturing

Above: **The later stages of the Battle of the Somme in the second half of 1916, revealing few gains for much blood spilled.**

Right: **A lucky British soldier with a bandaged head, showing the hole made by shrapnel in his helmet. His rifle is covered to protect it from the rain and mud of the Western Front.**

explosives. When the mines were detonated at 'zero hour', they had the effect of small earthquakes and the Germans immediately above them were obliterated. The many who were not killed saw it simply as a warning of the attack. 'This explosion,' states one German report, 'was a signal of the infantry attack, and everyone got ready and stood on the lower steps of the dug-outs, rifles in hand, waiting for the bombardment to lift. In a few minutes the shelling ceased, and we rushed up the steps and out into the crater positions. Ahead of us wave after wave of British troops were crawling out of their trenches, and coming forward towards us at a walk, their bayonets glistening in the sun.'

Despite the failure to silence German opposition and the subsequent heavy casualties, the first day of the offensive was not completely without achievement. In the southern part of the central sector, several German positions were captured, including Montauban, Mametz and Grandcourt. Elsewhere, however, the attacks had been blunted.

ADVANCE BOGGED DOWN

The shock of the losses on the first day did not dissuade Haig from continuing what was to become a five-month-long battle. However, some lessons were quickly learned and General Rawlinson gave an indication of the employment of more efficient tactics with his assault on 14 July on the second line of German defences at Longueval Ridge. His troops advanced under cover of darkness. A brief, five-minute bombardment preceded the assault and it was aimed at a far smaller area of

Above: **General Haig, commander of the British forces at the Battle of the Somme. Long derided as a poor commander, he spent much effort in developing new tactics and weapons in order to deal with the challenges of war on the Western Front.**

Above right: **British artillery at the Western Front. Their failure to destroy German bunkers and barbed wire on the first day of the Somme led to the tremendous casualties suffered by the British infantry.**

delays meant that only 32 of these new weapons were ready by September. Nevertheless, Haig pushed them into battle, and although they were dogged with mechanical faults, their first appearance on 15 September was sufficient to create panic among the Germans, who had been unaware of their development. At Thiepval, only three tanks were needed to terrify the Germans and capture the village. They were not sufficient to establish a breakthrough, but they did point to a new kind of warfare in the future.

BLED WHITE

The Battle of the Somme finally came to an end in November when the Allies captured the German defences at Beaumont Hamel and Beaucourt. In total, the British had lost 420,000

casualties, with the French losing 205,000. The Germans had been bled white with losses of 680,000. All this bloodshed was for an Allied advance of just 3km (5 miles).

Neither side would forget the horror of this battle, and both armies developed tactics which concentrated on more tightly defined objectives, using a variety of weapons and vehicles to support the infantry. It led to the birth of stormtrooper assaults as well as the use of the creeping barrage in which artillery dropped a curtain of fire just in front of the advancing infantry. The battle also demonstrated that the Germans were not invincible, and many British soldiers felt that although it would be costly, the Germans would eventually be beaten. A matching loss of confidence was noted in the German forces. The tide had turned.

ERNEST SHEPHARD, 1ST DORSETS

MACHINE GUN FIRE
'At 6.30am our artillery were bombarding intensely, a most awful din. At 7.30am, we moved to "the attack" by companies at 200 yds [180m] intervals... We had a terrible dose of machine gun fire sweeping us through the wood, could not understand why... We were told to cross as quickly as possible. I went on ahead, Gray the Company Orderly behind, and No.5 platoon behind him. How I got over I cannot imagine, the bullets were cracking and whizzing all round me. I got bullet holes through my clothing and equipment in several places and was hit in left side. The ground was covered with our dead and wounded...'
Quoted in *The Somme* 1916 by Michael Chappell (Windrow & Greene, 1995)

YPRES, 1917

What should have been an impressive demonstration of the new tactics and technology embraced by the British Army was turned into a muddy nightmare with enormous casualties. Advances were bogged down by excessive rain and the Flanders landscape was transformed into a sea of mud. If the Battle of the Somme had been the trauma that finally spurred the British Army into developing new tactics to deal with the stalemate of the Western Front, then surely the Third Battle of Ypres, launched in summer 1917, should have seen the fruits of this hard-won experience? And yet, after five months of fighting which culminated in the assault on Passchendaele (giving the battle its alternative name), the British suffered one-third of a million casualties and their strategic position was little changed. The name of Passchendaele rings almost as loudly as the Somme in the annals of 20th-century military tragedy.

This paradox is even more surprising when one considers the events of two previous battles in 1917. At the Battle of Arras and Vimy Ridge in April, several new tactics and weapons were employed: heavy but precise use of artillery, the creeping barrage, concentrated machine gun fire, gas projectors and tanks – all supported the infantry – who advanced to the front line under cover of tunnels, with the additional lucky elements of rain and snow to obscure their movements. The result was a swift victory in which the objectives were seized with minimal losses.

At the Battle of Messines in June, several mines tore apart the German front line and their use was accompanied by concentrated artillery fire and mastery of the sky by the Royal Flying Corps. Again, all the objectives were taken quickly and the Allied high command began to think that a breakthrough was possible by applying the same lessons on a larger scale. This was to be accomplished at Ypres.

SUCCESS BOGGED DOWN

In April 1917 the French had launched a major attack north of Reims, called the Nivelle Offensive, but it had failed in its objectives and some 130,000 Frenchmen were lost in the first five days. The failure snapped the sorely stretched morale of the French Army and mutinies broke out. France was on the edge of defeat and the British needed to launch a new offensive to distract the Germans. With the successes of Arras and Messines behind him, General Douglas Haig looked to the Flanders town of Ypres. The British position was a salient that bulged out into the German lines with Ypres at its rear. A ridge of high ground 11km (7 miles) east of Ypres, which contained the village of Passchendaele, was the target for Haig's assault.

With the lessons of the new tactics in mind, the attack began well on 31 July. A massive artillery bombardment from three

thousand guns placed almost five tons of shells on each metre of the enemy line. Reconnaissance had been provided by the Royal Flying Corps, which then managed to maintain air supremacy over the battlefield. As a result of this all-arms coordination, the Allied infantry were able to rush forwards and capture many of their objectives on the first day, including the ridges of Bixschoote, Pilckem and St Julien. Nearly 2km (1 mile) of the German front line was taken at a cost of relatively light casualties.

Amid this success, however, there were seeds of discord. General Gough was the main battlefield commander in charge of the Fifth Army, but his sense of operational detail was poorer than that of either Plumer (the victorious commander at Messines) or Rawlinson, who had hoped for the position. On top of this, the assault had been delayed by six weeks and had missed the good summer weather. When the Allied advance began to meet determined opposition from German strongpoints deeper in the lines, the autumn rains began and did not let up.

The tactical implications of the poor weather at Ypres are best explained by a geologist who has made a study of the landscape of the Western Front. 'The Flanders plain is composed mostly of blue clay,' says Peter Doyle. 'This clay produces a very sticky, heavy soil well known to people struggling with their gardens in London. Clay is impervious, repelling water, and this means that any rain that falls accumulates on its surface.'

Above: **British troops in hastily dug trenches wait for the signal to attack during the Allied offensive of the Third Battle of Ypres. The paint on their helmets is improvised camouflage.**

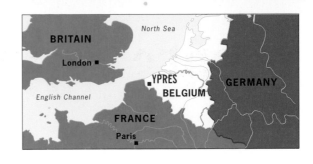

BRITAIN
North Sea
London ■
English Channel
YPRES
BELGIUM
GERMANY
FRANCE
Paris ■

Above: **A wrecked tank stands among the mud-filled craters that brought the Allied offensive to a halt. Excessive rain was unable to drain through the clay of Flanders.**

Left: **Australian troops in a trench during the Battle of Ypres.**

STAFF NURSE MACFIE

HAIR TURNED YELLOW

Women served on the Western Front as nurses and were frequently exposed to the same dangers as the men they helped. Staff Nurse Macfie recalled the effect of treating men exposed to mustard gas during the Third Battle of Ypres:

'The poor boys were helpless and the nurses had to take off these uniforms, all soaked with gas, and do the best they could for the boys. Next day all the nurses had chest trouble and streaming eyes from the gassing. They were all yellow and dazed. Even their hair turned yellow and they were nearly as bad as

the men, just from the fumes from their clothing. And all the time, of course, the bombs were falling, night after night.'
Quoted in *They Called It Passchendaele* by Lyn Macdonald (Michael Joseph, 1978)

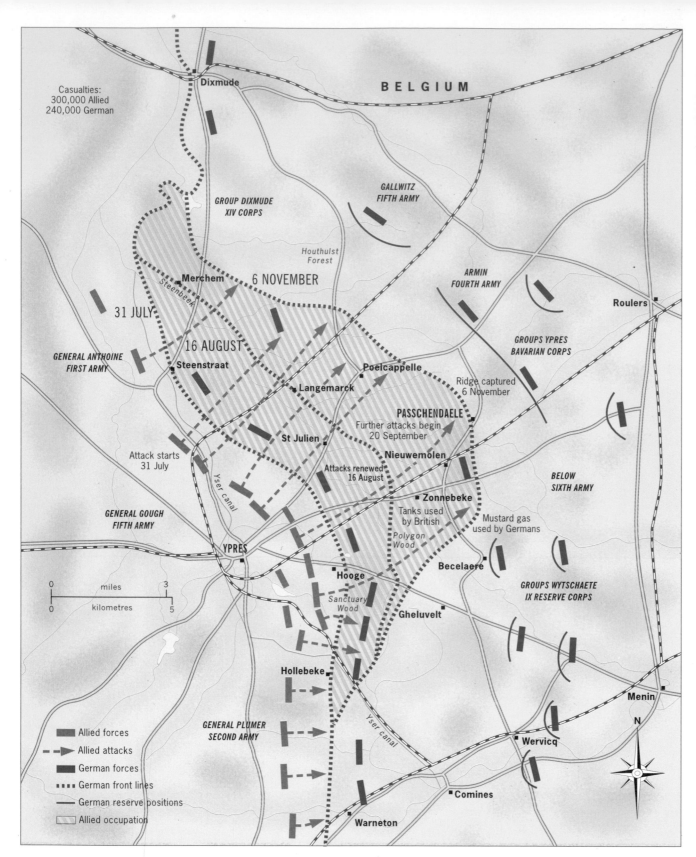

Casualties:
300,000 Allied
240,000 German

BELGIUM

Dixmude

GROUP DIXMUDE
XIV CORPS

GALLWITZ
FIFTH ARMY

Houthulst
Forest

Merchem

6 NOVEMBER

ARMIN
FOURTH ARMY

Steenbeek

31 JULY

Roulers

GENERAL ANTHOINE
FIRST ARMY

16 AUGUST

GROUPS YPRES
BAVARIAN CORPS

Steenstraat

Poelcappelle

Ridge captured
6 November

Langemarck

St Julien

PASSCHENDAELE
Further attacks begin
20 September

Attack starts
31 July

Nieuwemolen

BELOW
SIXTH ARMY

Yser canal

Attacks renewed
16 August

GENERAL GOUGH
FIFTH ARMY

Zonnebeke

Tanks used
by British

Mustard gas
used by Germans

Polygon
Wood

YPRES

Becelaere

Hooge

Sanctuary
Wood

GROUPS WYTSCHAETE
IX RESERVE CORPS

Gheluvelt

Hollebeke

Yser canal

Menin

GENERAL PLUMER
SECOND ARMY

N

Wervicq

Allied forces
Allied attacks
German forces
German front lines
German reserve positions
Allied occupation

Comines

Warneton

Above: **A tinted contemporary postcard showing a British soldier on observation duty on the Western Front.**

Left: **The British offensive in Flanders in 1917.**

Drainage in the Ypres area depended on the canals constructed by the local farmers, but this system was destroyed by the artillery shells, which had churned up the ground into a myriad of craters. The inevitable result was that as the rain continued, the battlefield at Ypres was transformed into a landscape of mud, splintered tree trunks and water-filled shellholes. This mud not only halted the progress of men and vehicles, but also swallowed many of them up; some forty thousand men were reported as missing, believed to have been drowned in the mud of Flanders.

ATTACK RESUMED

The initial downpour lasted two weeks and the Germans used the lull to strengthen their positions. On 16 August, the Allied attack resumed and Langemarck was captured. But then it began to rain again. Haig accepted that the offensive had ground to a halt and wanted to consolidate his gains.

Engineers used the cover of darkness to construct roads over the sea of mud using planks and logs, but in daylight the Germans submitted them to bombardment and the roads had to be built again and again. Despite the seemingly endless rainfall, the water it provided was contaminated by gas-filled shells and dead bodies and therefore drinking water had to be brought in daily.

William Sharpe, a private in the 8th Lancashire Fusiliers, gives an indication of what it was like to advance across the system of 'duckboards' laid over the mud at Flanders. 'In the pouring rain we started to march to supports,' he recalls, 'along a duckboard track – for there is not a spare yard of ground in front of Ypres that is not pitted with a shell hole... I will never forget this march, pouring down with rain, we made fairly good progress until it became dark and then fellows fell off the duckboards into shell holes and had to be got out, and suddenly the duckboards would be broken and the whole company would have to wade waist deep in mud and try to regain the duckboards.'

Haig replaced Gough with the more meticulous Plumer, who was now charged with the assault on the high ground around Passchendaele. The change in command and the subsequent reorganization of troops and artillery took a further three weeks, which coincided with a dry period in which the mud hardened and gave everyone cause for optimism. On 20 September, British and Australian troops resumed their advance by moving towards Polygon Wood and Gheluvelt in the south and Zonnebeke in the centre.

As they crossed the Gheluvelt plateau, the Australians had the novel experience of being caught in a duststorm caused by German artillery shells kicking up the dried mud. It was a cruel deception, however, for at the beginning of October the rain resumed and Allied soldiers had to march across 4km (2½

miles) of wooden tracks to approach the village of Passchendaele. Leading military historian Paddy Griffith describes the impact mud had on the efficiency of the new tactics: 'HE [high-explosive] shells became buried and smothered in it. If they could fly at all, aircraft could not tell friend from foe since the uniforms of both had been equally discoloured by it. Mortar base plates sank into it every time a bomb was fired, and tanks bogged down into it as soon as they left the roads. Small arms became hopelessly clogged by it within an hour of opening fire - and the wounded often drowned in it.'

The Germans fought back with fierce counter-attacks and used mustard gas for the first time. The poison gas lingered in muddy craters, making the two a deadly cocktail of threats to a soldier's life. 'Gas shells were bursting over me,' recalled one Canadian soldier, 'and I couldn't see where I was going. All of a sudden, my foot slipped on the slippery plank and I went right into a muddy hole. I was up to the neck in mud and couldn't get out... At last, two fellows came with a rope and hauled me up and lay me on the muddy ground. Then, I got three buckets of water thrown on me and was left there. I was choking with gas and couldn't see.'

It was Canadian soldiers who finally seized the key point of Passchendaele on 6 November, pushing the Germans off the ridge and gaining the high ground. The Third Battle of Ypres was undoubtedly a victory, but the appalling weather conditions had wrecked the well-laid plans of Haig and his generals. The swiftness of previous victories had been denied to them by the simple obstacle of mud.

Back in Britain, the tactical improvements developed by the British Army meant little to the politicians, who were confronted merely with an enormous casualty list of some three hundred thousand men. The Germans had lost at least 240,000 men but they still occupied Belgium and the war would continue for another year. It may have been a victory, but it seemed to many like another defeat.

Below: **A German machine-gun crew on the Western Front.**

Below right: **British soldiers covered in mud from the Western Front. They have adapted their clothing in order to cope with the mud.**

CAMBRAI, 1917

New assault tactics were demonstrated decisively at Cambrai by the British with a tank-led breakthrough, the first ever. It looked like a welcome victory, but German counter-attacks led by stormtroopers revealed a newly efficient edge to the German fighting on the Western Front, one that threatened to prolong the titanic struggle.

Quantity not quality was increasingly becoming understood as the key to battlefield success in the First World War. Brusilov had demonstrated this on the Eastern Front and British victories in early 1917 had made the same point. Liddell Hart, one of the first authorities on armoured warfare, thought this particularly true of the Battle of Cambrai, 'where the use of only 378

tanks and some 4,000 tank-men to assist a mere six divisions of infantry, produced a greater gain of ground and a greater shock to the enemy at a cost of some 5,000 casualties, than the use of several dozen divisions had achieved at Ypres in a three months' effort at a cost of 400,000 casualties.'

'LANDSHIPS'

The idea of an armoured, tracked, mobile gun platform was first considered as early as autumn 1914. Various prototypes were explored and the Royal Navy proposed a 'landship'. Within the Admiralty, Churchill favoured the idea and encouraged its development. Eventually the US-built Holt caterpillar tractor was

Above: **British tanks spearhead the dawn advance at Cambrai in this painting by W. L. Wyllie.**

selected as the basis for the chassis and General Haig was sufficiently impressed to call for it to be put into production. Britain's minister for munitions, David Lloyd George, gave the project the go-ahead and Mark I tanks began to arrive in France in the summer of 1916, described as 'water tanks' so as to hide their true purpose (see pp.72-73).

The battlefield performance of the first tanks was constantly overestimated, largely for propaganda reasons. Progressing little faster than the infantry, they were highly susceptible to breakdowns and frequently got stuck in the mud of the Western Front. The crews were highly vulnerable to carbon monoxide poisoning, and a desire for them to lay down fire while moving proved difficult to enact in practice. Enthusiasm remained undented by their poor performance, however, because they raised the morale of troops who had become anxious to believe in any machine that could make their lives easier. Newspapers built up their reputation to this end and a separate Tank Corps was formed to bolster their image. Tanks toured towns in Britain raising money for the war – perhaps their most useful campaign until they saw action at Cambrai.

By summer 1917, more of the improved Mark IV had been produced and 190 were deployed, albeit disappointingly, in the Third Battle of Ypres. Heavy mud and the piecemeal way they were used were put forward as the reasons for their failure, and in November 1917 Haig had become sufficiently convinced of their merits to decide to bring all the tanks together and use them in a mass attack across solid ground at Cambrai. The attack was originally conceived as an artillery assault and it has been suggested that the main purpose behind the presence of the tanks was to use them as barbed-wire breakers, thereby saving the artillery from having to undertake the task. If a breakout was to occur, then it would be the old-fashioned cavalry that would pursue it. Whatever the truth of this, certainly the tank commanders were keen to prove their worth once and for all.

MAXIMUM SURPRISE

To achieve the utmost surprise, General Byng, commander of the British Third Army, went without the usual devastating preliminary barrage and on the morning of 20 November his tanks broke cover. Mist covered their advance and a creeping barrage rained down just in front of them. Unsettled by the approach of these clanking monsters, the majority of Germans fled their trenches and the front line was penetrated by 8km (5 miles) in just 10 hours.

The tanks worked in teams of three, with the first one breaking through the barbed wire and then halting in front of the

enemy trench to guard the others by raking the trench with machine gun fire. A second tank then dropped a bundle of sticks into the trench and machine-gunned it. A third tank used the fascine to cross the first trench and then dropped its own bundle of sticks on the support trench and machine-gunned that. The first tank then crossed both trenches and dropped its own bundle of sticks on a third trench. That way, the trenches

MAP LABELS:

FRANCE

29 NOVEMBER British take Bourlon Wood

Bourlon

Bourlon Wood

Moeuvres

Cambrai

Fontaine

Canal de l'Escaut

MARWITZ SECOND ARMY

3 DECEMBER German counter attacks

Germans retake Bourlon Wood and British withdraw

German counter-attacks

Second Siegfried Line

5 DECEMBER Marcoing

Masnières

Havrincourt

First Siegfried Line

Couillet Wood

Havrincourt Wood

20 NOVEMBER Tanks advance with infantry over German lines

Canal de St Quentin

Bantouzelle

Gouzeaucourt

Gonnelieu

BYNG THIRD ARMY

Gauche Wood

Honnecourt

5 DECEMBER

3 DECEMBER German counter attacks

N

■ British armies
┅► British attacks
◣ Tank battalion
▨ British gains
■ German armies
┅► German attacks
┅┅ German front line
── German defensive lines

0 miles 2
0 kilometres 3

Epéhy

Vendhuille

Above: **The British offensive at Cambrai of November 1917 and the German counter-attacks of the following month.**

were both breached and cleared. At Flesquières, however, a German gun position held its nerve and managed to destroy seven tanks before it was overrun.

But how much had the tanks actually achieved? The German positions were known to be weak at this point, which is why they were chosen for attack, and the British artillery had quickly dominated the 34 German guns facing them. The Germans also chose to defend their front line in depth, with reserves readily available to stem any breakthrough. As the tanks ran out of steam towards the end of their initial advance, the Germans gathered their reserves to contest any further gains. Despite tanks breaking down and getting stuck, the British pressed on with their attack until 28 November, by which point they had taken some ten thousand prisoners and seized two hundred guns.

GERMAN COUNTER-ATTACK

The Allies enjoyed their success only briefly. On 30 November, the Germans led a major counter-attack that regained virtually all the ground that had been taken by the tank assault. Since 1916, the Germans had learned that they had to develop new tactics. Part of the outcome of this was a flexibility in defence, which meant that soldiers were taught not to stand or die, but to achieve a more flowing battle, one in which they could retreat before an Allied assault while outposts of machine guns formed a net in which Allied soldiers would be ensnared. As the enemy attack was blunted by this intersecting fire, the most

experienced German troops and the majority of the artillery were kept in reserve for the main effort of a counter-attack.

This flexible approach was extended to the development of stormtrooper tactics, by means of which small units of highly trained men, armed with hand-grenades, mortars, flame throwers and machine guns, were used to overrun weaker enemy positions, while leaving any strongpoints to be dealt with later (thus not holding up the momentum of an attack). As specialist troops who headed up any assault, the stormtroopers began to be regarded as an élite by the rest of the army and this helped to raise their morale when going into battle. It was the stormtroopers who spearheaded the counter-attacks at Cambrai and their success was noted by German generals, who used them extensively in the battles that followed in 1918.

Exhausted by the efforts of a sustained assault, Allied soldiers frequently had little power left to resist a concerted counter-attack by the Germans. Captain Neville of the 52nd Light Infantry described the impact of an incoming enemy artillery round during the German counter-attack at Cambrai: 'There was no way of escape; we could not dodge the brute, as we were far too cramped for space. With a tearing, rushing, mighty roar as of an express train screaming at top speed through an enclosed station, it crashed in the next bay from me, right in the middle of my platoon! I darted round the corner and found a shambles. It had fallen plumb in the centre of the trench.'

By the end of the German counter-attack on 6 December both sides had lost approximately forty-five thousand men

Below left: **Canadian troops on the Western Front. Soldiers of the Empire proved an invaluable source of manpower for the British and won high regard for their performance in battle.**

Below: **Stormtroopers like this led the German counter-attack at Cambrai. Wearing the new steels shrapnel helmets, these troops used hand-grenades to storm enemy trenches.**

Above: A British tank armed with machine guns. These machines worked in teams of three to cross enemy lines, laying down fire as other tanks filled in the trenches. Their frightening impact on the enemy was offset by their frequent breakdowns.

and they were back to square one. The failures of both Ypres and Cambrai cast a gloomy atmosphere over Allied command, which had put much effort into developing a new method of warfare with which to break the old stalemate. The brief triumph of the tank at Cambrai served more as a propaganda success than a real strategic achievement. It is noticeable that despite their enthusiasm for the tank, the Allied high command did not pursue any more mass tank assaults throughout 1918. The time of the tank had yet to come. The moment of the stormtrooper, however, was here and German commanders took much more encouragement from their counter-attack at Cambrai, thinking that their new tactics had been perfected to the point where they could risk a major offensive.

PRIVATE CHRIS KNIGHT, 6TH DRAGOON GUARDS

HORSES AMONG TANKS

Although the British high command was keen to exploit the use of new weaponry such as tanks, they also relied upon the mobility of more traditional units such as the cavalry. Chris Knight was a private in the 6th Dragoon Guards at Cambrai, waiting to make the most of any breakthrough, and described a wonderfully old-fashioned array of horsemen around him:

'I had never seen so many horses and men together at one parade. It was an awe-inspiring sight. Dragoons, Lancers, Hussars — they were all there, as well as Indian mounted troops. The "saddle-up" went for an Indian brigade first. By this time the bombardment was heavy. Tanks and infantry were well on their way to the Hindenburg Line, the supposed impregnable trench... At last the orders came: "Half-sections right, walk march! Form sections! Head, left wheel! Draw swords! Trot! Form troop! Form column of half squadron! Gallop!" The village lay about three-quarters of a mile away [1km]. We galloped fiercely to the outskirts, rapidly formed sections and got on to the road, numbers 1 and 2 troops cantering into the village first. Donelly, the Irishman, went raving mad, cutting and thrusting wildly at retreating Germans.'

Quoted in *Everyman at War* edited by C.B. Purdom (London, 1930)

GERMANY'S 'BLACK DAY', 1918

Left: German stormtroopers advance with a flamethrower and a captured British tank.

Below: German stormtroopers with machine guns counter-attack on the Western Front in 1918.

When Germany's final great offensive of the First World War ground to a halt, it was indeed Germany's blackest day. Stormtrooper tactics failed to break Allied resistance, and British and Commonwealth troops advanced in tanks behind a creeping barrage. It was too much for the Germans, whose morale crumbled. It was the beginning of the end for the Kaiser's army.

If the British could not win at Ypres or Cambrai, with all the benefits of new weaponry and tactics, what chance did they ever have of a breakthrough? Lloyd George, by now Britain's prime minister, could see little point in pursuing yet more costly offensives on the Western Front and he favoured a shift of resources to other areas of combat elsewhere in Europe. More British soldiers were sent to the Italian Front and the numbers of reinforcements in Flanders and France were reduced. The Americans had joined the war effort and soon their troops would help swing the balance of numbers against the Germans. In the meantime, the Allies would absorb any German attacks, just as the Germans had earlier blunted their assaults.

General Erich von Ludendorff, Germany's supreme commander, was feeling more confident. His troops were now experienced in the new, more flowing form of assault led by stormtroopers who would bypass the enemy strongpoints and infiltrate the lines (see Cambrai, pp.78–81). Most importantly, Ludendorff finally had the advantage of numbers, for Russia was out of the war, immersed in revolution, and he could shift

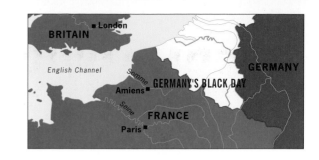

GERMANY'S BLACK DAY

trainloads of soldiers westwards from the Eastern Front. He saw an opportunity to strike before the Americans became fully involved in the fighting. The results were the Ludendorff Offensives of spring 1918.

SPRING OFFENSIVES

Ludendorff chose as his point of attack the place where the British and French armies were positioned on the old Somme battlefield, between Arras and La Fère. The British had taken over responsibility for some of the French front line and their soldiers were spread thinly. As with the British at Cambrai, the Germans used precision and surprise. On 21 March, a five-hour bombardment opened their assault, which then occurred under the cover of mist as well as gas and smokeshells.

Led by rapid-moving stormtrooper units, 65 German divisions took on nearly 100km (60 miles) of the British front

Right: **The British counter-attacks against German defensive lines on the Western Front in France during 1918.**

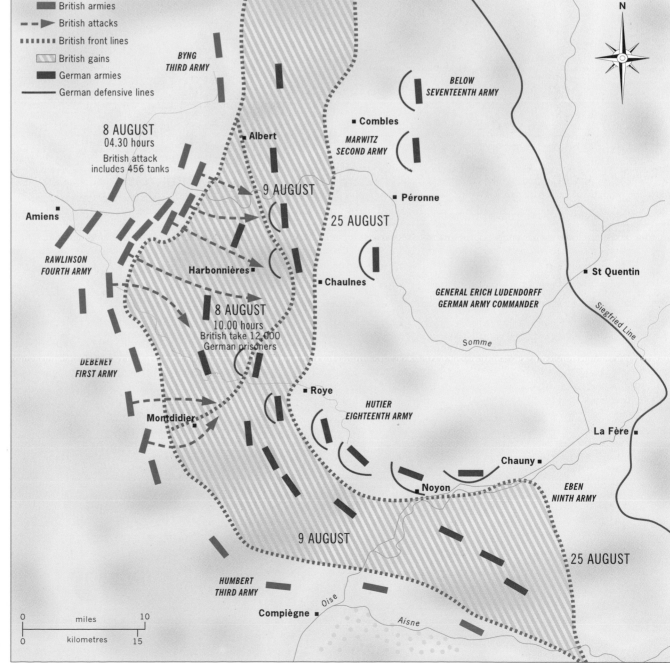

Above: **German prisoners taken on the Western Front in 1918. Many Germans were quite relieved to fall into Allied hands. Their morale had plunged severely after they failed to break through in their spring offensive.**

his finest stormtroopers. On the British side, the remains of the Fifth Army were taken over by the Fourth Army.

In April, Ludendorff began a new offensive near Ypres aimed at securing the Channel ports and cutting off the British from the French. The Germans chose another weak point, this time manned by Portuguese troops, and punched a hole in the Allied lines. After further assualts, all the ground lost in the Third Battle of Ypres was taken back. Only hard fighting by the British, Belgians and French managed to stop it becoming a major breakthrough and by the end of the month the ferocity of these counter-attacks forced Ludendorff to call off the offensive.

On 29 May, Ludendorff aimed another massive blow at the Allies, this time selecting the French on the River Aisne. Again the Allies crumbled before them and the Germans made a salient 30km (20 miles) deep. On this occasion the Germans were held by a new force in the region – the Americans. In June, two more German assaults pummelled the Allied lines, but were contained by French and American armies that were better organized in depth. Allied aircraft and artillery bombed the German-held bridges and thus destroyed their supply lines. Time was running out for Ludendorff. Tactically, the Germans had proved their strength, but a strategic victory eluded them. Ludendorff's losses were enormous and the will to continue the war was seeping away from his soldiers. In the meantime, three hundred thousand Americans were arriving every month.

'BLACK DAY'

'8 August was the black day of the German Army,' Ludendorff later wrote in his memoirs. 'Everything I had feared and of which I had so often given warning, had here, in one place, become a reality. Our war machine was no longer efficient.' By the beginning of August, Ludendorff was no longer taking the initiative. This had passed to the Allies and they delivered a massive surprise attack. Rawlinson's British and Commonwealth Fourth Army had been almost doubled in size. Secrecy had been maintained by moving the troops at night, so that not even most of the Allies knew of the forthcoming attack.

Before sunrise on the morning of 8 August, shrouded by a low mist, some 456 tanks and British, Canadian and Australian troops advanced behind a creeping barrage across land south of the River Somme at Amiens. Weakly enforced, the German line collapsed and fell back 13km (8 miles). Demoralized, the Germans fought back less fiercely this time and twelve thousand prisoners were taken on this first day, with Allied casualties low. Sergeant Witherby of the 20th Lethbridge Battery describes the mood of the Germans he encountered: 'The mist and smoke were lifting fast now, and we could see further around us – on our right was a shallow trench used by the Germans that morning, and some dead Germans lying there. Bunches of prisoners were coming across country, in some cases absolutely unattended, only too glad to get out of the battle.'

It was this recognition of a declining fighting spirit that worried Ludendorff most and made him claim this as his

line. The overstretched British Fifth Army was completely overwhelmed and, unlike its German adversaries, did not have the resources to defend itself sufficiently in depth to weather the storm. The mist added to the sense of confusion and fear. To the north, the British Third Army had better defensive lines and it held the German assault. Haig appealed to the French to help him plug the gap, but Pétain was more interested in defending Paris, which was now coming under long-range artillery attack. Having forced a bulge some 65km (40 miles) deep into Allied territory, the German armies began to outstrip their supply lines and came to a halt. Although highly successful, this first offensive had been costly for Ludendorff; the Germans had 250,000 casualties, the Allies slightly fewer. The breakthrough had not been a decisive one; in fact it had merely lost him some of country's 'black day'. Among the thousands of German soldiers who gave up during the initial attack were 281 officers. They offered token resistance and then simply threw down their weapons. They had had enough. The war of wills had been won by the Allies.

As always, such advances seem to have surprised both sides, and they rumbled to a halt only because supplies and communication could not keep up with the furthest troops. 'Command and control broke down too quickly on both sides,' concludes Paddy Griffith, 'once fully open warfare had replaced the static certainties of trench life. The artillery often failed to keep in touch with its infantry; lateral communications between formations tended to break down every time there was a move.' Nevertheless, it had been a solid blow.

On 21 August the British Third Army followed up with another thrust further north. With the pressure off, the Fourth Army resumed its advance. Overlapping attacks by successive Allied forces seemed to be the key to pushing back the Germans. Infiltration tactics were used by the British as effectively as the Germans. 'When in doubt go ahead,' said a British training manual. 'When uncertain do that which will kill most Germans. Don't fear an exposed flank.' Such an attitude ensured movement on the battlefield.

ENDING THE WAR

With the end of Ludendorff's final gambles, the Allied counter-offensive swung into action with crushing blows. The US First Army under General Pershing proved its professionalism and courage in an assault on the Meuse–Argonne region in September. The French regained a little national self-esteem when they recaptured Sedan, the scene of their humiliation in the Franco-Prussian War. In the north, British forces assaulted the Hindenburg Line and penetrated it on 5 October.

The German high command was in a state of panic. Ludendorff was convinced he had been 'stabbed in the back' by a lack of support in Germany, a legend that was to grow in strength after the war, accounting for some of the support given to Hitler and the Nazis. German leaders considered asking for a ceasefire. The British kept on the pressure with further attacks

Above: **Armistice is signed between Germany and the Allies, ending the First World War on 11 November 1918, in a railway carriage at Rethondes in the forest of Compiègne.**

in October, breaking the German defences on the River Selle. The Germans then asked the United States's President Wilson for a negotiated peace, but Wilson said he would not negotiate with a military dictatorship. On 27 October, Ludendorff resigned. Two days later, the German High Seas Fleet mutinied and demonstrations broke out across Germany - the public had been suffering slow starvation since a poor harvest in 1917.

The German government had little choice but to accept defeat. In the final months of the war, Germany had lost a further half a million men. The kaiser abdicated and fled to the Netherlands. Germany became a republic and an armistice was proclaimed at the eleventh hour on 11 November 1918 – a moment that is forever commemorated in Britain every year as Remembrance Day. The German Army withdrew to its pre-1914 frontiers and the First World War was over.

LIEUTENANT EDWIN TRUNDLE, 2ND AUSTRALIAN DIVISION

GETTING THE WIND UP

'I caught eight Huns myself... I saw these fellows about ten o'clock running away... I immediately yelled after them whereon they threw up their hands and ran towards me in a mob. At the time I was standing at the door of a dugout and soon found myself inside and alone, confronted with eight big burly

Boche. The first of them dropped his hands to his side, perhaps to come to attention on seeing I was an officer, or to get to his pockets, I don't know which. Anyway it made me feel a bit uncomfortable for a while as I didn't even have a pork sausage to point at him. A pick was lying at my feet so I grabbed this up and threatened to stick

it through his "napper". This had the effect of putting the wind up the mob and they all threw up their hands again and fell on their knees.'
Quoted in 1918 *Year of Victory* **by Malcolm Brown (Sidgwick & Jackson, 1998)**

NANKING, 1937

With its capture of the then Chinese capital at Nanking, Japan had soundly defeated its Chinese Nationalist opponents and made itself master of crucial parts of the Chinese mainland. However, the barbaric behaviour of Japanese troops shocked the world. Dreadful tales of massacres and rape heralded an age of grotesque atrocities against prisoners and civilians caught up in war.

The Second World War began in Asia, not with Pearl Harbor, but with the Japanese invasion of China in 1937, which was the culminating phase of Japan's campaigns of aggrandizement.

These campaigns had begun with the Sino-Japanese War of 1894–95 and continued through the Russo-Japanese War of 1904–05 and the First World War, in which Japan seized German colonies.

Civil war had racked China during the 1920s and Japan had exploited its weakness by invading Manchuria in 1931. A plot was fabricated called the Mukden Incident, in which it was claimed that China wanted to blow up the railway between Mukden and Port Arthur. The Japanese seized the province and called it Manchuko. Pu Yi, the last emperor of China, was then

Above: **Japanese infantry approaching the Chinese capital of Nanking through flooded farmland.**

set up there as the puppet ruler. China responded with an effective boycott of trade to Japan and in retaliation a Japanese army landed at Shanghai. A fierce battle followed, with China eventually agreeing to end its boycott. Tension between the two nations grew markedly.

Japanese society was becoming increasingly militarized and in 1936 a group of army officers tried to take over the government and press on with the conquest of China. The coup was crushed, but the rebels did not have long to wait for their wishes to be fulfilled.

THE INVASION OF CHINA

On 7 July 1937, Japan fabricated another clash in northern China – at the Marco Polo Bridge near Tientsin – as an excuse to launch a full-scale invasion of China. In the titanic struggle that would follow, the odds favoured Japan. Japan was the most modern power in Asia, with a highly effective navy and air force; the army was three hundred thousand strong and equipped with the latest weapons. The massive Chinese alliance ranged against Japan was poorly equipped and trained, and possessed neither naval nor air forces. The main Chinese army was the Nationalist force led by General Chiang Kai-shek, which numbered two million men and was based around the capital at Nanking. In northwest China there was a guerrilla army of 150,000 troops belonging to the communists. The two Chinese factions agreed to unite against Japan, but it was an uneasy alliance.

In summer 1937, Japanese armies captured Peking and Tientsin, then marched west and south, overcoming all Chinese opposition. By the autumn, however, resistance from the Chinese population as well as its military forces had begun to slow down the Japanese and their supply lines had become stretched. A second assault on Shanghai was met with strong resistance and it took several months of Japanese amphibious landings and aerial attacks to clear the city. In September, a Japanese division was defeated by a communist division in northwest China, greatly raising the morale of the Chinese and consolidating communist power in that part of the country.

The Japanese had thought the conquest of China would be easy, but they had been given a much harder time than they expected. This frustration and anger was carried westwards by the conquerors of Shanghai as they marched towards the Nationalist capital of Nanking.

PLUNGE IN MORALE

In November 1937, three Japanese armies raced towards Nanking. Their mood was ruthless and they annihilated the vil-

***Above*: Japanese assault teams breaking through the wall surrounding the Nationalist capital of Nanking.**

lages and towns in their way. For example, Suzhou was an historic city on the east bank of Tai Hu Lake, famous for its ancient canals and bridges, which had earned it the name of 'the Venice of China'. On entering the city, the Japanese massacred its inhabitants, burned down its historic landmarks and took away thousands of women to act as sex slaves for Japanese soldiers. In days, the population was reduced from 350,000 to less than 500. Sadly, this was just the beginning.

On 7 December, the Japanese armies closed in on Nanking itself. The defending Chinese army of three hundred thousand

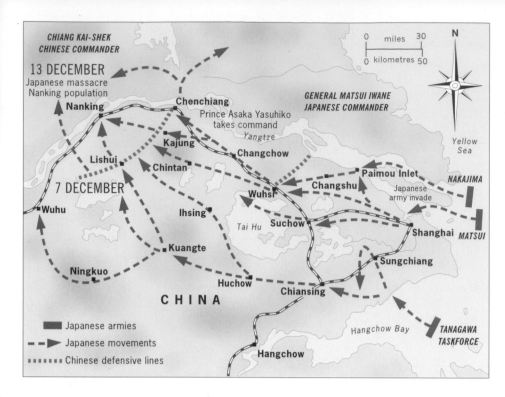

Above: **The progress of the Japanese campaign from Shanghai to Nanking in 1937.**

and the Chinese soldiers were bound and led off for execution. Such an easy, unexpected victory meant that any lingering respect the Japanese military might have felt for their Chinese captives disappeared completely. It was the beginning of a holocaust.

THE 'RAPE OF NANKING'

Having feared the Chinese earlier in the campaign, the Japanese soldiers now despised them for their cowardice. Heavily outnumbered, the Japanese subdued the Chinese by breaking them into small groups, binding their arms and then leading them off to the killing grounds. Huddled together, the Chinese were then machine-gunned to death. So many soldiers were murdered that there were not enough pits to bury them in and some were half burned or thrown into the River Yangtze.

With the execution of the Chinese soldiers, the Japanese army poured into Nanking and inflicted a crazed orgy of savagery on its civilians. Men, women and children were shot at random. When the bullets ran out, swords and bayonets were used. Piles of corpses built up on every street. The execution of civilians became a sport and soldiers competed to see who could kill the most in the shortest time. When the killing became boring, hideous tortures were invented. Many Japanese took photographs of one another, holding severed heads and grinning, enjoying the torture and the slaughter.

Females of any age were subjected to brutal sexual assaults by gangs of Japanese soldiers, who then mutilated and killed them. The actions were sickening and barbaric, but they continued for days, with officers encouraging their soldiers.

The horror subsided on 17 December when General Matsui rose from his sick bed and entered the city. He was shocked by what he heard of the behaviour of his troops, but it was too

was trapped by the River Yangtze behind the city and could offer little decisive resistance. Chiang Kai-shek ordered a chaotic, last-minute retreat from the city. For those soldiers remaining, thoughts turned to surrender. General Matsui Iwane was in overall command of the Japanese forces in this region and he saw the conquest of the capital as his crowning glory. He regarded it as an international showcase for the Japanese Army and he gave strict orders that entry into the city should be conducted in a disciplined manner that would impress the Chinese and the rest of the world. Plunder and bad behaviour were not to be tolerated and guards were to be posted to protect the citizens. Such grand plans were sunk by his own illness and a change in command.

Emperor Hirohito placed his uncle Prince Asaka Yasuhiko in command of the Japanese forces at Nanking. As a member of the royal family, his authority was superior to that of any other commander in the field. Asaka was influenced by the ruthless General Nakajima and a counter-command was issued to the troops, which instructed them to execute all prisoners of war. Before dawn on 13 December, a mere fifty thousand Japanese troops broke through the walls of Nanking and found themselves in charge of ninety thousand Chinese soldiers and half a million civilians.

Why, especially with superior numbers, did the Chinese not demonstrate the same resistance they had shown at Shanghai? It appears that the Chinese army in Nanking may well have been exhausted by its retreat from Shanghai, and the offers of fair treatment seemed much more attractive than earlier on in the campaign. Many of the soldiers threw away their weapons and offered themselves up for arrest. There appears to have been little coordinated action from the Chinese commanders in the city. A catastrophic plunge in morale had given the Japanese their greatest victory in the campaign. Tragically, the offers of fair treatment were false

Below: **Japanese aerial bombardment of Nanking resulting in a direct hit on a Chinese ammunition store.**

Above: Victorious Japanese soldiers parade through Chungsun gate into Nanking. Terrible torture and slaughter would follow for Chinese citizens

NAGATOMI HAKUDO, JAPANESE SOLDIER

SMILING PROUDLY

'I remember being driven in a truck along a path that had been cleared through piles of thousands and thousands of slaughtered bodies. Wild dogs were gnawing at the dead flesh as we stopped and pulled a group of Chinese prisoners out of the back. Then the Japanese officer proposed a test of my courage. He unsheathed his sword, spat on it, and with a sudden mighty swing he brought it down on the neck of a Chinese boy cowering before us. The head was cut clean off and tumbled away on the ground as the body slumped forward, blood spurting in two great gushing fountains from the neck. The officer suggested I take the head home as a souvenir. I remember smiling proudly as I took his sword and began killing people.'
Quoted in *The Rape of Nanking* by Iris Chang (Basic Books, 1997)

late for the 250,000 Chinese men, women and children who had been massacred or the 80,000 women who had been raped. Despite Matsui's disapproval, the atrocities went on for weeks afterwards.

The 'rape of Nanking' is one of the great war atrocities of the 20th century. The Japanese government tried to bury the incident and to a certain extent it has succeeded, because the horror of it has not implanted itself in Western sensibilities to the extent of German and Russian atrocities. The lack of punishment of the soldiers involved meant that such barbarity was considered to be acceptable behaviour among the Japanese Army for the rest of the Second World War, its conquering soldiers treating civilians and prisoners of war in the most appalling ways. For the Chinese, the lesson was clear: they could expect no mercy. Their war of resistance was to continue for many more years.

FRANCE, 1940

The swift defeat of France at the beginning of the Second World War gave Hitler his greatest trophy. It was a ruthless display of blitzkrieg warfare in which motorized columns in combination with air power overwhelmed a more static foe. Poorly equipped and badly led, the French were both surprised and outmanoeuvred by an armoured thrust through the Ardennes Forest. The Battle of France was the culmination of Hitler's blitzkrieg in western Europe and it ended Continental opposition to the Nazis.

As the decades have passed since the end of the Second World War, it has become easier to see that terrible and most destructive war as the culminating phase of a series of conflicts that convulsed the first half of the 20th century. The conflicts – begun by Germany in 1914 and only ended in 1945 with Germany's total defeat – have been referred to as the 'second Thirty Years War', and from a military point of view it makes sense to bring the two world wars in Europe together. Both wars repeat basic strategies, with Germany turning first to defeat the Western powers and secure its industrial heartland before then turning to the main business of conquering eastern Europe and defeating Russia.

In terms of military techniques, the lessons learned in 1916 and developed through to 1918 were continued throughout the 1930s and bore fruit for Germany in its swift conquests of 1939 to 1941. At the core of these victories was the stormtrooper and as a concept he had been born in the trenches of the Western Front (see Cambrai, pp.78–81). Adolf Hitler himself had fought in the trenches and considered it one of the defining moments of his life. 'I wouldn't feel I had the right to demand of each man the supreme sacrifice,' he later said in 1942, 'if I hadn't myself gone through the whole 1914–18 war in the front line.' And initially, the Nazis had found their power base among the disaffected veterans of the first war.

Above: **A German motorized column spearheads the advance through a devastated French town. Such columns gave the attacking Germans tremendous impetus, although their support troops often arrived at the speed of their horse-drawn supply vehicles.**

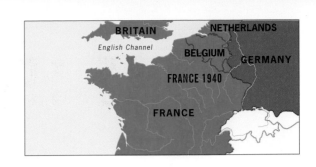

BLITZKRIEG

Nazi Germany's colonialism in central and eastern Europe began with the annexation of Austria in March 1938 and then Bohemia and Moravia the same month. Hitler's invasion of Poland in September 1939 left France and Britain with little choice but to declare war and so the Second World War began. The German Army entered Poland at speed and had captured Warsaw by the end of the month. This victory has been portrayed as the first triumph of Germany's blitzkrieg, establishing the legend of Germany's irresistible military system. This is only a partial truth; the Polish Army put up a fierce resistance and stopped the Germans on several occasions, but the latter had the tremendous advantages of having invaded without warning and in greater strength. Added to this, the Soviet Army had honoured its pact with Nazi Germany by invading eastern Poland in the middle of the same month. Against such odds, bravery was not enough and Poland had little choice but to concede defeat. In the wake of this triumph, everyone, including Hitler, now considered that the Germans were military geniuses, thus adding supreme confidence to their armoury.

Right: **German dive-bombers, such as this Junkers Ju87, opened the German blitzkrieg campaigns of 1940, dropping bombs on strategic points.**

Below: **The dynamic advance of German motorized columns in their blitzkrieg assault on France in March 1940.**

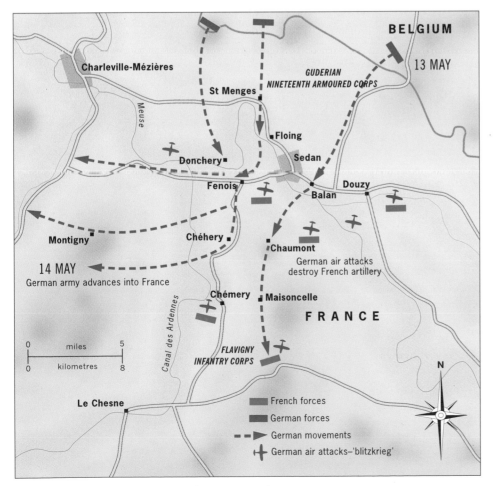

German strategy and tactics in the first years of the Second World War were based on lessons learned in the latter half of the First World War. Combined-arms assaults were the key to success, with the emphasis on manoeuvre and maintaining impetus. Fighter and bomber aircraft were swift to dominate the air space and bomb the opposition. Armoured motorized columns followed up, punching holes in the enemy lines. Infantry tactics were those of the stormtroopers, with autonomous groups of highly trained, heavily armed soldiers attacking targets in rapid assaults, supporting one another until contact, then pressing in on weak points. The technical

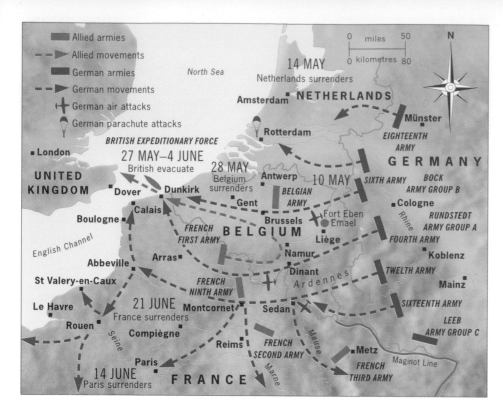

Map labels:
- Allied armies
- Allied movements
- German armies
- German movements
- German air attacks
- German parachute attacks

North Sea

14 MAY Netherlands surrenders

Amsterdam · NETHERLANDS

Münster

Rotterdam

BRITISH EXPEDITIONARY FORCE

London

27 MAY–4 JUNE British evacuate

28 MAY Belgium surrenders

10 MAY

UNITED KINGDOM

Dover · Dunkirk

Antwerp · Gent

EIGHTEENTH ARMY

GERMANY

SIXTH ARMY · BOCK ARMY GROUP B

Calais · Boulogne

BELGIAN ARMY

Cologne

English Channel

FRENCH FIRST ARMY

BELGIUM

Brussels · Fort Eben Emael · Liège

RUNDSTEDT ARMY GROUP A

Rhine

Abbeville · Arras

Namur

FOURTH ARMY

St Valery-en-Caux

Dinant · Ardennes

Koblenz

Le Havre

FRENCH NINTH ARMY

TWELTH ARMY

Rouen

21 JUNE France surrenders · Montcornet

Sedan

Mainz

Compiègne

Reims

FRENCH SECOND ARMY

SIXTEENTH ARMY

Paris

Meuse

Metz

LEEB ARMY GROUP C

Seine

FRENCH THIRD ARMY

Maginot Line

14 JUNE Paris surrenders · FRANCE

Marne

0 miles 50 / 0 kilometres 80 · N

Above: **Hitler's conquest of the Low Countries and France, culminating in the evacuation of Allied troops from Dunkirk and capture of Paris on June 14 .**

Right: **German infantry advance through a village some 40km (25 miles) from Dunkirk.**

improvement in aircraft and armoured vehicles in the twenty years since 1918 greatly improved the execution of such tactics, yet we must not overestimate the modernism of the German Army in 1939.

The vast majority of German military transport was horse-drawn. Each regiment had 683 horses, as opposed to just 73 motor vehicles. A total of almost three million horses were employed by the German Army throughout the war. Although German propaganda films liked to focus on the role of tanks smashing through enemy lines and troops racing behind them on motorbikes, the majority of its forces advanced at the pace of a horse, just as the armies of the First World War had. Attempts to embrace modernism and overcome this inherent slowness were not always successful. Germany's much-vaunted paratroopers were soundly defeated in Norway and heavy losses in Crete saw them reduced to the role of élite infantry.

CONQUERING THE WEST

Having conquered Denmark and Norway in order to outflank Britain's attempts at a maritime blockade, Germany finally turned to face its principal Western enemies a good nine months after the beginning of the war. In the meantime, why did France not attack the Rhineland, the industrial heart of Germany? The short answer was that the shadow of the First World War hung heavily over the Allies. Neither the British nor the French wanted another world war. Both had suffered too much in the first and went to great political lengths to accommodate Germany's territorial ambitions. In the inter-war period they had not modernized or increased the size of their armies to the same extent as Hitler had in Germany.

Should a war come, the Allies expected it to be a replay of the Western Front, fought from largely static defences. To this

end, France had invested vast sums in a string of fortifications called the Maginot Line. It believed that Germany's own lines of defence, the Westwall, were similarly impregnable and the human costs of invading the Rhineland would be too high. Thus, France and Britain decided to fight a war of defence, using the delay to rearm and expand their armies as best they could. They even refrained from the idea of the aerial bombardment of Germany, hoping by this restraint not to escalate the war. The Allied wish that Belgium and the Netherlands would join them in a defensive coalition evaporated because both of the smaller countries similarly wished not to provoke Hitler. Even so, the day of reckoning came in May 1940.

On 10 May, German armies invaded the Netherlands and Belgium. Rather than withdrawing towards the Allies, the Dutch Army was cut off in the north of the country. The main northern Belgian defensive line, anchored at the fortress of Eban Emael, was overwhelmed after stiff fighting. A terror bombardment of Rotterdam then convinced the Dutch to surrender. The ferocity of the assault against the civilian population relieved the Allies of any restraint during future bombing raids and in Britain Winston Churchill became the prime minister following the resignation of Neville Chamberlain. The German advance through Belgium reassured the French that this was a repetition of the First World War strategy and that they were right to wait behind their defences. But this was exactly what Hitler, overall director of the military campaign, wanted them to believe.

THE FALL OF FRANCE

'It had been a clever piece of work to attack Liège,' Hitler later recalled in 1941. 'We had to make them believe we were remaining faithful to the old Schlieffen Plan.' Advancing to the

the movement of French troops. The French Air Force, in contrast, was poorly equipped and could not match the Germans in the skies. French planning had been proved to be fatally flawed: committed to a defensive ground strategy along the Maginot Line, the French now had to witness the main German attack coming from the north, ignoring their magnificent fortresses completely.

Caught in the open, the French were no match for the better-equipped and more determined German soldiers. Their morale collapsed and by 9 June German panzer divisions had reached the River Seine to the west of Paris. A few French forces resisted fiercely and launched counter-attacks, but overall they achieved little and failed to stem the German advance. On 13 June, Paris fell and the French government moved south. Three days previously, Italy had joined Germany and declared war on France, putting further pressure on its politicians. German armoured divisions roared on towards the Atlantic coastal ports and central France.

On 17 June, France's prime minister, Reynaud, refused to join with Britain in continued resistance to Germany and resigned. His place was taken by the First World War veteran General Pétain, who asked the Germans for an armistice. On 21 June, the formal capitulation of France was signed by France's General Huntziger, who met Hitler in the railway carriage in the Compiègne Forest where the original armistice had been agreed in 1918. For Germany, it was sweet revenge and Hitler later had the carriage destroyed to prevent any further symbolic acts.

In less than a month, France had been knocked out of the war. It was a humiliating defeat, even greater than that in the Franco-Prussian War (see Sedan, pp.36–37), and convinced the rest of the world that the German war machine was invincible. Certainly, Germany had achieved the ambition held since 1870 of being undisputed master of western Europe, leaving it free to turn east and pursue territorial ambitions. British intervention had been soundly defeated and the ease of this operation now tempted Hitler to consider invading Britain. His overconfidence in blitzkrieg warfare also promoted his decision to invade Russia in 1941.

Above: Captured British and French soldiers at Dunkirk.

Below: Hitler the conqueror poses in front of the Eiffel Tower after his rapid defeat of France.

Belgian frontier, the wrong-footed French were little prepared for an armoured thrust through the Ardennes Forest by General Rundstedt. The Germans crossed the River Meuse and, aided by relentless Ju87 Stuka dive-bomber raids, smashed the French flank. The Germans then broke through to the Channel ports and divided the Allied armies. The British Expeditionary Force that had come to aid the Belgians found itself pushed back to the English Channel. Hitler withheld his ground troops from capturing the British at Dunkirk in order to allow his air force to destroy them on the beaches, but this failed and more than three hundred thousand British, French and Belgian soldiers were evacuated back to Britain. Cut off from their allies, Belgian forces had no choice but to surrender.

With the conquest of Flanders achieved and Britain expelled from the Continent, German armies regrouped and struck southwards. The Luftwaffe helped to disrupt rail links and slow

---

GERMAN GENERAL BLUMENTRITT, RUNDSTEDT'S OPERATIONS CHIEF DURING THE BATTLE OF FRANCE

THEY WERE BRAVE!

'In the 1940 campaign the French fought bravely, but they were no longer the French of 1914–18 – of Verdun and the Somme. The British fought much more stubbornly, as they did in 1914–18. The Belgians in part fought gallantly; the Dutch, only a few days. We had superiority in the air combined with more up-to-date tanks than the French. Above all, the German tank troops were more mobile, quicker and better at in-fighting, and able while in movement to turn wherever required by their leader. This, the French at that time were unable to do. They still thought and fought more in the tradition of the First World War. They were not up to date either in leadership or in wireless control. When they wanted to change direction on the move, they had to halt first, give fresh orders, and only then were they able to start again. Their tank tactics were out of date — but they were brave!'

Quoted in _The Other Side of the Hill_ by B.H. Liddell Hart (Cassell, 1948)

BATTLE OF BRITAIN, 1940

Britain's defiant use of air power to block Hitler's projected invasion of the country is a remarkable case study for the importance of mastering the newest military technology. Göring overestimated the ability of his aircraft to bomb Britain into submission and his losses mounted day by day. The Spitfire fighter plane had never had a better opportunity to show off its capabilities. The Battle of Britain halted Hitler's plans to invade Britain and gave the British time to strike back at Germany in occupied Europe.

The Battle of Britain was, as Winston Churchill declared, the finest hour of the British people. At their most vulnerable point in more than two hundred years, they faced the very real threat of invasion by Europe's most effective military conqueror since Napoleon. German armies had swept through eastern and western Europe, and with the modern technology available to them it seemed in the summer of 1940 to be only a matter of weeks before they would cross the English Channel.

Before Hitler could deliver the final blow, he had to master the air above Britain. Göring had failed to crush the British Army at Dunkirk with his Luftwaffe, but now he promised to deliver Britain to Hitler in a brief but devastating air campaign. He had

access to all the airfields along the North Sea coast and so could take all his aircraft to within range of British targets. In contrast, Britain's Royal Air Force (RAF) could muster only 650 fighter aircraft – it was outnumbered by almost four to one.

The ensuing conflict has been characterized as a David versus Goliath struggle, with inspired English amateurism pitched against cool German efficiency, but recent historians have questioned this legend and made the point that Göring's campaign was a classic example of German overconfidence. Although the numbers were unequal, the Germans were used to dealing with the old-fashioned, poorly equipped air forces of Poland and France, not the professional and skilled RAF. Technically, the Germans placed too much faith in long-range twin-engined fighters, while Britain's Spitfire with its eight machine guns was truly an awesome piece of high technology.

FROM SCAPEGOATS TO HEROES

An indication of what was to come was demonstrated by the fighting in the skies over Dunkirk as the RAF sought to protect the evacuating British troops from the attacks of the Luftwaffe.

Above: **British pilots run to their Spitfire fighter planes in the winter of 1940.**

Right: **An ARP warden searches a wrecked bedroom for survivors after a bombing raid. The German decision to switch their attacks from airfields to civilian targets saved the RAF but put the British people on the front line of the war.**

'There was a victory inside the deliverance,' Churchill told Parliament. 'It was gained by the Royal Air Force.' The troops on the beaches saw it with different eyes. They complained about the lack of RAF cover and to an extent they were correct. Air Chief Marshal Sir Hugh Dowding refused to risk all his aircraft in the fighting over Dunkirk and so those that were sent were stretched thinly, but the Spitfires performed well, proving more versatile than the German Me109s and Me110s. German pilots were beginning to get the message. 'From the British fighters we met heavy resistance,' remembered Ju87 Stuka pilot Rudolf Braun. Back in England, however, the reputation of the RAF was at an all-time low.

Dunkirk gave British pilots the battle experience they were soon to need in earnest. As part of the preparations for Operation Sealion, the invasion of Britain, Göring's campaign for air domination began on 10 July. The first stage was the Kanalkampf, or Channel Battle, in which German aircraft assaulted English coastal towns and merchant shipping for three weeks. Göring hoped to draw the British aircraft into a killing zone, but the RAF, demonstrating its cool professionalism, shot down twice as many as it lost. Hitler had hoped this display of air power would encourage the British to accept peace on his terms, but the Luftwaffe's failure in these opening encounters did little to discourage Churchill, and Hitler ordered a massive air assault on the mainland. In total, the Luftwaffe could call upon some 860 bombers, 250 dive-bombers and 850 fighters.

Eagle Day on 13 August was the day chosen for the crushing blow: 1,485 German aircraft roared into the skies

Above: **German and British aircraft bases during the Battle of Britain in 1940.**

and headed for RAF airfields with the intention of destroying British aircraft on the ground. Events went badly, however, almost from the start. A radio message to the German fighter escort informed them that the raids had been called off and they returned to base, but no one told the bombers and they continued without protection. The RAF shot down 45 aircraft for a loss of only 13 fighters. On the next day, 70 German planes were brought down for a loss of 27. This killing ratio continued for two more days, but many of the

German bombers had got through and destroyed some 16 British aircraft on the ground. The British public could see in the skies above it the RAF fighting for the country's survival and the reputation of the RAF soared, making the darker days of Dunkirk a distant memory. When Churchill broadcast his famous phrase – 'Never in the field of human conflict was so much owed by so many to so few' – everyone heartily agreed.

BEGINNING 'THE BLITZ'

Göring was not used to his air force sustaining heavy losses and these were wounds that could not be healed easily. Bomber pilots needed two years of training and their losses in the Battle of Britain would impact on the effectiveness of German bombing raids in future campaigns. German aircraft production was not as efficient as it could have been, and at the height of the battle, British factories, on the other hand, were producing five hundred fighters a month, twice the number being built by the Germans. Also, those machines that were built by the Germans were often not produced to optimum fighting effectiveness.

Three twin-engine machines could be produced for every two four-engine bombers and Göring subscribed to a belief that Hitler 'will not ask how big the bombers are, but how many there are'. The invention of radar, however, meant that British air defences possessed the decisive advantage, for it told them exactly where the approaching Germans were so that the British fighters, fewer in number, could be aimed precisely at incoming aircraft.

British fighters operated during the day, while British bombers attacked Hitler's soldiers at night as they waited in their barges for the signal to cross the English Channel. Having failed to down sufficient British aircraft, Göring resumed his assault against RAF airfields. Several fighter stations were put out of action between 24 August and 6 September, with the RAF losing 290 aircraft. The Luftwaffe was still incurring greater losses, but the draining of the RAF's manpower was beginning to assume dangerous proportions, with almost a quarter of its one thousand pilots having been killed or wounded. The replacement pilots were keen but inexperienced, making them more vulnerable in the sky.

This was the point at which Britain's air defences were at their weakest and if Göring had continued with this strategy, the attrition might well have brought him success. But Göring was impatient and Hitler had lifted his ban on bombing London. The British attacked Germany's cities in retaliation and this rapidly escalated events, to the point where Göring switched his plans and directed massive bombing raids against the British capital. By shifting focus away from the airfields, Göring gave the RAF the breathing-space it needed. It was a decisive German error.

The first mass air raid took place on 7 September when 650 bomber aircraft dropped more than 670 tons of high explosive on London's docks along the Thames, killing 458 civilians. The

Below: **Luftwaffe Dornier bombers fly from France to bomb Britain in the summer of 1940.**

Above: Young RAF Hurricane fighter pilots rest between combat engagements.

SQUADRON LEADER GARVIN, BATTLE OF BRITAIN PILOT

BREAKING POINT
'The strain had almost reached breaking point. The usually good-natured George was quiet and irritable; Colin, by nature thin-faced, was noticeably more hollow-cheeked; Desmond, inclined to be weighty, was reduced to manageable proportions; and I, though I had no way of knowing how I appeared to others, was all on edge and practically jumped out of my skin when someone shouted unexpectedly over the R/T. But still we continued to operate – there was no alternative.'
Quoted in *The Most Dangerous Enemy* by Stephen Bungay (Aurum Press, 2000)

bombing reached a climax on 15 September when more than a thousand bombers subjected the city to a tremendous raid. It came at a heavy cost for the Germans with the RAF downing 56 planes for a loss of 26 aircraft. Enough was enough and the Luftwaffe refused to undertake any more daytime raids, preferring the protective cover of darkness. The bombing continued in what Londoners called 'the Blitz', a terrifying experience for the city's civilian population, who took to the cover of air-raid shelters dug in their gardens or the deeper protection afforded by underground train stations. But Hitler had had enough as well. Winter and its poorer weather was coming and on 17 September he postponed Operation Sealion for ever. The Battle of Britain was won and the threat of invasion lifted, but the terror bombing continued, putting British civilians on the front line of the war far into 1941, with a total of 43,000 civilians dying in raids on London and other British cities. It was savage revenge for the German failure to break the spirit of British resistance.

CRETE, 1941

The German attack on the island of Crete was the first great airborne assault in history. Thousands of highly trained German paratroopers descended on British Army positions. It was a remarkable demonstration of air power, one that forced the British from the island and back to North Africa, but the high numbers of casualties endured by the Germans meant such an operation would never be tried again.

In 1941, as Hitler planned Operation Barbarossa (see pp.100–103), he felt the need to secure Germany's southern European flank. An agreement in March 1941 with Prince Paul, regent of Yugoslavia, for his country to join the Axis alongside Romania and Hungary had been overturned within days by a *coup d'état*, which rejected any such alliance and aimed to preserve Yugoslavia's neutrality. The arrival of British troops in Greece further threatened Hitler's hold over the Balkans and he decided to invade Yugoslavia and then Greece. Both operations were carried out brilliantly by his troops in less than a month with few losses and huge gains. Yugoslavian and Greek resistance would grow over the years, but the immediate aftermath of these two conquests was to increase greatly Hitler's faith in his own abilities and those of his soldiers.

Just over fifteen thousand British soldiers retreated from Greece to the island of Crete. Although defeated, this force still posed a threat to Germany's control of the Balkans and Hitler needed to deliver one final blow against the Allies to drive them

Right: **German paratroopers descend from Junkers Ju52 transport aircraft during the aerial invasion of Crete.**

Below: **The German aerial assault on Crete in May 1941.**

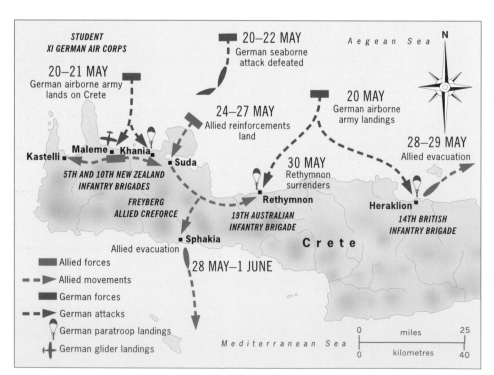

out of southern Europe. For this, he would use a new kind of warfare that had proved itself in western Europe during the victorious blitzkrieg campaign of 1940: airborne assault.

THE AIRBORNE ELITE

Hitler's airborne troops were one of his élite units. Highly trained and motivated, the paratroopers had enjoyed spectacular success in 1940 during the German invasion of Belgium and the Netherlands. They landed on the massive Belgian fortification of Eban Emael and captured it after hard fighting, striking a major blow against the Allied defences in this region. Similar airborne raids were later carried out successfully against strategically important positions in the Netherlands. Hitler was now keen to use the paratroopers again in a major campaign.

Hitler's operation against Crete was code-named Merkur (Mercury). The aim was to capture the island's airbases. It was planned as a purely aerial assault with some ten thousand paratroopers, under the command of General Kurt Student, being carried in 75 gliders and 500 transport aircraft protected by bombers and fighter planes. The invasion would be carried out in two phases, with the first wave descending on Maleme, Khania and Suda Bay. The transport planes would then return to take in the second-phase troops for an assault on the airfields at Rethymnon and Heraklion. British and Allied troops on Crete were joined by twelve thousand reinforcements from Egypt

STUDENT XI GERMAN AIR CORPS

20–22 MAY German seaborne attack defeated

Aegean Sea

N

20–21 MAY German airborne army lands on Crete

24–27 MAY Allied reinforcements land

20 MAY German airborne army landings

28–29 MAY Allied evacuation

Kastelli ■
Maleme ■ Khania ■
■ Suda

5TH AND 10TH NEW ZEALAND INFANTRY BRIGADES

FREYBERG ALLIED CREFORCE

30 MAY Rethymnon surrenders

■ Rethymnon

Heraklion ■

19TH AUSTRALIAN INFANTRY BRIGADE

14TH BRITISH INFANTRY BRIGADE

■ Sphakia

Allied evacuation

28 MAY–1 JUNE

C r e t e

■ Allied forces
▪ ▪ ▶ Allied movements
■ German forces
▪ ▪ ▶ German attacks
German paratroop landings
German glider landings

Mediterranean Sea

miles 0 – 25
kilometres 0 – 40

and a fourteen thousand-strong Greek garrison. They were commanded by New Zealander Major General Bernard Freyberg. Unfortunately, German air raids forced the few RAF aircraft on the island to withdraw, leaving the Allies without air cover. It was a grave error.

Following a heavy aerial bombardment, the invasion began at dawn on 20 May 1941. 'I reached the door,' recalled Oberjäger Lingg. 'The slipstream made me gasp. I jumped, tumbling two or three times as I plummeted earthward until my parachute opened with a sharp jolt. "Thank God!" was all I could say. So far, so good. But the worst had yet to come.' The paratrooper was correct, for below him Allied soldiers were ready and waiting. Thanks to the Ultra intercepts of German coded signals, the Allies were fully aware of the coming German invasion and had prepared themselves. Alerted to the beginning of events by the preceding air raids, the Allied troops in position fired upwards as the airborne soldiers descended. Hundreds of paratroopers were killed before they reached the ground; some were lost at sea without even reaching the island.

NEVER AGAIN

By the end of the first day, the airborne assault had failed to capture any of the Allied airbases, although some outskirt defences outside Maleme had been taken. Despite the horrendous losses, Student persisted with the attacks and a further drop of paratroopers on the second day enabled him to gain control of Maleme airfield. Reinforcements were now sent in, consisting of the 5th Mountain Division, but many of their planes crashed in the approach. Enough survived, however, for them to hold on to Maleme.

Further reinforcements were flown in over the next few days and although more casualties were taken, the German force slowly but surely extended its control over the island. The sky continued to be the only way into Crete because the Royal Navy controlled the sea, destroying two attempts to send reinforcements by sea. By 27 May, most of the Allied troops had evacuated the island and German paratroopers captured the final airfield at Heraklion. The remainder of the British and Greek forces surrendered.

The price of the German victory was high. At least one in four of the paratroopers had been killed, with a great many more injured – a total of some 5,670 casualties. Student called Crete the 'grave of the German paratroopers'. Hitler himself was shocked by the losses endured by his favoured soldiers. 'Crete has shown that the day of the paratroopers is over,' he told Student as he awarded him a medal. 'Paratroopers are a weapon of surprise, and the surprise factor has been overplayed.' Never again would Hitler order a large aerial assault to be conducted. The majority of German paratroopers would now function as élite infantry on the eastern and western fronts.

Below: British soldiers are taken prisoner by German paratroopers during the invasion of Crete.

GENERAL KURT STUDENT, COMMANDER OF THE GERMAN AIRBORNE FORCES

BITTER MEMORIES

'For me, the commander of the German airborne forces, the very name Crete conjures up bitter memories. I miscalculated when I proposed the operation, and my mistake caused not only the loss of very many paratroopers – whom I looked upon as my sons – but in the long run led to the demise of the German airborne arm which I had created.'
Quoted in *Hitler's Green Devils* by I.M. Baxter (Military Illustrated, 2001)

BARBAROSSA, 1941

Although the invasion of the Soviet Union was Hitler's greatest gamble, it was the culmination of his political career. He regarded the coming war not just as a means to seize vast amounts of *lebensraum* ('living space') for the German people, but also as a crusade against the 'Bolshevik' Slav people. 'The safety of Europe will not be assured until we have driven Asia back behind the Urals,' he told friends in 1941. 'No organized Russian state must be allowed to exist west of that line. They are brutes, and neither Bolshevism nor Tsarism makes any difference – they are brutes in a state of nature.' He imagined that Nazi Germany's destruction of Russia would be his gift to the rest of Europe and as a consequence he expected all the other states to support him. And to a certain extent, his idea of a pan-European army was realized.

On the day Germany invaded the Soviet Union, Italy honoured its treaty obligations to Germany and declared war too. Romania then joined the fighting, as did Hungary and Finland, all of them sending numerous divisions of troops. Spain raised an expeditionary force and a foreign legion of volunteers was recruited from Norway, Denmark, the Netherlands, Belgium, France and Yugoslavia. Unlike previous campaigns in the war, idealistic young men saw

***Above*:** German armoured vehicles halt on the Russian steppes during the invasion in 1941.

***Right*:** A German infantryman, armed with a Kar 98k rifle, advances during Operation Barbarossa.

Operation Barbarossa was Hitler's long-awaited invasion of the Soviet Union and it very nearly succeeded in its aims. The operation began the most destructive and brutal war of the 20th century, fought between the two leading ideological superpowers of the day. German armoured divisions raced ahead and encircled massive numbers of bewildered Russian soldiers, tens of thousands of whom surrendered. Stalin was devastated, but Germany's initial success ran foul of the Russian weather and increased military resistance by the Soviet Army.

this as a just war against communism. Even the Pope, Pius XII, lent his support to the struggle, which had taken on the spirit of a medieval crusade. Under the circumstances, the code-name chosen by Hitler for the operation was the entirely appropriate one of Barbarossa, a medieval German crusader king.

A DIFFERENT KIND OF WAR

The army that Hitler assembled was one of the greatest ever seen and the war on the Eastern Front was the most destructive fought in the 20th century. More than three million soldiers and three thousand tanks were assembled along a 1,700-km (thousand-mile) frontier running from the Baltic to the Black Sea. The attack began before dawn on 22 June 1941. Hitler had briefed his generals on the behaviour he expected in the campaign: 'The fight will be very different from the fight in the west. In the east harshness is kindness towards the future. The leaders must demand of themselves the sacrifice of overcoming their scruples.' It was a speech that implied a bloodbath.

Behind the advancing German army followed the Einsatzgruppen, soldiers who specialized in the extermination of Jews and 'Bolsheviks'. Not trusting to chance the 'scruples' of his generals, Hitler put these death squads under the separate command of Heinrich Himmler, who had already proved his capacity for efficient brutality in Germany and Poland. It was the Einsatzgruppen that carried out the infamous order of 6 June in which Hitler identified the political commissars of the Red Army as 'authors of barbarously Asiatic methods of fighting' who 'when captured in battle or in resistance are on principle to be disposed of by gunshot immediately'. The war in the east was to be war without mercy.

Under the cover of a tremendous aerial bombardment, three main army groups moved across Soviet territory. Their three main objectives were the cities of Leningrad, Moscow and Kiev, with the intention of establishing a German frontier from Archangel in the north to the Caspian Sea in the south. Panzer divisions drove deep into the Soviet Union, an advance which carved up the Red Army and allowed the slower-moving artillery and infantry to finish off any resistance. The speed and tactical efficiency of the German forces shocked the Soviets. 'They were firing into our rear lines,' recalled one Russian soldier, 'which had a big effect on our morale. We realized we were surrounded. Our soldiers were shouting "we're surrounded". As they started shooting with machine guns, the German tanks came in. In the confusion, our officers grabbed rides on passing vehicles although they were

completely packed. We ended up in a situation with no commanders and there was nothing we could do.'

When German troops had entered the Soviet Baltic states, they had been greeted as liberators. In Riga, Latvian resistance fighters appeared to fight street battles with Red Army troops. In Estonia, anti-communist groups took the opportunity to strike

Below: **The initial German invasion of Russian territory during Operation Barbarossa.**

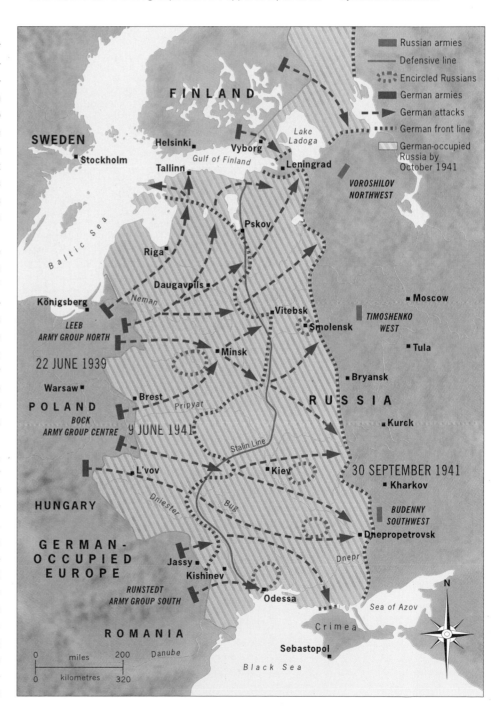

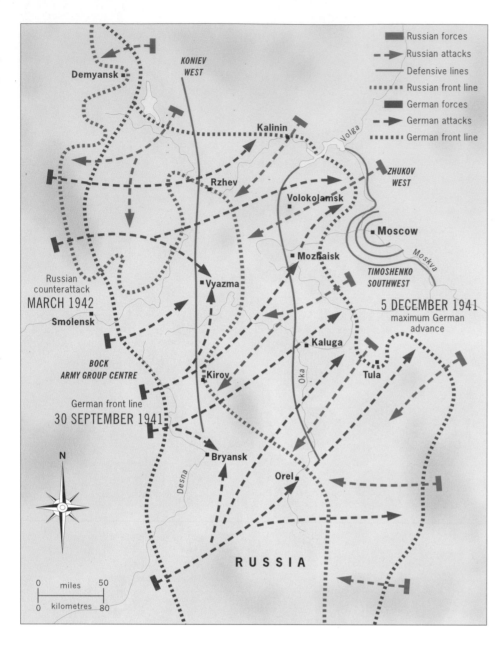

Russian forces
Russian attacks
Defensive lines
Russian front line
German forces
German attacks
German front line

Demyansk

KONIEV
WEST

Kalinin

Volga

Rzhev

ZHUKOV
WEST

Volokolamsk

Moscow

Mozhaisk

Moskva

Russian
counterattack
MARCH 1942

Vyazma

TIMOSHENKO
SOUTHWEST

Smolensk

5 DECEMBER 1941
maximum German
advance

Kaluga

BOCK
ARMY GROUP CENTRE

Kirov

Oka

Tula

German front line
30 SEPTEMBER 1941

N

Bryansk

Desna

Orel

RUSSIA

0   miles   50
0   kilometres   80

Above: **The final stage of Operation Barbarossa; while German troops halted outside Moscow. Soviet armies would use the winter to prepare a counter-attack.**

Right: **A German convoy of motorized transport and horses advances through a Russian village.**

a blow against the departing Red Army. Within weeks of the beginning of the Nazi occupation, many of these Baltic peoples also turned their anger against local Jewish populations and committed massacres and atrocities with the full connivance of the Germans. In the Ukraine, peasants flocked to the German tanks, cheering and applauding, happy to be liberated by 'Christian warriors'.

THE DRIVE TOWARDS MOSCOW

By the middle of July, the German Army Group Centre had captured Minsk and seized some 290,000 prisoners and 2,500 Soviet tanks. Continuing onwards to Smolensk, the panzer divisions scooped another one hundred thousand prisoners and two thousand tanks. Both flank groups, however, were finding the going harder, with the enormous distances putting a strain on supplies as well as the stamina of the tank divisions. Hitler halted Army Group Centre and detached divisions from it to transfer to the other army groups. This helped Army Group

South but frustrated Army Group Centre, which had, critically, to delay its advance on Moscow. By 26 September, on the southern front, five Russian armies were trapped in a bend of the River Dnieper near Kiev, with the result that some 665,000 Soviet soldiers surrendered. Further south, German troops reached the Crimea.

Army Group North laid siege to Leningrad in October. The Luftwaffe had command of the skies, shooting down some 4,500 Soviet Air Force planes for the loss of less than half that number of its own. Army Group Centre had been ordered to resume its march on Moscow and had reached to within 65km (40 miles) of the Soviet capital before it encountered stiffer resistance. The autumn rains then turned the roads to mud and this slowed down the German advance. Soon the rain had turned to snow as winter began to set in. Marshal Georgy Zhukov headed the defence of Moscow, and a Russian counter-attack succeeded at Rostov. More massive counter-offensives followed in December using one hundred new Soviet divisions. Kalinin was retaken on 15 December and the German offensive ground to a halt. Hitler was furious with his generals and relieved many of them of their commands, taking direct control of the campaign from Berlin by radio.

SOVIET PANIC

Operation Barbarossa had thrown the Soviet Union into a panic. Its armies had suffered more than three million casualties, half of whom were prisoners whose treatment was so bad that most did not survive to return home. Stalin faced the greatest

crisis of his life, but even though he was shaken by the rapid Nazi advance, he would not leave his capital and his solidly defiant mood spread through his army.

Hitler had undoubtedly bitten off more than he could chew. The German armies' initial advances had been helped by the fact that many of the states they passed through regarded the German soldiers as liberators from the Soviet regime, but as Nazi occupation rule became more oppressive, this support evaporated. The cost of Operation Barbarossa had been great as well, losing Hitler some eight hundred thousand men. He had gambled on the Soviet state collapsing in the face of the German onslaught, just as Poland and France had. But the Soviet Union was too vast and the Russians in particular too determined, being prepared to face annihilation rather than to surrender. Hitler's troops were wholly unprepared for a war lasting into the winter. They froze in their summer uniforms and their tanks became immobile with ice. Barbarossa now turned into a war of attrition, one that would ultimately drain the German Army of its manpower and leave Hitler's land empire vulnerable to an Allied counter-attack.

Above: As the bitter Russian winter descends, German troops try to keep themselves warm. Anticipating a quick victory, many troops did not have winter clothing.

Above: Many Russian soldiers were quickly surrounded and captured by German troops during opening strike of Operation Barbarossa.

CURZIO MALAPARTE, ITALIAN JOURNALIST

BURYING THE DEAD
'The retreating Soviet troops do not abandon their dead on the battlefield, nor do they bury them on the spot. They take them away. They bury them twelve, twenty miles [20–30km] further east, in the heart of a wood, or in the depths of a valley. They bury them in huge communal graves: and on the graves they plant no crosses, nor do they leave any marks of identification. They trample down the newly-turned earth and cover it with leaves, grass, branches of trees, sometimes with heaps of manure, so that none may ever be able to violate these secret tombs.'
Quoted from *The Volga Rises in Europe* by Curzio Malaparte (Birlinn, 2000)

PEARL HARBOR, 1941

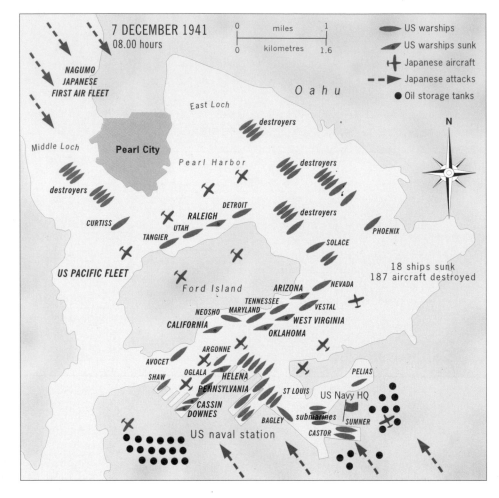

7 DECEMBER 1941
08.00 hours

| | miles | 1 |
| 0 | kilometres | 1.6 |

- US warships
- US warships sunk
- Japanese aircraft
- Japanese attacks
- Oil storage tanks

NAGUMO
JAPANESE
FIRST AIR FLEET

O a h u

East Loch

Middle Loch

Pearl City

Pearl Harbor

N

destroyers

destroyers

destroyers

CURTISS
RALEIGH   DETROIT
UTAH
TANGIER

destroyers

PHOENIX

SOLACE

US PACIFIC FLEET

18 ships sunk
187 aircraft destroyed

Ford Island   ARIZONA   NEVADA
TENNESSEE
NEOSHO MARYLAND   VESTAL
CALIFORNIA   WEST VIRGINIA
OKLAHOMA

ARGONNE
AVOCET
SHAW   OGLALA   HELENA
PENNSYLVANIA   ST LOUIS   US Navy HQ   PELIAS
CASSIN
DOWNES   BAGLEY   submarines   SUMNER
US naval station   CASTOR

Above: The Japanese aerial assualt on US battleships anchored around Ford Island at Pearl Harbor on 7 December, 1941.

Japan's surprise attack on the United States was a perfectly executed pre-emptive assault with devastating results. Swarms of Japanese aircraft bombed and torpedoed American battleships at their moorings. But American aircraft carriers were not there and the Japanese attack failed to destroy US naval power. Japan's intended knock-out blow, far from discouraging the United States from declaring war on Japan, brought relief to the Western allies because the United States was now brought into the war and could help them to defeat Japan and Germany.

In 1940, the militaristic Japanese government felt that war with the United States was inevitable. In September, it had agreed an Axis alliance with Germany and Italy, with Germany giving Japan permission to acquire all its former colonies that had been taken over by the Allies after the First World War. The Japanese believed they had enough supplies, including oil, to carry on with their war in China, move south to acquire European colonies and fight the United States. Their relationship with Germany would help solve any problems with the

Soviet Union, which had soundly beaten Japan in a short war in 1939, and later, when the situation in Europe changed, Japan signed a non-aggression pact with the Soviet Union in April 1941 that suited both sides very well.

At the end of September 1940, Japanese troops began to occupy northern Indochina, taking advantage of French weakness there. This was done despite warnings from the United States for Japan not to get involved, and the result was an embargo on the shipment of steel to Japan. The continued Japanese occupation of Indochina forced the United States in July 1941 to freeze Japanese assets in the USA. In September, the US government gave tacit approval to the formation of a volunteer group of American pilots who flew as the Flying Tigers in support of the Chinese in their war against Japan.

As tension mounted, ambassadors on both sides sought to defuse it, but in October General Hideki Tojo became chief of the government in Tokyo and he was in no mood for compromise. He initiated Japanese war plans against the United States and the European colonies. Faced with US demands for withdrawal from China and Indochina, Tojo could see no alternative to war.

THE PRE-EMPTIVE STRIKE

Japan's unannounced act of aggression against the US naval base of Pearl Harbor was nothing new in Japanese strategy. Japan struck first in its war against Russia in 1904, with torpedo boats wrecking the Russian fleet in Port Arthur before any formal declaration of war. In 1941, the torpedoes were delivered by aircraft.

Rear Admiral Isoroku Yamamoto was the mastermind behind the assault. He knew the future of naval warfare lay with the aircraft carrier and he instigated a carrier-building programme in Japan in the 1930s. He also encouraged the construction of the famous Mitsubishi A6M2 Zero fighter. Yamamoto had served as a naval attaché in Washington, D.C., and he knew the strength of the United States at first hand. He opposed the idea of a war with the United States, but when the decision was made, he knew it had to be through a knock-out blow.

Minoru Genda worked on the details of the attack, taking as a model the British raid at Taranto in November 1940, when British bombers had taken off from carriers and sunk Italian ships. He worked alongside Commander Mitsuo Fuchida, one of Japan's most experienced aviators, who would actually lead the attack. Genda designed new torpedoes and bombs for the task.

The Japanese First Air Fleet, which included six aircraft carriers and supporting battleships and submarines, set sail under the command of Vice Admiral Nagumo on 26 November 1941.

A S I A — UNITED STATES

JAPAN
Tokyo
San Francisco
Hawaiian Islands
PEARL HARBOR Honolulu

Pacific Ocean

Japan's plans for war were known to US intelligence, which had broken the Japanese codes, but the expectation was for the blow to fall against Malaya or the Philippines. US code monitors lost touch with Nagumo's fleet because it was maintaining strict radio silence.

TORA! TORA! TORA!

On the morning of 7 December 1941, Nagumo's fleet sailed to a point 440km (275 miles) north of Oahu in Hawaii, home of the US Navy base of Pearl Harbor. The power Nagumo could call upon was impressive: 104 Nakajima B5N2 torpedo bombers, 135 Aichi D3A1 dive-bombers and 81 Mitsubishi A6M2 Zero fighters. At 06.00 hours, the first wave of aircraft set off towards Oahu. 'Tora! Tora! Tora!' screamed the pilots – *tora*, meaning 'tiger', being the code-word for the attack. Two hours later, as US navy crewmen were rousing themselves for a day's work, the Japanese aircraft began to drop their bombs on the battleships moored around Ford Island.

On board the USS *Nevada*, Oden McMillan was conducting a US Marine band playing The Star-Spangled Banner as the Japanese aircraft attacked, shooting up the ship around him. Clearly disbelieving what was happening, McMillan kept on conducting. 'The years of training had taken over,' Walter Lord later wrote in *Day of Infamy*, 'it never occurred to him that once he had begun playing the national anthem he could possibly stop. Another strafer flashed by. This time McMillan unconsciously paused as the deck splintered around him, but he quickly picked up the beat again... Not a man broke formation until the final note ended. Then everyone ran wildly for cover.'

Genda's specially designed torpedoes had been modified to function in the harbour's shallow water and there were no defensive nets to intercept them. The resulting destruction was tremendous. Fuchida, who led the attack, flew over the fleet moored around Ford Island and could not believe his luck. 'Even in the deepest peace,' he recalled, 'I have never seen such ships anchored at a distance of less than 500 to 1,000yds [450–900m] from each other. The picture down there was hard to comprehend.'

Oden McMillan's *Nevada* was struck by a torpedo that ripped a huge hole in its port bow. It tried to escape by

Below: Admiral Isoroku Yamamoto, commander of the Japanese fleet that sent out the air strike against Pearl Harbor.

Right: A contemporary painting of Japanese aircraft preparing to take off from an aircraft carrier. Carriers transformed the war in the Pacific, enabling fighters and bombers to strike anywhere, without the need for land bases.

Right: A Japanese
photograph taken during
the aerial assault on
Pearl Harbor, showing
Ford Island and US
battleships moored
beside it.

Below: The first phase of
the Japanese attack
virtually destroyed the
US air defences, leaving
the fleet completely
vulnerable.

steaming out of the harbour, but its captain had to make the difficult decision to beach the ship rather than have it sink and block the harbour entrance. The *Arizona* was hit by both torpedoes and bombs, exploding like a fireworks display. The *West Virginia* was struck by six torpedoes and sank to the bottom of the harbour. The *Oklahoma* keeled over as it was pounded by torpedoes. The *Maryland* and *Tennessee* were shielded from torpedoes by the other ships anchored beside them, but bombs hit them from above and fire spread from the *Arizona* to the *Tennessee*. The *California* was hit twice and the *Pennsylvania* received one bomb as it lay in dry dock. All in all, eight battleships had been devastated.

The morning attack caught the US air defences completely off guard. Aircraft parked on Oahu's five airfields were virtually all destroyed, so there was nothing with which to contest the skies over the harbour. Forty-five minutes later, a second wave of Japanese aircraft dropped explosives on the ships below. The smoke from the burning fleet hindered the pilots' vision, so their aim was less keen, but more than three thousand American servicemen were killed in the onslaught and a total of 18 ships and 187 aircraft were lost. From the Japanese point of view, it was a brilliantly executed raid, one that had been delivered at a long distance from the fleet's homeland and yet it had caught the US Pacific Fleet completely unawares. No longer would the patronizing view be held by either the Americans or the British that Japanese pilots were no good because they wore spectacles.

The US Pacific Fleet was neutralized for six months after the attack, which left Japan free to attack Hong Kong,

Above: US battleships burn and sink during the Japanese attack.

JOHN CHARMLEY, HISTORIAN

SLEEP OF THE SAVED

Although the attack on Pearl Harbor shocked the United States and made it feel vulnerable, across the Atlantic there was a sense of relief. Historian John Charmley describes Winston Churchill's response to the news:

'Once Churchill had digested the fact that the Japanese had attacked the American Fleet at Pearl Harbor, he ordered a call to be put through to Roosevelt. After a few minutes, Roosevelt came through and Churchill asked him: "Mr President, what's all this about Japan?" "It's quite true," he replied. "They have attacked us at Pearl Harbor. We are all in the same boat now." Roosevelt said that he was going to ask Congress to declare war on the morrow, and Churchill pledged himself to the same in the Commons... Churchill retired to bed and, "being saturated and satiated with emotion and sensation", he "slept the sleep of the saved and thankful".'

Quoted from *Churchill – The End of Glory* by John Charmley (Hodder & Stoughton, 1993)

Malaya and the Philippines before the year was out. Even though it seemed a devastating blow at the time, the attack on Pearl Harbor did do the Allied cause some good. The United States was now in the war, which came as a great relief to Britain. Its entry into the war was consolidated when Hitler declared war on the United States shortly afterwards. The raid itself was not as destructive as it first looked. Luckily, all three US aircraft carriers were absent from the harbour at the time of the attack and these were to be the key weapons in the war in the Pacific. In addition, only two of the wrecked battleships would never sail again; the others were raised from the shallow waters and repaired. The United States had been stirred to anger and was ready to fight a bitter war against Japan and Germany. In the long-run, Japan had miscalculated its ability to wage war against the United States.

SINGAPORE, 1942

The conquest of Singapore and Britain's defeat at the hands of the Japanese was a humiliation and it signalled the end of Western supremacy in the Far East. Japanese soldiers broke through the supposedly impenetrable jungle to storm positions where most of the big guns were pointing the other way. Thousands of British and Commonwealth soldiers were condemned to years of misery as Japanese prisoners of war.

If Pearl Harbor was the greatest blow delivered by the Japanese against the Americans in the Second World War, then the fall of Singapore was the greatest setback for the British. Britain's wartime leader Winston Churchill called it 'the worst disaster and largest capitulation in British history'. Singapore came hard on the heels of Pearl Harbor, finally dispelling any latent prejudices held by the Western powers that the Japanese Army was not as effective as any of their own. It was the culmination of Japan's process of military modernization that had begun in the latter part of the 19th century, and finally the invincible aura of Western imperialism was broken, opening the way for numerous other Asian powers to offer a challenge.

Above: Australian soldiers in Malaya were sent to reinforce the Allied garrison at Singapore.

Left: A contemporary Japanese print show its assault force in action, with the naval support close by.

JAPANESE BLITZKRIEG

Days after Pearl Harbor, Japanese armies swept through southeast Asia. On 8 December, Japanese forces broke into Hong Kong Island and by 25 December the city had been bombed into submission. Also on 8 December, a Japanese army of one hundred thousand soldiers, commanded by Lieutenant General Tomoyuki Yamashita, executed an amphibious invasion of northern Malaya, a British colony. Lieutenant General Percival was in command of a force of one hundred thousand British, Australian and Indian soldiers whose express purpose was to defend Singapore, a vital naval base and trading centre at the southern tip of Malaya. Sweeping aside the light British forces in the north of Malaya, the Japanese quickly advanced through the country, descending southwards towards Singapore.

The British battleship *Prince of Wales* and the battlecruiser *Repulse* sailed north to attack the Japanese fleet that was supporting the invasion, but the British vessels were spotted by Japanese aircraft and on 10 December were sunk by bombs and torpedoes. With the exception of the three US aircraft carriers that survived Pearl Harbor, the Allies now had no major battleships in the Asia/Pacific region. It also meant that Singapore had no naval protection.

Japanese forces pressed on and the British-led defenders fell back before them, their morale plunging as the experienced Japanese soldiers overwhelmed them in jungle fighting, outflanking and infiltrating their positions. By January 1942, the British and Commonwealth army manned a defensive line just 40km (25 miles) north of Singapore. On

Above: **A Manchester Regiment machine-gun crew at practice before the battle at Singapore.**

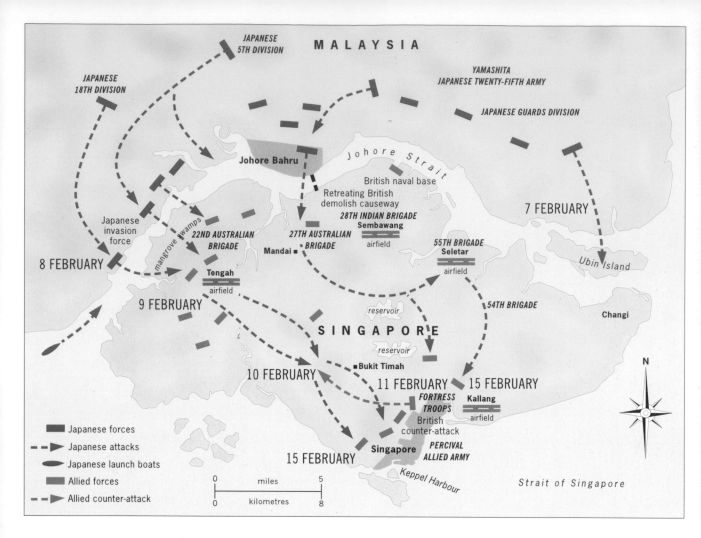

Japanese forces
- - -▶ Japanese attacks
◉ Japanese launch boats
Allied forces
- - -▶ Allied counter-attack

MALAYSIA

JAPANESE 5TH DIVISION

JAPANESE 18TH DIVISION

YAMASHITA JAPANESE TWENTY-FIFTH ARMY

JAPANESE GUARDS DIVISION

Johore Strait

Johore Bahru

British naval base

Retreating British demolish causeway

7 FEBRUARY

Japanese invasion force

28TH INDIAN BRIGADE
Sembawang

8 FEBRUARY

mangrove swamps

22ND AUSTRALIAN BRIGADE

27TH AUSTRALIAN BRIGADE

airfield

55TH BRIGADE
Seletar

Ubin Island

Mandai

Tengah
airfield

9 FEBRUARY

airfield

54TH BRIGADE

reservoir

Changi

S I N G A P O R E

reservoir

N

10 FEBRUARY

Bukit Timah

11 FEBRUARY 15 FEBRUARY

FORTRESS TROOPS
Kallang
airfield

British counter-attack

15 FEBRUARY Singapore *PERCIVAL ALLIED ARMY*

Keppel Harbour

Strait of Singapore

miles 0 ___ 5
kilometres 0 ___ 8

Above: The Japanese assault on the island garrison at Singapore. The British did not expect a major attack to come from the land through the jungle.

15 January, this position was breached and the British withdrew to Singapore itself, crossing the Johore Strait and demolishing the causeway behind them.

IMPREGNABLE FORTRESS

Following Japan's success in the Russo-Japanese War (see Tsushima, pp.54–57), the British government rightly considered that the only threat it faced in the Far East was from the Imperial Japanese Navy. As a result, the British decided to turn Singapore into their major fortified naval base in Asia. With construction under way in the 1930s, an array of 29 big guns were sited around the base, pointing out to sea in order to defy the approach of any enemy navy. With the base completed, the British felt confident that their position was impregnable. The guns were not sited northwards to defend against a land approach because the jungle was thought to be impenetrable by an army. Of course, the Japanese were to demonstrate that this was not so, but the legend that the big guns at Singapore could not then be turned on a land-attacking army is not true and many of the guns were turned round to face the Japanese invaders.

Unfortunately, by 1941 Britain had many other demands on its resources. As Peter Elphick put it in *Singapore: The Pregnable Fortress*: 'Overnight the Far East slid from the number three position in Churchill's scale of defence priorities to number four; it was now behind Great Britain itself, the Middle

East, and Russia.' This meant that British forces in Malaya were not well equipped or supplied. Some 676 aircraft and 446 tanks had been sent to Russia in the six months prior to the assault on Singapore and if these had been directed towards Asia, they might well have helped, but the Japanese assault was so sudden that such supply decisions could not have been made in time. That said, the defending force in Singapore still greatly outnumbered the thirty thousand soldiers that Yamashita could muster for his final assault on the city. Yamashita had only two hundred pieces of artillery against the four hundred guns in Singapore. Although the Japanese had the advantage in morale and training, they did not possess superior numbers or supplies and Yamashita did not feel confident in the task facing him.

THE ATTACK BEGINS

Percival was uncertain where the Japanese would attack and he spread his forces thinly along the northern coast of Singapore. His weakest point was a stretch of mangrove swamp in the northwest. This was where the Japanese attacked on the night of 8 February, when just three Australian battalions found themselves under attack from sixteen Japanese battalions. The Australians inflicted heavy casualties on the Japanese but a third wave managed to gain a toehold on the island.

Colonel Tsuji was one of the Japanese commanders responsible for planning the assault on Singapore and he describes an

Above: **Mother and daughter cry in the street after being caught in a Japanese air raid during the attack on Singapore.**

The Japanese used their aerial supremacy to bomb the island but suffered a self-inflicted setback when blazing oil from wrecked storage tanks drifted into the sea and incinerated Japanese soldiers caught in its way. So far, the defenders were more than holding their own. Although the Japanese had secured a beach-head they were suffering high casualties, but then the Australian commander, Bennett, passed on a message to his officers in which he explained Percival's contingency plan for retreat to a defensive line north of the city. His troops misunderstood this as an order to retreat and the Allied soldiers withdrew, allowing the Japanese to cross the strait unhindered. The causeway was repaired and Japanese tanks rolled across it.

The Japanese swiftly took control of most of the island but bitter fighting broke out around the city's water reservoirs. 'Realising that this was a battle to finish the British Army defending Singapore,' recalled Tsuji, 'we poured all our fighting strength into the battle line.' The big guns of the naval base could do little to stop the Japanese as their shells were designed to hole ships and not shower infantry with shrapnel. When the reservoirs fell, the Japanese closed in on the city.

Panic seized Singapore and there were disgraceful scenes when Australian deserters got drunk and started looting. Civilians were being evacuated and some drunken soldiers used their guns to force their way on to ships in order to escape. Percival was instructed by Churchill to fight to the death, but the capture of the reservoirs weighed heavily on him. He believed there was only 24 hours' worth of water left. This, combined with a severe lack of fighting spirit, saw him veer away from a last stand towards approaching Yamashita under a flag of truce.

At that moment, the Japanese commander was outnumbered three to one and running low in supplies, with only enough ammunition for a few more hours' fighting. If Percival had fought on as recommended he could have turned the tide, but his weakness encouraged the Japanese to persist. Yamashita kept up the bluff with renewed fighting and Percival surrendered unconditionally on 15 September. It was a dreadful and unwarranted decision, condemning tens of thousands of British and Allied soldiers to years of horrifying captivity, during which prisoners were starved, worked and tortured to death. It was Britain's blackest hour in the Second World War and it ended two centuries of respect for its empire and feats of arms.

example of Japanese determination during this first assault: 'Troop Leader Lance-Corporal Yamamoto, standing at the bow of a raft made of three launches lashed together, was continually drenched with spray thrown up by enemy shells hitting the water around the boats. While fully loaded with men of the second line of assault troops, a shell burst on the gunwale of the launches composing the raft, killed the two other coxswains and severely damaged their boats. Yamamoto was the only man left capable of handling the launches, which had fifty men aboard. He landed them on the enemy shore and then collapsed like a falling tree. When the squad commander of the troops lifted him in his arms he saw his lungs protruding through his ribs.'

PETER ELPHICK, HISTORIAN

HOSPITAL ATTACKED

When the Japanese broke into Hong Kong, their troops unleashed an orgy of violence against the inhabitants. At Singapore, its civilians feared the same treatment and historian Peter Elphick records one such incident:
'During that day's fighting [13 February]

a group of Indian soldiers, falling back before the enemy and still firing their weapons, entered the grounds of Alexandra Military Hospital. The Japanese took this for an excuse to commit one of their worst atrocities. Attacking the hospital they bayoneted to death a number of staff and patients,

including one lying on an operating table. They then herded 150 staff and patients into an adjoining building, and massacred them the following morning.'
Quoted from *Singapore: The Pregnable Fortress* (Hodder & Stoughton, 1995)

MIDWAY, 1942

Above: Admiral Chester W. Nimitz, commander in chief of the US Pacific Fleet.

Left: A US navy Grumman TBF Avenger torpedo-bomber attacks Japanese ships in a painting by Bud Parke.

At the Battle of Midway the United States gained its first revenge for Pearl Harbor. Japanese battleships were pounded by American aircraft in a battle where aircraft carriers were the most important weapons. It was a decisive US victory and signalled the beginning of the American advance across the Pacific. The Battle of Midway demonstrated that the United States could strike back at Japan in the new age of aircraft carriers.

Pearl Harbor (see pp.104–107) signified the beginning of a new kind of naval warfare. Japan had demonstrated by that action that the aircraft carrier could win conflicts at sea without battleships even seeing one another. Swarms of aircraft launched from the decks of carriers were capable of overwhelming the defences of any battleships. Fortunately for the US Navy, its three aircraft carriers were absent during the devastating raid at Pearl Harbor and it retained significant air power at sea.

For the moment, Vice Admiral Nagumo dominated the seas off southeast Asia and he struck next at Darwin, Australia, with 188 aircraft that caused such damage to the military base that Australia feared an imminent invasion. From there, Nagumo sailed into the Indian Ocean, where his five carriers took on three carriers of Britain's Royal Navy. Outnumbered in aircraft, the Royal Navy put up a good defence but lost one carrier and was forced to withdraw to East Africa. The Japanese fleet appeared unassailable and its commander in chief, Admiral Yamamoto, was determined to finish off all opposition by means of a decisive battle like Trafalgar or Tsushima. He planned to execute this victory at the islands of Midway, in the middle of the Pacific near the islands of Hawaii.

CORAL SEA CLASH

Before Yamamoto could move against Midway, he had to secure the eastern peninsula of Papua New Guinea and the Solomon Islands. He presumed this would attract American interest and made preparations to fight the first carrier against carrier battle. The Allies, however, had one major advantage: they had broken the secret code of the Japanese and therefore knew in advance what moves the Japanese would make. US Rear Admiral Frank Fletcher was sent to the Coral Sea with two carriers. Bad

weather hindered visibility in the initial conflict and both sides sent large air strikes against unimportant targets. On 8 May, the main battle took place and American inexperience meant that its fleet came off worse, with one carrier sunk. Yamamoto therefore remained confident he could deliver a knock-out blow at Midway.

Despite winning the battle at sea, the Japanese had decided not to land at Port Moresby, Papua New Guinea, and the end of this threat meant that Admiral Nimitz, commander in chief of the US Pacific Fleet, could withdraw his ships from the area and face the new threat at Midway. Yamamoto intentionally signalled his attack against the island because he wanted to draw the US Navy into an ambush and a decisive defeat. The *Yorktown* had survived the battle at Coral Sea and aircraft that had been on board the sunk *Lexington* were reallocated. The US Navy partly overcame its inferiority in fighter aircraft by bringing in upgraded, folding-wing F4F Wildcats. Yamamoto was overconfident and despite two of his carriers being repaired, he decided to proceed to Midway with only four carriers. It was still the largest armada seen in the Pacific, with some 165 warships and 18 submarines.

Yamamoto secretly planned a simultaneous invasion of the Aleutian Islands to the north of Midway and he sent three small carriers loaded with 90 aircraft to accomplish the task. Nimitz presumed this was a diversionary attack and largely ignored it. The shortfall in aircraft that this left for Yamamoto would be noticed. Allied code-breakers informed Nimitz that Nagumo was to attack Midway from the northwest. Nimitz therefore placed his carriers *Enterprise* and *Hornet*, under Rear Admiral Spruance, and *Yorktown*, under Fletcher, to the northeast.

DECISIVE DAYS

The first phase of the Battle of Midway began early on the morning of 4 June, when Nagumo launched a 108-strong aircraft strike against Midway in preparation for a landing. So confident was he that there were no US carriers in the region that he changed the armaments on a second wave of aircraft, removing their anti-ship bombs and replacing them with weapons for mounting attacks against targets on land.

American aircraft took off from the landing strips on Midway, but were too slow to compete effectively with the Japanese fighters and were shot down in great numbers, unable to touch the Japanese carriers. As the Japanese were rearming their planes for another land assault, a reconnaissance craft spotted the US fleet to the northeast. Nagumo changed the direction of his fleet to face the new threat and hurriedly tried to change back the armaments on his aircraft.

US aircraft then took off from their three carriers and attacked the Japanese carriers – but with little success. As at

Coral Sea, American inexperience showed as dive-bombers overshot their targets and US torpedo bombers attacked without fighter escorts, with almost all of them being easily shot down and not scoring one direct hit. Nagumo thought victory was close to hand as he carried on rearming his aircraft to strike back at the US carriers. But the American dive-bombers returned and this time they were spot on target. By 10.25 hours, three Japanese carriers were on fire.

The surviving Japanese carrier sent its aircraft against the *Yorktown* and struck it with three bombs. Rearmed torpedo bombers also hit the *Yorktown*, and Fletcher had to abandon his hopelessly listing ship. In retaliation, 24 US dive-bombers found

Above: **A painting by G.B. Coale depicts US dive-bombers attacking Japanese aircraft carriers.**

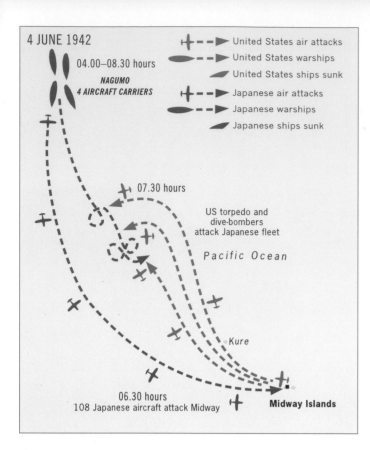

4 JUNE 1942

04.00–08.30 hours

NAGUMO
4 AIRCRAFT CARRIERS

- ✈ ➝ United States air attacks
- ⬭ ➝ United States warships
- ⬮ United States ships sunk
- ✈ ➝ Japanese air attacks
- ⬮ ➝ Japanese warships
- ⬮ Japanese ships sunk

07.30 hours

US torpedo and dive-bombers attack Japanese fleet

Pacific Ocean

○ *Kure*

06.30 hours
108 Japanese aircraft attack Midway

Midway Islands

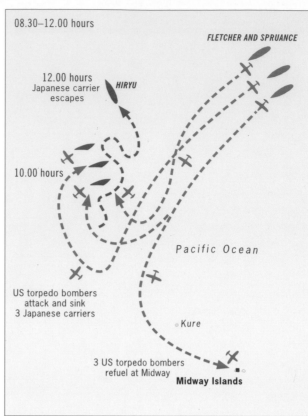

08.30–12.00 hours

FLETCHER AND SPRUANCE

12.00 hours
Japanese carrier escapes

HIRYU

10.00 hours

US torpedo bombers attack and sink 3 Japanese carriers

Pacific Ocean

○ *Kure*

3 US torpedo bombers refuel at Midway

Midway Islands

Far left: The first phases of the battle – the Japanese attack on the Islands of Midway and the first counter-attack on the Japanese carriers.

Left: By mid-morning, the second wave of US aircraft had succeeded in destroying three of the Japanese cruisers.

Below: American aircraft carrier USS *Yorktown* begins to sink after being struck by Japanese dive-bombers.

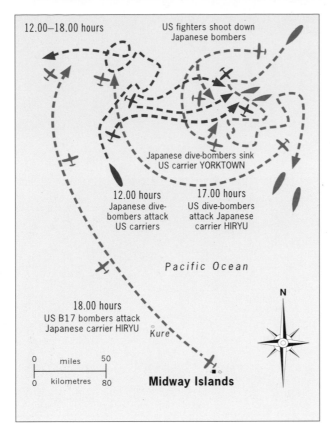

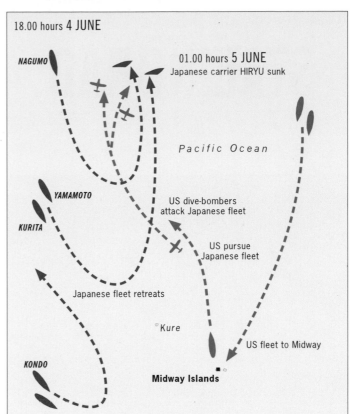

Right: During the afternoon of 4 June, aircraft from the remaining Japanese carrier, *Hiryu*, crippled the USS *Yorktown*. US aircraft then found and neutralized the *Hiryu*.

Far right: The remaining Japanese battleships followed the US fleet until they realized that they could not catch them. The US ships then turned and pursued them.

the remaining Japanese carrier and submitted it to a relentless assault until it, too, burst into flames. By the end of the afternoon, the Japanese fleet had lost all four of its carriers, while the US fleet still had two in service.

Yamamoto had in part been the architect of his own defeat, having split his massive naval force into several non-supporting elements. He now sent his awesome battleships against the smaller US fleet, but Spruance realized the danger and sent his carriers away, sailing eastwards. Accepting that he could not catch the US fleet and aware of his lack of air cover, Yamamoto finally decided to withdraw westwards. The US fleet turned back and pursued the Japanese fleet for two days, inflicting further damage. The *Yorktown* was towed back to Pearl Harbor but was sighted on the way by a Japanese submarine and sunk. Along with an accompanying destroyer, these were the main US losses, as opposed to four Japanese carriers and one heavy destroyer. The United States had lost a total of 132

aeroplanes, but the Japanese losses were more than double this, with 275 planes destroyed and 3,500 men killed.

Midway was a truly decisive battle in that the Japanese had entered it as the dominant naval power in the Pacific, only to be suddenly reduced to a navy without aircraft carriers. From now on, the Japanese Navy was on the defensive, giving the United States a huge advantage in its desire to reconquer the Pacific. Nagumo's fatal decision to rearm his planes half-way through the battle meant that his decks were crowded with vulnerable craft, making them easy targets for the US counter-attack. The loss in aircraft could be replaced, but the loss in talented and experienced naval pilots left a greater gap in Japan's naval strength. The Americans had been greatly helped, to say the least, by their mastery of Japanese codes, which gave them the element of surprise. The battle also provided them with valuable experience in carrier warfare. The tide of the war in the Pacific had turned, but a similar victory was needed by the Allies in the west.

SNELLING ROBINSON, ENSIGN, USS COTTEN

ENEMY PLANE APPROACHING

'At 11.55 I saw a single dive-bomber plunge down on Enterprise... The enemy pilot released his bomb, which exploded in the water close aboard the bow, then pulled out of his dive and came on toward Cotten in a high-speed attempt to escape. A moment later he came within range, and Sky 1 ordered, "Enemy plane approaching from port quarter. Commence firing when on target!" Our gunners opened up, firing seventy-six 40mm rounds and three hundred 20mm projectiles as the plane screamed close by on our port side. When he was abeam to port, some thousand yards [900m] away, a shell hit his right wing; it immediately came off, and he commenced a rolling, burning dive over us, hitting the water and exploding about two thousand yards [1,800m] off our starboard bow.'
Quoted in *200,000 Miles* by C. Snelling Robinson (Kent State University Press, 2000)

STALINGRAD, 1942

Above: General Georgy Zhukov was responsible for the defence of Stalingrad. Rather than interfering for political reasons, Stalin left him alone to conduct the battle.

Left: Russian soldiers in winter uniform combat the extreme cold as well as the Germans in the rubble of Stalingrad.

Stalin refused to give up the city in southern Russia that bore his name and the Germans were encircled in a crushing pincer movement. A German army became trapped inside the wrecked remains of the city, fighting a bitter house-to-house battle for survival. It was the beginning of the end for Hitler's war against the Soviet Union.

The German war machine had come to a halt outside Stalingrad and the Soviet Union had begun to gain the initiative in the most terrible war of the 20th century.

The contest for Stalingrad has often been called the most decisive battle of the Second World War. Before it, German armies had conquered most of Europe and they seemed poised to complete Hitler's long-desired conquest of the east. In the ruins of Stalingrad, however, the Red Army halted the German advance and so weakened the resolve of Hitler's army that from then onwards it was more or less in retreat back to Berlin.

One decisive aspect of the battle was that it revealed the limits of political power. It demonstrated to two of the biggest ideological dictators of the 20th century that war could not be fought by politicians alone and that military command was best left to generals. But only one of the dictators was to learn the lesson.

THE FAILURE OF DICTATORS

Up until this point in the great clash between the Nazi and Soviet regimes, each leader had believed that his own political will was enough to bring victory to his armies. Hitler and Stalin were convinced they knew better than their generals. In order to secure his grip on power, Stalin had fatally weakened the Red Army with purges of its officers and placed it directly under political influence. After war broke out, humiliating defeat on all fronts was the result of his paralysing efforts, and when faced with annihilation in 1942 Stalin was forced to concede

command of the Stalingrad campaign to one of his generals, Georgy Zhukov, and let him get on with it.

Hitler, on the other hand, was intoxicated with victory. He believed his generals were too timid and constantly pushed them onwards, until he fatally overextended Germany's military and logistical capacities. When two of his generals protested, they were relieved of their commands and Hitler took direct control of the fighting in southern Russia. The remaining generals were too afraid to counter Hitler's commands and they and hundreds of thousands of soldiers were sacrificed to his vanity. After Stalingrad, Hitler no longer dined with his high command. He ate alone, with only assistants to perpetuate his delusions.

HITLER TAKES COMMAND

At the beginning of 1942, the Russians launched a winter counter-offensive, but the Germans were too strong to be affected by it and maintained their lines from Finland to the Crimea. In the spring, the German armies pressed forward, forcing the Russians on to the defensive once again.

Hitler's generals recommended that the German and Axis armies combine in one powerful thrust southwards along the Don and Donets valleys to capture Rostov and Stalingrad and then move into the Caucasus to assume control of its immense oil reserves. Hitler was impatient, however, and decided on simultaneous thrusts against Stalingrad and the Caucasus. This meant dividing his armies and the creation of a considerable gap between the two forces. Hitler's generals complained that

Right: **The progressive advances of the Soviet forces as they broke through and surrounded the German troops fighting inside Stalingrad.**

Below: **Russian soldiers in snow camouflage advance through a ruined factory at the heart of the fighting.**

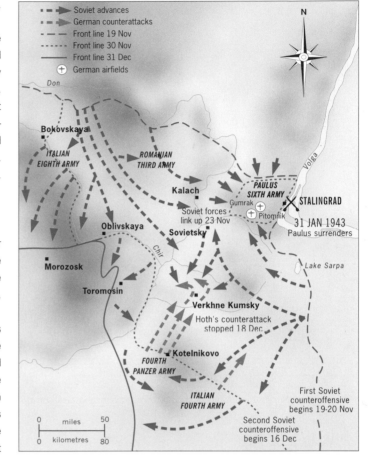

this would put severe pressure on their fighting and supply abilities. Hitler dismissed two of his generals and took direct command of Army Group A, communicating his orders from his headquarters in East Prussia 1,900km (1,200 miles) away.

In August 1942, Hitler concentrated his troops in order to capture the city of Stalingrad astride the River Volga. He issued commands to General Friedrich Paulus and his Sixth Army, which took on the brunt of the fighting. In the meantime, Army Group B held the line to the north of Stalingrad, while Army Group A led the line to the south, with a gap of 380km (240 miles) between them maintained by only one German motorized division and some less than reliable allies.

Georgy Konstantinovich Zhukov had survived Stalin's purges in the 1930s to emerge as his leading general, having been awarded the honour of Hero of the Soviet Union for his victorious battle against the Japanese in Manchuria. Stalin now looked to him to defend Stalingrad and, for once, let his general deal with the situation without political interference. Zhukov made a very accurate analysis of the situation, believing, as

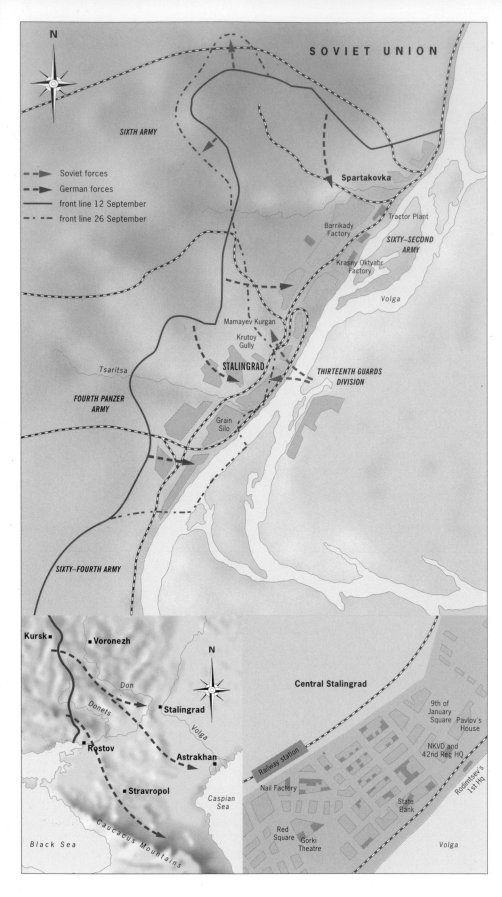

N

SOVIET UNION

SIXTH ARMY

- - ▶ Soviet forces
- - ▶ German forces
—— front line 12 September
—·—· front line 26 September

Spartakovka

Barrikady
Factory

Tractor Plant

SIXTY–SECOND
ARMY

Krasny Oktyabr
Factory

Volga

Mamayev Kurgan

Krutoy
Gully

STALINGRAD

THIRTEENTH GUARDS
DIVISION

Tsaritsa

FOURTH PANZER
ARMY

Grain
Silo

SIXTY–FOURTH ARMY

Kursk

Voronezh

Don

Donets

Stalingrad

Volga

Rostov

Astrakhan

Stravropol

Caspian
Sea

Caucacus Mountains

Black Sea

N

Central Stalingrad

9th of
January
Square

Pavlov's
House

NKVD and
42nd Reg HQ

Rodimtsev's
1st Hq

Railway station

Nail Factory

State
Bank

Red
Square

Gorki
Theatre

Volga

***Top*: During the fight for the city, front lines swung back and forth as each side made gains one day only to lose them again the next.**

***Above left*: Germany's strategic offensive in the Caucasus region of southern Russia meant that Hitler's troops were dangerously stretched.**

***Above right*: Central Stalingrad, where the rubble of bombed-out buildings slowed the German advance towards the Volga.**

Hitler's own generals had argued, that the German forces around the city were greatly overextended. Zhukov also observed that the flanks of the German thrust into Stalingrad were protected by Italian, Romanian and Hungarian troops, men who were less well armed than the Germans and less committed to the cause. Zhukov's plan was to hold Stalingrad until he could muster sufficient forces to launch counter-attacks against the weaker German flanks.

STREET FIGHTING

The bitter fighting inside Stalingrad dragged on for months and into the winter of 1943. The Soviet Sixty-second Army was surrounded in the centre of the city but refused to give up. A second Soviet army, the Sixty-fourth, maintained a small bridgehead on the River Volga, over which supplies could be sent to the desperate defenders. Soviet artillery and aircraft based on the other side of the Volga kept up a relentless barrage against the attacking Germans.

The rubble created by the fighting stopped tanks from advancing swiftly and led to hand-to-hand fighting. Snipers took up positions in the many broken buildings. The daily pressure on both sides was tremendous, and hungry, cold, frightened and exhausted soldiers found themselves reduced to desperate animals, depending on a primeval desire to survive.

General Vasily Chuikov, the tough son of a peasant, took on the terrible task of battling with Paulus's men in the ruins of the city. Paulus was less resilient and his health began to deteriorate during the months of fighting. The morale of his troops had slumped considerably too. 'Stalingrad is hell on earth,' wrote one German officer in September. 'We attack every day. If we capture twenty yards in the morning, the Russians throw us back again in the evening.'

Despite being more poorly armed, the Soviet soldiers fought for every square metre of the city. Building by building they were forced back towards the Volga, but it was a costly and slow victory for the Germans. And as the Germans slogged it out inside the city, Zhukov was gathering his forces for a counter-attack outside.

ZHUKOV STRIKES

On 19 November, Zhukov sprang his attack. More than a million men, with almost a thousand tanks, struck north and south of Stalingrad, taking the Germans completely by surprise. Zhukov had judged the opposition just right: the flanking Romanian armies and German reserves crumbled before the determined offensive, with many quickly surrendering. Soviet tanks executed swift advances, just as the Germans had shown them in earlier battles, and rapidly surrounded the German Sixth Army inside Stalingrad. By 22 November, Soviet forces had linked up. Realizing the danger of encirclement, Paulus wanted to pull his men out of Stalingrad and break through to safety, but Hitler was obsessed with beating Stalin and refused Paulus permission to retreat. The Sixth Army was trapped.

News of this development coincided with the Allied victory in North Africa over Rommel at El Alamein. For a moment, Hitler was struck by uncertainty. The Luftwaffe promised to relieve the trapped soldiers by delivering 500,000kg (500 tons) of supplies a day, but in reality it could barely manage 100,000kg (100 tons). Soviet aircraft enforced a blockade of the city. Panzer divisions attempted to break through, but were met by stiff resistance from Soviet tank crews. Elsewhere, the Italian and Hungarian armies collapsed under further Soviet aggression. The Red Army had finally learned to coordinate its elements and concentrate its power against the weakest aspects of the enemy. Having found its strength, the Red Army would now take the war to Germany.

Almost a quarter of a million German soldiers remained inside Stalingrad, but by late December they were in a poor state. They were short of food, medical supplies and ammunition. Worn down by constant Soviet bombardment, German soldiers began to lose the will to resist. On 10 January, Zhukov gathered his forces to crush the remaining opposition. The fierce resistance they met surprised the advancing Red Army

forces because the number of Germans left inside the city had been wildly underestimated. The Germans now fought with the same sort of desperation that had been characteristic of the Soviets. Eventually, though, German nerves gave way and on 31 January Paulus surrendered his army to Zhukov. The day before, Hitler had promoted Paulus to the rank of field marshal; now, on 1 February, Hitler condemned him for his betrayal.

Stalingrad was a costly defeat. At least 147,000 German soldiers were dead and 91,000 taken prisoner, many never to return. Thousands of German tanks, aircraft and guns had been destroyed. Germany's allies had suffered a trauma they would not forget. Soviet morale was lifted immensely: the depression of their earlier defeats was forgotten and it had been demonstrated that they had learned the lessons of war. The Soviets now believed they could win this awesome struggle. Stalin took back control of the war, but he was more open to the advice of his generals. Even Hitler seems to have been cowed by his massive defeat and allowed his generals to plan counterattacks from 1943 onwards.

Above right: **Soviet T34 tanks in action against the Germans in southern Russia.**

Above: **A Russian soldier raises the Red Flag as a signal of victory as the German army surrenders inside Stalingrad.**

GUY SAJER, GROSSE DEUTSCHLAND DIVISION

VICIOUS WAR

All wars are bitter and cruel, but the German invasion of the Soviet Union in 1941 unleashed a warfare of absolute brutality, one in which atrocities and massacre were commonplace, with civilians suffering as much as soldiers. Guy Sajer was a French member of the Grosse Deutschland Division posted to the Eastern Front and recalls his experience of this routine brutality:

'Every [Russian] prisoner caught robbing a German body was immediately shot. There were no official firing squads for these executions. An officer would simply shoot the offender on the spot, or hand him over to a couple of toughs who were regularly given this sort of job. Once, to my horror, I saw one of these thugs tying the hands of three prisoners to the bars of a gate. When his victims had been secured, he stuck a grenade into the pocket of one of their coats, pulled the pin, and ran for shelter. The three Russians, whose guts were blown out, screamed for mercy until the last moment.'

Quoted from *The Forgotten Soldier* by Guy Sajer (Cassell, 1999)

EL ALAMEIN, 1942

Below: **The British offensive at El Alamein, first breaking through the defensive lines of the Germans and Italians and then throwing them back.**

Rommel's invincible German army in North Africa seemed to be on the verge of capturing Cairo when the British staged a major counter-attack and threw the Germans and Italians backwards. Using devastating artillery bombardments to open his attack, Montgomery followed through decisively with aircraft to pound the German panzers.

The Allied victory in North Africa marked a significant turning point in the war. Control of the Mediterranean was vital to

British imperial interests. The Suez Canal in Egypt provided a short sea route to India and Australia. Mussolini, the Italian Fascist leader, was keen to demonstrate his own mastery of the region by capturing the canal. On 13 September 1940, Italy invaded Egypt but Britain's desert force, commanded by General Wavell, beat off the larger Italian army and threw it out of Egypt. Wavell then captured the Italian colonies in North Africa. Mussolini was in dire danger of being humiliated and Hitler sent him help in the form of General Erwin Rommel and his Afrika Korps.

Rommel's force was a completely different quality of opposition and the British and Commonwealth forces were soon thrown on to the defensive at Tobruk. The British and Commonwealth desert force was renamed the Eighth Army and at the end of 1941 it struck back at Rommel, halting the German advance. Rommel withdrew and built up his reinforcements for another offensive in 1942, receiving better supplies than the British could manage for their forces.

In January 1942, Rommel launched his second offensive and pushed back the Eighth Army to Benghazi. German tanks proved adept at threatening the Allied positions and the Eighth Army withdrew to Egypt. Tobruk fell and the situation began to look perilous for the British and Commonwealth troops. Rommel dominated the region and one more blow would give him Egypt, but the enormous distances travelled meant the German lines of supply were stretched. Hitler urged Rommel to capture the Suez Canal, but he failed to give him any extra support because he was fully committed to the war in the Soviet Union.

THE 'DESERT RATS'

In August 1942, Lieutenant General Bernard Montgomery was made commander of the Eighth Army, or 'Desert Rats' as it became known. Montgomery would never have been put in charge if General Gott had not died in an air crash. He was the second choice for command. Somewhat puritan in his personal habits – he did not drink alcohol or smoke and retired to bed no later than 21.30 hours – he knew that good morale lay at the heart of a successful army, and with a force that had been pushed back to Egypt he knew this was particularly true of his desert troops. He spent much time getting to know them and keeping them informed about the situation. He created a character for himself – Monty – by wearing distinctive headgear and being highly visible in the media. 'Not the least of Montgomery's achievements,' writes leading military historian Gary Sheffield, 'was to turn the Eighth Army into a "brand name" with which soldiers and civilians could identify and of

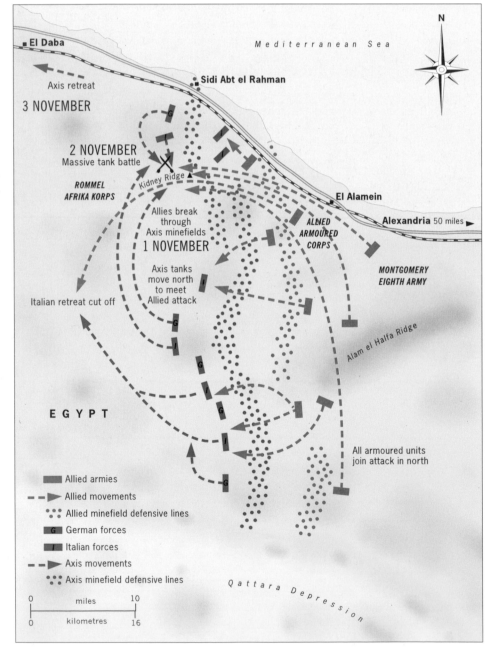

Top: Erwin Rommel, German commander of the Afrika Korps, stands on the road to Cairo in 1942.

Above: General Montgomery, victor at El Alamein, painted by Captain Neville Lewis in December 1942.

Above right: British soldiers fire a six-pounder anti-aircraft gun during the battle of El Alamein.

which they could be proud.' Most importantly, he knew that a little victory was needed immediately.

Since July 1942, Rommel had been only 160km (100 miles) from the vital British naval base at Alexandria. A state of emergency had been declared in Cairo and Rommel anticipated the final stage of his long journey to Egypt. He hoped to catch the British off guard with a sudden panzer thrust on 31 August, but Montgomery was waiting for him. The German tanks initially overlapped the British left flank but were stopped by a tank brigade dug in at Alam el Halfa. The British armoured unit repulsed the panzers, and with support from British aircraft it pushed the Germans back.

Montgomery was cautious and did not counter-attack straight away, preferring to prepare his knock-out blow methodically. Suddenly, the situation was not looking so good for Rommel. After 17 months of desert fighting, his 96,000-strong army was below strength and suffering from illness, and it possessed only 600 tanks against the Allies' 1,114. Montgomery's victory at Alam el Halfa lifted the morale of his

troops tremendously and he used the pause to reinforce them, bringing their strength up to 150,000. The British Desert Air Force had complete mastery of the skies and relentlessly attacked the German positions. Rommel himself fell ill and flew back temporarily to Germany, leaving General Stumme in command. Montgomery would not be rushed. A minefield separated the two armies and neither could have flanks turned. To the north was the Mediterranean coast and to the south was the impassable Qattara Depression on the edge of the Sahara Desert.

THE BEGINNING OF THE END

Montgomery began his major assault on the evening of 23 October. He had been trained as an officer during the First World War and knew the value of good artillery. The battle began with a massive thousand-gun barrage along a 10-km (six-mile) front. It lit up the night sky. Rommel himself was impressed by its impact, later writing, 'Never before had we experienced such rolling fire in North Africa, and it continued

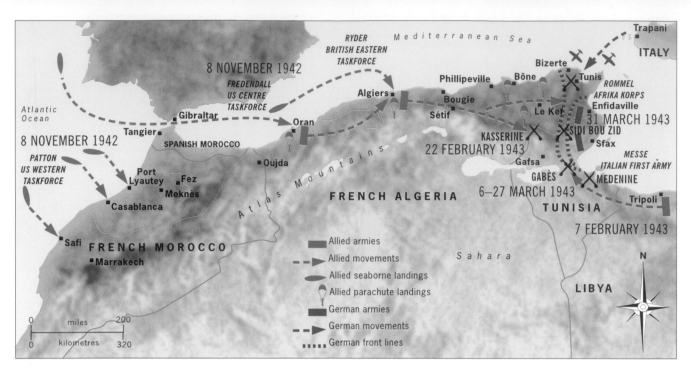

Above: Montgomery's victory at El Alamein in October 1942 allowed Allied troops to land and reoccupy North Africa in an offensive called Operation Torch. This gave them a base from which to invade Italy.

throughout the entire course of the battle at El Alamein. With extraordinary accuracy, British gunners shelled our positions, resulting in very heavy casualties.' Montgomery had prepared his attack perfectly.

Some twenty minutes later, a diversionary attack surged forwards near the Qattara Depression, but the main assault came in the north when the Allied Armoured Corps struck the weaker Axis left flank defended by Italian forces. British infantry opened two corridors through the minefields along which tanks could advance. The Italians fought harder than expected and a German panzer counter-attack nearly halted the advance.

Stumme, the German commander, had a heart attack and died, but Rommel resumed command on 25 October.

On 26 October, Montgomery halted his diversionary attack in the south and put all his efforts into pressing ahead along the coast. The Australian 9th Division held the German 164th Division against the sea, while tanks battled away at each other for a week. But aerial superiority helped the Allies tremendously and as their planes and tanks pounded the German panzers, the armoured power available to Rommel declined rapidly. Rommel could not keep up with the demand for fuel, ammunition and new vehicles. His supplies had been difficult to begin with and now he was stretched to breaking point. With the Australians nearly surrounding the German 164th Division, he pulled back his troops to a new defensive line on 1 November.

BREAKTHROUGH

This time Montgomery left no time for rest, knowing that impetus was important at this stage of the battle. He quickly regrouped his soldiers and plunged ahead south of Kidney Hill, using a creeping barrage to shield the New Zealand 2nd Division as it carved a route through the minefields for more tanks to follow. Panzers fought a last-ditch action to stem the advance, but with only 35 tanks left at the end of the day, there was little they could do. Allied aerial bombardments and artillery fire silenced the previously deadly German 88mm anti-tank guns. Rommel wanted to withdraw but Hitler insisted he face the British.

Two more days of fighting bled the Afrika Korps dry and Montgomery's forces finally broke through at Kidney Hill, leaving Rommel no choice but to disregard Hitler and retreat, leaving the Italians behind. Reverting to caution, Montgomery halted, but the battle was over and German resistance had been destroyed. Some fifty-nine thousand Germans and Italians were killed, wounded or captured, and more than five hundred tanks and four hundred guns had been destroyed. Montgomery had casualties of thirteen thousand, with 432 tanks destroyed. He had been careful not to waste his men in needless attrition but had not been faint-hearted when aggression was needed.

Although the fighting in North Africa was a sideshow compared to the colossal struggle on the Eastern Front, the Battle of El Alamein was a decisive victory because it ended Axis aggression in the Mediterranean region. It provided a turning point for the Allies, allowing troops to land in North Africa as a prelude to invading Italy and the opening of the much-needed second front against Hitler (thus relieving pressure on the Red Army). It had a huge effect on Allied morale too, with Churchill claiming, not exactly accurately, 'Before Alamein, we never had a victory. After Alamein, we never had a defeat.' The tide had turned for the Allies and Hitler was on the defensive.

Above: British soldiers of the Eighth Army fire on retreating Germans.

Above right: An Afrika Korps motorcycle combination. Although well equipped, the Germans could not replace their losses fast enough to avoid defeat.

HEINZ WERNER SCHMIDT, LIEUTENANT, AFRIKA KORPS

DEADLY CHRISTMAS TREES
'We moved through the Sidi Barrani region by night. The track was sandy and in places almost impassable. Several times we nearly capsized trucks and guns. An hour or two before midnight the first parachute flares opened above us. I never saw them, but they struck me as emerging from the darkness with an almost idiotic exultancy. In a few minutes the heavens were filled with "Christmas trees", the countryside was lit as though by limelight, and bombs thundered down from the low-flying planes. At times we raced madly amidst the thunder and the flashes. If we halted and went to ground the aircraft attacked even solitary soldiers whom they caught erect: their grotesque shadows danced revealingly across the ground as the flares flamed down to low levels. If we were not prone, we were visible.'
Quoted from *With Rommel in the Desert* by Heinz Werner Schmidt (George Harrap & Co., 1951)

BATTLE OF THE ATLANTIC, 1943

A second 'battle of Britain' was fought between 1939 and 1945, one that took place beneath the waves of the Atlantic Ocean. 'The Battle of the Atlantic,' declared Winston Churchill, 'was the dominating factor all through the war. Never for one moment could we forget that everything happening elsewhere, on land, at sea, or in the air, depended ultimately on its outcome.' This second 'battle of Britain', in which German U-boat submarines threatened to cut the trade between Britain and North America, was a brilliant example of how Allied air and sea power worked together to defeat an almost undetectable foe. Used to almost unrivalled mastery of the sea, German U-boats began to be picked off by aircraft attacks and ship-launched depth-charges.

In 1939, the Royal Navy had mounted an effective North Sea blockade of Germany. Germany retaliated by sending

Below: *Prince Robert*, a cruiser of the Royal Canadian Navy, depth-charges a submerged U-boat.

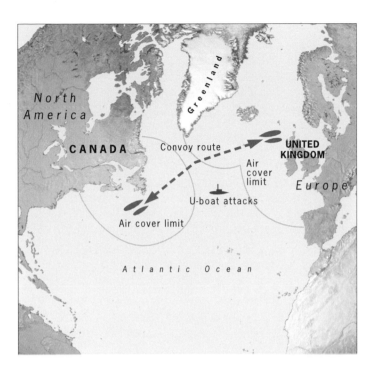

U-boats to attack British merchant ships sailing between North America and Britain. In the first year of conflict, Germany sank 677 merchant ships, totalling nearly 4,600,000 tonnes (4,500,000 tons). If such losses continued, Britain would be deprived of food, weapons and other valuable supplies, strangling its ability to continue the war. Trade was Britain's lifeblood and without it Britain could not win the war. Churchill understood this.

In 1940, following the fall of France, Germany obtained ports on the Atlantic and constructed bomb-proof shelters for its U-boats. U-boat activity then increased dramatically. In 1941 alone, some 3,760,000 tonnes (3,700,000 tons) of shipping was sunk and there seemed to be little the Allies could do to strike back against the elusive foe. German submarines could cruise up to 19,000km (12,000 miles), and when the United States entered the war, its merchant ships became targets for the U-boats that hunted off the eastern coast of the United States. In 1942 nearly 500 ships were sunk. The situation was becoming critical for the Allies, who could not produce enough shipping to keep up with the losses.

ATTACK! ADVANCE! SINK!

On 1 May 1943 the largest fleet of German submarines assembled in the war entered the Atlantic – some 134 U-boats. Their orders were simple: 'Angreifen! Ran! Versenken!' ('Attack! Advance! Sink!') They were intended to strike a devastating blow against Allied shipping. In the first twenty days of March 1943, German U-boats had sunk 72 ships, 60 of them in Royal Navy-protected convoys. German radio broadcasts boasted of it as the greatest convoy battle of all time, particularly because only one submarine had been lost. Officials at Britain's Admiralty were alarmed, later declaring that the 'Germans never came so near to disrupting communication between the New World and the Old as in the first twenty days of March 1943'. If the convoy system, which had proved its worth in the First World War, was failing to protect Allied shipping, what could the Royal Navy do?

The fact was that the convoy system was working and that losses would have been even worse if ships had scattered and sailed independently. The Royal Navy had slowly been improving its ability to detect U-boats and destroy them, and in May 1943 its progress would be fully tested. Breakthroughs had been made in several areas: for example, air cover and weaponry. Air cover had been improved dramatically and by April 1943 RAF Coastal Command had added long-range B-24 Liberator bombers to its inventory of Sunderland and Catalina flying boats. These Liberators could cover all areas of the convoy routes and they carried a new secret weapon: the Mark 24 Mine. More a torpedo than a mine, the Mark 24 had a homing device that targeted the noise made by a submarine's propeller, so scaring

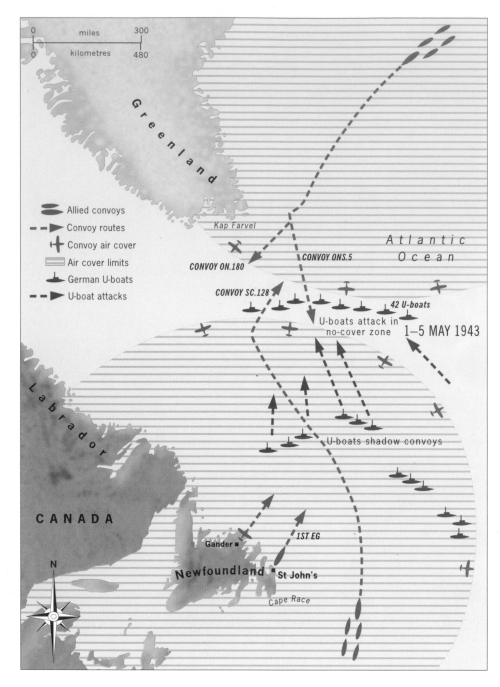

G r e e n l a n d

A t l a n t i c
O c e a n

Kap Farvel

CONVOY ONS.5

CONVOY ON.180

CONVOY SC.128

42 U-boats

U-boats attack in
no-cover zone 1–5 MAY 1943

Allied convoys
Convoy routes
Convoy air cover
Air cover limits
German U-boats
U-boat attacks

U-boats shadow convoys

L a b r a d o r

C A N A D A

1ST EG

Gander

Newfoundland St John's

Cape Race

N

BLACK MAY

On 1 May 1943, convoy ONS.5 was struck by bad weather as it sailed from Britain to North America. The formation began to break up, but Commander Peter Gretton stuck by the merchant ships and rounded them up, continuing westwards. U-boat packs had been following the convoy and skirmished with it, but on 4 May, 42 submarines regrouped to launch a massive assault. They attacked at night and six broke through the escort fleet and sank seven ships. It looked as though history was going to repeat itself.

The next day, Allied code-breakers picked up German orders instructing the U-boats to renew their attacks. This pinpointed *U-192* and it was promptly sunk by HMS *Pink*. Three huge air bubbles broke the surface of the sea, the sign of a submarine kill, followed by numerous small bubbles, making the sea appear to boil. 'The water in the vicinity [was] considerably aerated in appearance and green and white like shallow water,' reported Captain Newfoundland on HMS *Pink*. 'Tangible evidence of destruction was greedily and most enthusiastically searched for, but nothing further was seen. It was realized that my little convoy was drawing away and was now some distance ahead and also unprotected, but I decided to risk this and to continue with the hunt.'

Eleven U-boats now entered the fray and sank three more merchant ships, but three of the attackers were also hit and sunk. HMS *Pelican* joined the battle and detected *U-438* on its radar. As the U-boat dived, the sloop sank it with depth-charges.

Above: **U-boat attacks on convoys in the western Atlantic during a five-day period in May 1943.**

Right: **The view from the conning tower of a surface-cruising U-boat.**

submarines into diving. Torpedoes could then be dropped into the sea to home-in on the U-boats, to devastating effect.

Three new escort aircraft carriers were introduced to the Atlantic theatre in April 1943. These were added to the support groups operated by Admiral Sir Max Horton, which raced to points of attack and fought the U-boats while the convoys sailed on. Escort ships were armed with new weapons such as the Hedgehog, which hurled 24 bombs in an oval pattern ahead of the escort ship, thus trapping the U-boats in a ring of fire. Intelligence about U-boat attacks was greatly improved by the breaking of U-boat codes, as well as the introduction of centimetric radar and radio direction-finding gear, which pinpointed the presence of submarine packs. This combination of improved air and sea power would suddenly bring dramatic results in May 1943.

Right: New German U-boats line up for inspection in 1943 before entering combat in the Atlantic.

Below: A US Navy PB4Y bombs a surfaced U-boat in the Bay of Biscay. Co-ordinated air and sea attacks on German submarines proved the turning point in the battle for the Atlantic. Painting by Dwight Shepler.

HMS *Spey* surprised another U-boat on the surface and shelled it, then depth-charged it as it tried to escape by diving. At the end of the battle, six U-boats had been sunk, five more badly wrecked and another twelve damaged. For the loss of only 12 merchant ships, this was a very bad result from the German point of view.

Admiral Horton was exuberant. He declared that it marked a 'turning point in the battle of the Atlantic'. U-boat crew morale plummeted and the submarines were withdrawn from action. As the weather cleared, Liberators, together with aircraft flying from escort carriers, inflicted further destruction. By the end of May, 41 U-boats had been destroyed and a further 37 damaged. For Germany, it was 'Black May'. In his report to Hitler, Admiral Dönitz ascribed the defeat to Allied aircraft and radar, claiming 'we don't even known on what wavelength the enemy locates us'. He concluded, 'We must conserve our strength, otherwise we will play into the hands of the enemy.'

Submarine attacks continued in the Atlantic, but the Germans no longer held the edge over the convoys and the importance of their attacks diminished. It was no longer a life or death struggle for the Allies.

HERBERT APEL, CREWMAN *U-439*

A SUNDERLAND CLOSES IN

'We once had an alarm owing to aircraft, a Sunderland flying boat. The fellow succeeded in forcing us to remain submerged for seven hours. He dropped a bomb every ten minutes to the second, and always near us. We couldn't surface. Either it was the same aircraft, though I don't imagine so, or it may have been relieved at intervals. A Sunderland. In the middle of the North Atlantic. We were about half-way between North America and Ireland. Exactly every ten minutes he dropped a bomb. It was quite extraordinary. The devil even tracked us from the air. That is an entirely new English discovery and I don't know if we know [about] it, at any rate it was quite unknown to us...'

Quoted in *Black May* by Michael Gannon (Aurum, 1998)

KURSK, 1943

Above: **Soviet infantry lanch an attack from entrenched positions at Kursk in 1943.**

Famous for being the greatest tank battle ever fought, Kursk crushed the German offensive in the Soviet Union once and for all. Thousands of tanks clashed, with Germany's awesome Tiger tank proving to be a ferocious fighting machine. But the Soviet T34s also proved their worth in almost suicidal assaults. From this point onwards, Hitler's forces were in retreat.

Hitler's war machine may have been shaken by its tremendous loss of men and material at Stalingrad, but it was far from finished. Six months after losing more than two hundred thousand men at Stalingrad (see pp.116–119), Germany assembled sufficient forces to attempt to encircle and break the Red Army at Kursk in southern Russia. Stalin had just seen his soldiers defeated at Kharkov and was wary enough not to risk a summer offensive in 1943. He was waiting for the western Allies to open their second front in the Mediterranean and would play a defensive strategy instead.

A Soviet spy ring called 'Lucy' gave Stalin full warning of Germany's intentions for an offensive at Kursk, code-named Zitadelle (Citadel). This gave the Russians good time to fortify the Kursk salient in depth, and over the course of three months more than half a million railway wagonloads of supplies were brought in. Hitler's delays in beginning the offensive helped too, although the reason was that he was waiting for the arrival of what he hoped would be a new generation of battle-winning 'supertanks': the Panther and Tiger. At Kursk, the Russians built three main fortified lines, which

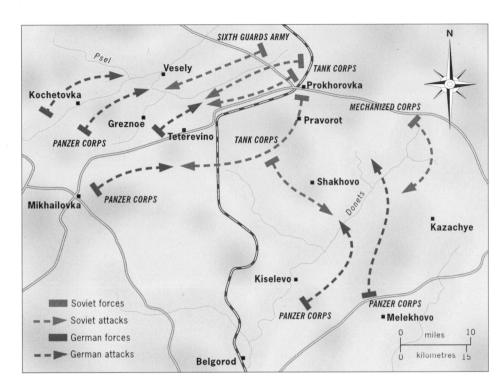

Above: **The intense armoured battle around Prokhorovka on the southern front at Kursk in mid-July 1943**

Right: **A Soviet poster from 1943 showing the avenging Red Army on the counter-attack against the Germans, following victories at Stalingrad and Kursk.**

As the Tigers advanced to meet the T34s, one German tank was struck by gunfire from behind, which typified the confusion the Soviets were trying to create. The Tigers ignored the gun and engaged the T34s. Their superior armament proved decisive, and several Soviet tanks were destroyed. Continuing to the second defensive line, Wittmann was to claim by the end of the day a kill of eight T34s and seven anti-tank guns. German pioneers helped to support the tanks by clearing paths through the minefields and over the anti-tank ditches, but this was just the start of the maze of defences planned by the Soviets.

The German advance stalled in front of the heavily fortified Soviet positions at Hill 220.5, having been confronted by an array of ditches, mines, concealed guns and dug-in tanks with only their turrets visible. Supported by aircraft and panzer grenadiers, it took the Tiger tanks almost five hours of fierce fighting to take the hill. It was a small victory for the Germans, but it came at a big cost, because it had reduced their troop

were protected by anti-tank ditches, minefields, concealed anti-tank gun emplacements, dug-in T34 tanks, tank traps, flame-throwers and artillery batteries. The idea was to channel the attacking armour into a web of flanking fire. Some 6,000km (3,750 miles) of trenches were dug, with more than 48,000 mortar and artillery positions. An average of 1,500 mines were laid per kilometre. An array of T34 tanks were held in reserve between the fortified lines to effect counter-attacks. It was the largest tank trap ever created and Hitler's forces were heading straight for it.

TIGER ATTACK

Operation Zitadelle was simple and direct, with a two-pronged attack from the north and south of the salient, which would meet at Kursk. The battle began on 5 July 1943, with a total of six thousand tanks and four thousand aircraft engaged on both sides. German tank ace Michael Wittmann was in command of the new Tiger tanks Hitler had such faith in. His 13 Kompanie of 1st SS Panzer Regiment operated in the south alongside the II SS Panzer Korps. On the first day, Michael Wittmann's Tiger tanks crossed the Soviet trenches and formed an attacking arrow formation, but they were driving into a trap, and camouflaged Russian anti-tank guns opened fire on them. The heavily armoured Tigers dealt with this first assault, destroying several of the guns. Their next challenge was a unit of T34s.

Above: Red Army General Malinin takes a smoke outside his bunker at Kursk Bulge.

Left: Russian soldiers clamber on a tank during the Soviet advance. Much fighting was at close hand with infantry attacking tanks.

Below: Soviet T34s roll into battle at Kursk. The Germans developed Panther tanks in response to the T34.

numbers and damaged their valuable tanks. This attritional fighting was repeated all over the battlefield, proving that although the Soviets would take heavy punishment, they had created an awesome defensive position in depth that would exhaust the German assault.

TANK CLASH AT PROKHOROVKA

Having broken through the first two defence lines and penetrated some 50km (30 miles) into the salient, the Germans were readying themselves for a final push towards Kursk. The Soviets now released their reserves for a counter-attack at Prokhorovka, hoping to isolate and destroy the German armoured spearheads. The Soviet counter-attack came before dawn on 12 July in the form of a massive frontal attack led by the 5th Guards Tank Army fielding some 830 tanks and self-propelled guns. The Germans assembled some five hundred tanks and assault guns, with Tigers leading the attack formations. The landscape was a gently sloping plain, perfect for large tank formations, and the stage was set for the largest tank battle of the Second World War.

The combat started with aircraft attacks and artillery barrages. The Fifth Guards Tank Army then crashed into the panzer forces while they were still preparing for their attack. Tank

historian Renato Niemis describes what happened to Wittmann and his Tigers: 'At first Wittmann and his Tigers could pick off tanks at long range but as the range rapidly closed the danger from the Russian tanks and infantry increased and Wittmann had to order the Tigers to advance to meet the threat head on... There followed a dance of death between the opposing tanks each trying to outmanoeuvre the other in the murky smoke-filled haze. To avoid the enemy tanks, Wittmann used his experience gained with Stug IIIs, making his driver turn the Tiger on the spot, changing directions rapidly to outwit the enemy and to bring his gun to bear on them and shooting whilst moving rather than offering a standing target.'

It was a savage encounter. Lieutenant General Rotmistrov, commander of the Fifth Guards Tank Army, gives his view of the fighting: 'The battlefield seemed too small for the hundreds of armoured machines. Groups of tanks moved over the steppe taking cover behind the isolated groves and orchards. The bursts of gunfire merged into a continuous, mighty roar. The Soviet tanks thrust into the German advanced formations at full speed and penetrated the German tank screen. The T34s were knocking out Tigers at extremely close range, since their powerful guns and massive armour no longer gave them an advantage in close combat. The tanks of both sides were in the closest possible contact... Frequently, when a tank was hit, its ammunition and fuel blew up, and torn-off turrets were flung through the air over dozens of yards.'

By the end of the day, the Germans had lost more than 60 tanks. The Soviets had lost 328 tanks, but both sides had failed in their objectives. The ferocity of the battle halted the German advance and there would be no breakthrough to Kursk. The new Tiger and Panther tanks had proved their worth, but they also possessed weaknesses and would not become the battle-winners Hitler had hoped for. Two days before the tank battle at Prokhorovka, the western Allies had successfully landed in Sicily. This, in combination with another Soviet offensive at Orel, convinced Hitler that he should call off the assault at Kursk, even though his generals in the field felt that they could grind a victory out of the fighting. With this battle, the Germans had lost the initiative on the Eastern Front and the Soviet Army would begin to push them back to Berlin.

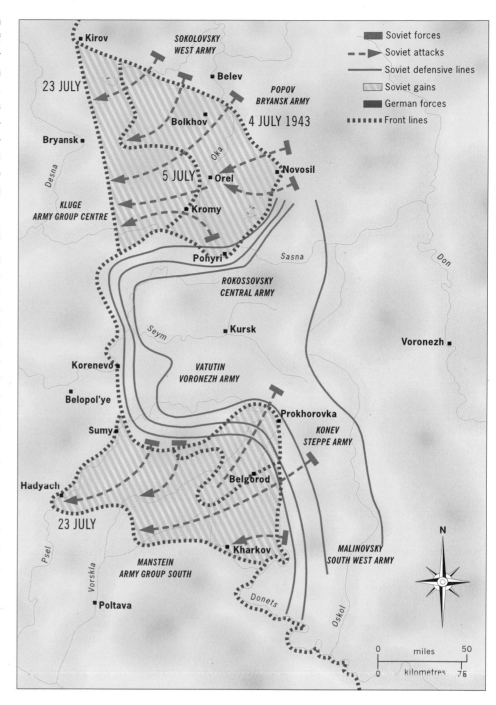

Above: The fighting around the Kursk salient in July 1943, showing the striking Soviet counter-attacks against German positions and their remarkably rapid gains.

GENERAL HEINZ GUDERIAN

IMPERFECT TANKS

'I gained an insight into the course that events were taking, the lack of our men's experience in the attack and the weakness of our equipment. My fears concerning the premature commitment of the Panthers were justified. Also the ninety Porsche Tigers, which were operating with Model's army, were incapable of close-range fighting since they lacked sufficient ammunition for their guns, and this defeat was aggravated by the fact that they possessed no machine-guns. Once they had broken into the enemy's infantry zone they literally had to go quail shooting with cannons. They did not manage to neutralise, let alone destroy, the enemy rifles and machine-guns, so that the infantry was unable to follow up behind them. By the time they reached the Russian artillery they were on their own.' **Quoted from *Panzer Leader* by Heinz Guderian (Michael Joseph, 1952)**

TARAWA, 1943

One of the bloodiest battles in American military history, the assault on Tarawa was a key battle in the island-hopping offensive of the war in the Pacific theatre. US Marines stormed ashore in the face of heavy Japanese resistance, a brave act that provided a hard lesson in frontal assault and one from which many things were learned and later utilized to great effect elsewhere.

A year after Pearl Harbor, the US Navy and US Army were readying themselves for the counter-offensive against Japan in the Pacific theatre. Troops, ships and aircraft were built up at bases in Hawaii, the Fiji Islands and the New Hebrides. Admiral

Nimitz commanded the US Fifth Fleet and with it a massive amphibious force consisting of more than one hundred thousand soldiers. His target was the Gilbert Islands. It was to be the first step in an island-hopping campaign that would take American air power closer and closer to Japan. Once the Gilbert Islands were captured, airbases would be built there for the assault on the Marshall Islands, and so on.

The Japanese understood this strategy and had heavily fortified the Gilbert Islands with major defence works at Makin and Tarawa atolls – clusters of islands surrounded by coral reefs. The assault began with an aerial bombardment of the Japanese

Above: **US Marines are pinned down on the shore at Tarawa under heavy fire from the Japanese.**

positions from 13 to 17 November. This was then followed by a substantial naval barrage before the landing forces left their ships. On 20 November, American infantry quickly overwhelmed the 250 Japanese soldiers on Makin, but Japanese submarines counter-attacked and sank an escort carrier. Makin, however, had been seized and American attention turned to Tarawa. A similarly smooth operation was expected, but the Americans were in for a terrible shock.

US MARINES GO IN

Tarawa was both a natural and a man-made fortress. The coral reef that ringed the island was a formidable barrier for ships, and the gaps in it had been laced with mines by the Japanese. Further in, the beaches were covered with barbed wire, and Korean slave labourers had been forced to build more than four hundred concrete gun emplacements and bunkers. These defences had the effect of channelling any attacking troops into the face of a terrifying array of heavy artillery, which included 20mm (8-inch) coastal defence guns taken from Singapore, as well as concealed field guns and dug-in tanks. Rear Admiral Shibasaki commanded a garrison

Above: **The route of the American amphibious assault on Betio Island in Tarawa Atoll.**

Left: **US troops of the 2nd Marine Division huddle on the beach at Tarawa. Pre-landing bombardments failed to destroy Japanese gun emplacements and they encountered heavy fire.**

force of 4,836 naval guards, of whom half were élite Special Naval Landing troops.

Surprise was felt to be the best way to overcome the Japanese defences at Tarawa and so a preliminary bombardment from the navy was declined. A similar idea that artillery might be landed on a nearby unoccupied island was also rejected. It meant the troops would go in without any softening of the enemy defences. The unit chosen for the task of attacking Betio Island in the southwestern corner of Tarawa Atoll was the 2nd Marine Division, commanded by Major General Julian Smith. The US Marines were masters of amphibious warfare and decided that the first assault waves should be transported by amphibious tractors (Amtracs), but only 125 were available. This meant that the other troops would have to be sent in by boat, and if their boats got caught on the coral reefs, they would

have to wade through the waters of the lagoon under enemy fire. The signs were not good and General Holland Smith later declared of those US Marines who went in, 'Their only armour was a khaki shirt!'

The attack began on the morning of 20 November 1943 with an assault on the northern shore of Betio Island. Soldiers descended into their Amtracs and the engines roared into action, propelling them across the coral reefs. A last-minute naval barrage had not silenced the Japanese artillery, and shells began to drop among the advancing landing craft, forcing the supporting ships away and leaving the US Marines alone. As their Amtracs approached the beach, the Americans were made frighteningly aware that their brief naval barrage had done little to blunt the Japanese defences. Artillery shells and machine gun fire raked the landing troops. Private Reder of the 2nd Marine Division describes the moments before hitting the beach: 'The last few minutes in the Amtrac were a jumble of sensations: mortar and artillery fire rocking the Amtrac with geysers of water; the Amtrac bouncing over the coral reef; machine gun fire ricocheting off its armoured sides; torpedo bombers and Hellcats streaking overhead to bomb and strafe the island, and then the shout: "Let's Go!"'

Above: US Marines leap out of an Amtrac caught on a coral reef to wade, under constant fire, through the water of the lagoon at Tarawa towards the beach. Painting by Tom Lovell.

Left: A US Marine at Tarawa takes a rest near a trench containing a dead Japanese soldier.

BLOODY TARAWA

The first battalion of US Marines lost 10 per cent of its troops before it even reached the beach, while the battalions that followed took about 20 per cent casualties in the water. When the surviving troops had reached the beach, they had to face the gunfire that erupted from pillboxes just above them. Some US Marines bravely assaulted the emplacements, destroying them with grenades and explosives. Staff Sergeant William Bordelon knocked out four pillboxes and rescued two wounded comrades before being killed, acts of heroism that led to his posthumously receiving the Congressional Medal of Honor.

With the Amtracs used up, subsequent waves of troops took to boats but were caught on the coral reefs and had to climb out and wade through water that went up to their chests. By midday, the US Marines were still pinned down on a strip of beach a mere 6m (20ft) wide. Some Amtrac drivers bravely took their craft back under fire to rescue soldiers caught on the coral reefs. Slowly but surely, reinforcements built up on the beach until five thousand men were ashore by nightfall. American soldiers then crept out over the coconut log sea wall to destroy the Japanese gun emplacements with explosives and flamethrowers. The landing had cost 1,500 casualties – proportionately one of the bloodiest encounters experienced by the US armed forces. Fortunately, the Japanese did not counter-attack and the US Marines used the cover of night to bring artillery ashore piece by piece.

The next day, a second American landing was met by withering fire, but more and more troops came ashore, and with the American artillery pounding the Japanese bunkers, the battle was on the way to being won. Two more days of fighting secured the island, but more than a thousand Americans had died in the assault – news that shocked the nation. Despite the great strength of the Americans in numbers and material, there would be no easy victory against the Japanese. Such frontal assaults had to be more carefully supported by naval and aircraft bombardments, and more Amtracs had to be made available when negotiating coral reefs. These were among the valuable lessons that helped the US Marines to capture a lot more island fortresses.

Above right: **US Marines with a captured Japanese soldier. Such was the animosity between the two sides that few prisoners were taken alive.**

US MARINE LIEUTENANT NYGREN, AMTRAC COMMANDER

BURNED AIR

'We had been told by the naval gunfire liaison officers and Naval Air Force people that there would be no opposition left. I thought that they were overly optimistic. It was very bright now. The colors were deep and vivid. We were 1,000 yards [900m] out from the island, in deep blue water. I could see only remnants of palm trees sticking up from low lying land. There were fires burning all along the shore. Black smoke welled up. The air was filled with wisps of burnt powder bags from our naval rifles. The air smelled burned. The sun blazed down and it was getting very warm... The tractors lurched and tossed as we climbed the coral heads. The troops in our open compartment were thrown about. Our three neat lines became ragged as we bounced and lumbered along the reef. Mortar shells from shore began to explode around us.'
Quoted in *Marine* by Ron Field (Military Illustrated, 1999)

CASSINO, 1944

Above: German paratroopers defend the ruins of Monte Cassino. The Allied bombing of the monastery at Cassino was a disaster as it created a defensive position even more difficult to storm.

Below: The Allied advance on the town of Cassino and the monastery in early 1944.

The monastery of Cassino stands on the road to Rome. The Allies had to take it, but by bombing it they turned it into a formidable stronghold. German paratroopers hidden among the rubble resisted attack after attack until Polish soldiers forced their way up the slopes to victory.

Britain and the United States opened up a second front in Europe in July 1943 when they invaded Sicily. Almost immediately after the landing, the Italian people overthrew their Fascist leader, Mussolini, who had taken them into a very unsuccessful war. His successor entered into negotiations with the Allies and a secret armistice was signed in September. The Germans were now left on their own to stem the Allied advance, and reinforcements were sent into Italy to achieve this.

The Allies invaded mainland Italy in September, landing at Salerno. Albert Kesselring, the commander in chief of Axis forces in the Mediterranean, made sure the Allied advance through Italy was very difficult indeed. The landing at Salerno alone cost the Allies 15,000 casualties. A second landing at Anzio was contested for three months. In January 1944 the US

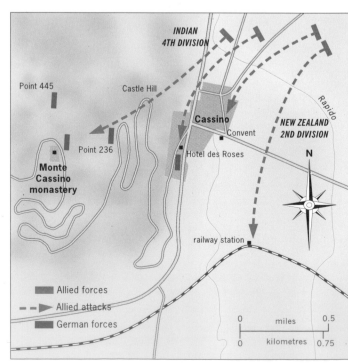

INDIAN 4TH DIVISION

Point 445

Castle Hill

Rapido

Cassino

Convent

NEW ZEALAND 2ND DIVISION

N

Point 236

Hotel des Roses

Monte Cassino monastery

railway station

■ Allied forces
▶ - - Allied attacks
■ German forces

| 0 | miles | 0.5 |
| 0 | kilometres | 0.75 |

34th Infantry Division approached the town of Cassino on the road to Rome. Above the little town, on a massive rock 520m (1,700ft) high, stood a centuries-old Benedictine monastery. The Allies had to take the town of Cassino to gain access to the Liri Valley and onwards to Rome. The Germans were determined to deny them this ancient gateway.

FANATICAL RESISTANCE

At first the Germans did not occupy the ancient monastery, not because of its antiquity, but because it was considered too obvious a target (although General von Senger gave a different view when in captivity; see panel overleaf). Senger was in command of the XIV Panzer Korps and he positioned his men in camouflaged positions at the base of the hill. It was a severe winter and the Allies were exhausted as they battled their way inland. 'Men fall asleep under shellfire,' recalled General Rene Chambre, 'in the midst of mines and bullets. They are killed almost before they realize it. Only wounds make them wake up.' The US 34th Infantry Division took days to move its tanks through the clogging mud.

Above: **The battered walls of Monte Cassino. Allied bombing turned it into a formidable stronghold of rubble hiding German snipers.**

Finally, upon reaching Cassino, the Americans were met by strong opposition and had to withdraw.

A second assault on the town took place in February, this time incorporating New Zealand, Indian and British infantry divisions. The Germans were reinforced by paratroopers fighting as élite infantrymen. Freyberg, the commander of the New Zealand Corps, wanted to open the assault with a crushing bombardment of the monastery, but Lieutenant General Clark, commander of the US Fifth Army, said it was a major cultural site and believed assurances by the Germans that they would not occupy it. Freyberg, however, was not convinced and he believed that all the treasures in Cassino were not worth the life of one Allied soldier. His views prevailed, and once the monks and all their treasures had been removed, the Allies

Above left: The skull of a German paratrooper killed during the defence of Monte Cassino.

Above right: US soldiers wearing layered winter clothing against the severe weather that afflicted the Allies in Italy in 1943–44.

GENERAL VON SENGER

BASTION OF DEFENCE
At the time of the Allied bombardment of the monastery at Monte Cassino, a statement was made that the Germans had already occupied it, thus making it a legitimate target. General von Senger denied this in an interview with Basil Liddell Hart:
'Field Marshal Kesselring had given express orders that no German soldier

should enter the Monastery, so as to avoid giving the Allies any pretext for bombing or shelling it. I cannot testify personally that this decision was communicated to the Allies but I am sure that the Vatican found means to do so, since it was so directly interested in the fate of Monte Cassino. Not only did Field Marshal Kesselring prohibit German soldiers from entering the Monastery,

but he also placed a guard at the entrance gate to ensure that his orders were carried out... [After it was bombed] as anyone with experience of street-fighting knows, it is only when buildings are demolished that they are converted from mouse-traps into bastions of defence.'
Quoted in *The Other Side of the Hill* by Basil Liddell Hart (Cassell, 1948)

dropped hundreds of tons of explosives on the monastery, reducing it to rubble. The action rebounded on the Allies, for the Germans now rushed to occupy a site that provided excellent cover for their men.

Crossfire from these new positions ravaged Freyberg's initial attacks. On the night of 16 February, Royal Sussex Regiment soldiers stormed the monastery slopes, but, strangely, a German paratrooper fired three green flares – the prearranged signal for the British to withdraw – and so the British troopers dutifully left their gains behind. When the mistake was realized, another attack failed to grab the position. New Zealanders tried to capture the town at the base of the hill, but German tanks drove them back. After three days of fighting, Freyberg had to call off the attack.

A third major assault on the town was planned for March. New Zealand and Indian divisions joined forces and it was preceded by a massive bombardment on 15 March that left not one building intact. The Allies pressed on through torrential rain and found themselves confronting a fanatical defence from the German paratroopers, who had survived the bombardment and were shooting at the attacking forces from every crevice. The sheer quantity of rubble left by the bombardment made it impossible for armoured units to support the Allied infantry in their advance. Once more, the bombardment had created more problems than it solved. Hand-to-hand fighting led to some positions being won, but by 23 March Freyberg had to admit defeat again.

SEND IN THE POLES

By spring, the weather in the area had improved and a major offensive was launched against the German Gustav Line, in which Cassino was a major strongpoint. On the night of 11 May, an enormous barrage of artillery erupted and was followed by Allied divisions advancing along a line from Cassino to the sea. North African troops made the breakthrough into the Liri Valley and the Gustav Line had been pierced. At Cassino, it was left to the II Polish Corps to take the monastery. Fifty thousand strong, the unit was led by Lieutenant General Władysław Anders and was composed of Polish soldiers who had escaped from the Nazi–Soviet partition of their country. They were hungry for vengeance against the Germans and were determined to take the position.

On the morning of 12 May, the Poles scrambled up the shell-cratered slopes. They took some positions but were held at others by the equally determined paratroopers. It took five days of hard, close-combat struggle before the Poles could push on up the hill and occupy all the positions around the monastery. On the morning of 18 May, a unit of Polish Lancers finally clambered into the ruins of the monastery. It was empty except for a few wounded Germans. The paratroopers had finally had enough and withdrawn. It was a sweet victory for the Poles and it ended five months of fighting. At least 45,000 soldiers had been lost in total. All along the Gustav Line, the Germans pulled back their forces and the Allies could now concentrate on the liberation of Rome.

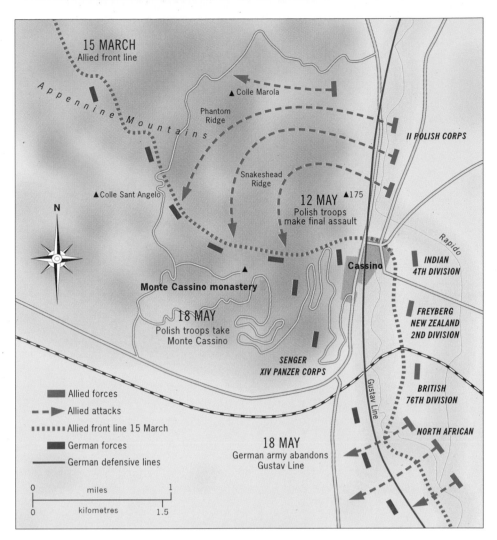

Above: **The final assault against Monte Cassino led by the II Polish Corps, took six days to seize the monastery.**

Left: **The front cover of** *Yank* **magazine showing the ruins of Monte Cassino abbey.**

KOHIMA, 1944

Dubbed the 'Stalingrad of the jungle', the Battle of Kohima halted the Japanese advance towards India. A fierce stand by British and Indian troops exhausted Japanese determination. It marked a turning point in Japan's prosecution of the war, forcing them to withdraw through Burma ahead of the Allied advance.

Burma was the gateway to India and by capturing it the Japanese threatened the heart of the British Empire in the east. The Japanese invasion of Burma began in January 1942, when it attacked from Thailand and captured Rangoon. With their supply lines severed, British and Chinese troops had been forced out of Burma by May. For nearly two years the Japanese occupied the country. In 1943, British troops, led by Major General Orde Wingate, returned as guerrillas and fought behind enemy lines. In 1944, a major British army was assembled under Lieutenant General William Slim along the Indian border with northern Burma. The Japanese pre-empted this build-up by attacking communication centres at Imphal and Kohima.

Lieutenant General Renya Mutaguchi commanded the Japanese Fifteenth Army, which consisted of three divisions

with a hundred thousand men overall. He had fought against the British in Malaya and at Singapore and he had a poor opinion of their fighting spirit. He did not therefore anticipate strong resistance from them in Burma. More than two-thirds of the British force consisted of Indian troops, many of them from the Punjab. They were protecting their homeland from invasion, and the Japanese were to find a very different attitude to that displayed earlier in the war in Malaya.

SIEGE WARFARE

The Japanese offensive began on the night of 7 March and advanced so swiftly across the River Chindwin that the 17th Indian Division at Imphal was virtually cut off. Another attack from the north of Imphal was held at bay by the 20th Indian Division, but the road to Kohima in the north was severed. The fighting was especially fierce, because neither side could afford to give way: the Japanese needed the supplies at Imphal for their survival, while the British and Indian troops knew that a defeat would leave India wide open to invasion. RAF airlifts dropped supplies to the British trapped at Imphal and siege warfare ensued, lasting for 86 days.

In the meantime, the little hill station at Kohima was attacked on 5 April by 12,000 men from the Japanese 31st Division, commanded by Lieutenant General Sato. General Slim was caught unawares by the attack, expecting it further north at the rail centre of Dimapur, to where he had sent a large body of troops to put up a defence. A smaller holding force had been

Above: **British soldiers fight a tough battle against the Japanese in Burma. Neither side could afford to give way and Kohima has been called the Stalingrad of the jungle.**

Left: **The Japanese advance through Burma towards India in March 1944 and the Allied lines of withdrawal.**

Map

Kohima
Jessami
SCRATCH ALLIED FORCE
30 MARCH
7 MARCH
N
SATO
31ST DIVISION
Sangshak
Homalin
Imphal
17TH INDIAN
DIVISION
Kabaw
INDIA
Palel
MUTAGUCHI
15TH ARMY
Chindwin
Tamu
BURMA
Manipur
Sittaung
British forces
British retreat
airborne supply
Japanese forces
Japanese attacks
Mawlaik
Tongzang
Tiddim
7 MARCH
0   miles   25
Kalewa
0   kilometres   40

Right: British Chindits fought a guerrilla war behind Japanese lines in Burma. Considering themselves masters of the jungle, the Japanese were surprised by the British mastery of the difficult terrain.

Above: General William Slim, commander of the British Fourteenth Army in Burma. Having halted the Japanese offensive at Kohima and Imphal, he then pursued the Japanese through Burma.

posted to Kohima, under the command of Colonel Hugh Richards, and given the order to hold it to the last man. And that is exactly what they did.

The defending force of 1,500 men consisted of soldiers from the Royal West Kents, the Assam Rifles, 7th Rajputs and Burma Rifles. The latter included Burmese-born Gurkhas, descendants of soldiers who had fought for the British in the 19th century and been given land in Burma as a reward. The defenders fortified the hillocks around the town as best they could, but when the Japanese arrived, they quickly took the commanding positions and slowly tightened their hold on the settlement, completely surrounding it and using the high ground to shoot down on the defenders. Japanese snipers made any movement during the day almost impossible, although the British deputy commissioner raised morale by strolling among the British and Indian soldiers wearing a Panama hat. Gradually, the British perimeter was reduced to just 36m (40yds).

Water became a problem because the Japanese cut the main supply and it had to be rationed to half a pint a day per man. Wounded soldiers were exposed to constant fire. The two sides were so close that artillery could not always be used, but mortars were and their explosions among the trees caused terrible wood splinters to fly about. Despite Japanese ground fire, the RAF managed to drop supplies of ammunition to the defenders, but it was their fighting spirit that kept them going in the face of constant close-quarter assaults.

John Wright was a young sapper officer during the Battle of Kohima and praises the many Indian troops who fought under him, including the Rajputs and the 'Punjabi Mussalmans who fought under me in Burma and are stolid, loyal and level-headed'. He blames poor officers for a panic among the Sher Gurkhas at Kohima. 'All 730 of them ran through us when mortared,' he recalls, 'and probably incurred many more casualties than we did over the 10 or so days of fairly continuous attack.' Above all, he remembers, 'no one can hold a candle to

Above: **Japanese troops take cover during an attack on a Burmese settlement near Kohima in 1944.**

Left: **The Japanese assaults of April 1944 on Kohima, followed by the British counter-attacks.**

the 4th Royal West Kents, a territorial battalion, who, outnumbered 13 to 1, still beat the Japanese at Kohima.'

Thirteen officers and 201 men of the Royal West Kents were killed or wounded in the process of resisting 25 infantry assaults mounted by the Japanese. Lance Corporal John Harman won a posthumous Victoria Cross when he saved his section from heavy fire by racing towards a Japanese machine gun crew and killing them with a hand grenade. He brought the weapon back on his shoulders. He then charged forward again to kill the crew of a second machine gun post with his rifle and bayonet. As he strolled back, he was killed by a third machine gun, telling his men with his last breath, 'I got the lot; it was worth it.'

THE TENNIS COURT BATTLE

On 14 April, a British relief force nearly broke through to Kohima. As they waited for more reinforcements, the Japanese launched desperate, suicidal attacks on the defenders, which ended in hand-to-hand fighting. Several outposts were captured but still the main line held. On 20 April, British forces finally broke through and the gallant Royal West Kents and Indian troops were relieved. But the fighting was far from over as Slim ordered more troops towards Kohima to prevent Sato's Japanese from sending any support to their forces at Imphal.

Map:

GROVER
BRITISH 2ND DIVISION

Zubza

0 — miles — 1
0 — kilometres — 1.5

N

14 APRIL
Japanese road-block cleared

Japanese flank turned

2 MAY

7 APRIL
Japanese surround Kohima

SATO
31ST DIVISION

Naga village

Jotsoma

Japanese road-blocks

Kohima

Terrace Hill

Tennis court battle
Kohima relieved
18 APRIL

British counter-attack
29 APRIL

- British forces
- British attacks
- Japanese forces
- Japanese attacks
- Japanese front lines

Above: British soldiers of the Royal West Kent Regiment visit the graves of their comrades killed at Kohima.

At the end of the month, the monsoon came and mud and rain added to the misery of the battle. Desperate close-quarter fighting continued as both sides fought for each bit of ground. Eventually, logistics let Sato down and his supplies dwindled. As the Japanese began to starve, the British and Indians gained the upper hand. The Allies took key positions, including a famous battle for the tennis courts belonging to the deputy commissioner's bungalow, during which a tank was hauled up the hillside to fire point-blank at the Japanese bunkers.

By the end of May, devastating air strikes were called in and General Sato had had enough. He withdrew his shattered and hungry soldiers back to Imphal, where the commanders of the Japanese Fifteenth Army realized their offensive had failed. The British and Indians had proved to be far tougher foes than expected. On 8 July the Japanese stumbled back towards Burma, more than sixty thousand of them having been killed or wounded. The British and Indians had suffered 17,587 casualties. General Slim had held the line and could now prepare his offensive into Burma.

MAJOR WATERHOUSE, 2ND DURHAM LIGHT INFANTRY

MIDNIGHT ATTACK
'The Japs attacked with about two companies. The leading men carried bags full of grenades but no weapons. They again broke through owing to sheer weight of numbers, got on the plateau, running around and shouting "Tojo! Tojo!"

[their wartime leader] before digging in. The Durhams counter-attacked at first light, led by Captain "Conky" Greenwell, blowing a hunting horn... A great sound, and they caught the Japs with their pants down... they packed up and ran and found cover in our own smoke, which

was blanketing Kuki Picquet. Fire support was first class... 3.7s, 25 pounders, our own mortars fired 1,300 rounds and caused the Japs heavy casualties.'
Quoted in *The Unforgettable Army* by Michael Hickey (Spellmount, 1992)

D-DAY, 1944

The day the Allies invaded Nazi-occupied Europe saw one of the greatest amphibious landings of all time. Meticulously planned and well supplied with vehicles and equipment, its success or failure still turned on the bravery of the men storming out of their landing craft and on to the beaches in the face of deadly machine gun and artillery fire. Although a triumph overall, the bloody events at Omaha Beach demonstrated the cost of war.

Winston Churchill, Britain's wartime leader, must have been plagued by doubt as he contemplated Operation Overlord, the Allied invasion of western Europe in 1944. The first great amphibious assault he had championed was Gallipoli (see pp.62–65) in the First World War and this had ended in dreadful failure. Other more recent attempts to probe Hitler's coastal defences, such as at Dieppe, had also ended in bloody defeat.

Churchill consoled himself during the months of preparation by considering proposals for imaginative devices that would assist the landing forces. One such innovation was the artificial harbour, code-named the 'Mulberry' harbour; he tested the principle of it in his bath. Less practical was the idea of creating aircraft carriers out of man-made icebergs.

The decision to invade Europe across the English Channel was made between 15 and 25 May 1943, when Churchill met US President Roosevelt at the Trident Conference in Washington, D.C. Planning began immediately and May 1944 was originally selected as the time for the attack. US forces were transported to Britain and intensive training began. A campaign of deception, called Operation Bodyguard, was created to confuse German intelligence, and this campaign included the construction of dummy installations and shipping as well as

Above: **Under heavy fire, US troops leave their landing craft to wade ashore at Omaha Beach.**

misinformation. It worked so well that even on D-Day, Hitler and his staff still expected a main attack to come from the Pas de Calais and he held up reinforcements to Normandy because of this perceived threat.

ALLIED ARMADA

Hitler's Atlantic Wall was an impressive obstacle for the invaders to overcome, stretching 2,600km (1,600 miles) from the Arctic Circle to the border with Spain. From 1940 onwards, massive concrete bunkers were built all along the French coast. In 1943 in one month alone, some 760,000 cubic metres (990,000 cubic yards) of concrete was poured during the

construction of the Atlantic Wall, with the average being around 200,00 cubic metres (260,000 cubic yards) per month until April 1944. Field Marshal Erwin Rommel took over command of the defences in 1943 and he directed efforts towards stopping an invasion force on the beaches, by having six million-plus mines laid there, many of which were not dug into the sand but raised on wooden posts to sink boats. Thousands of obstacles known as 'hedgehogs' – large steel spikes to halt the progress of enemy tanks – were sunk into the sand.

Delayed by poor weather, the Allied landings finally took place on D-Day, 6 June 1944. An armada of 4,000 ships set sail carrying 176,000 men. The landing area chosen consisted

Below: **Having secured their hold on Omaha Beach, American troops and supplies move inland.**

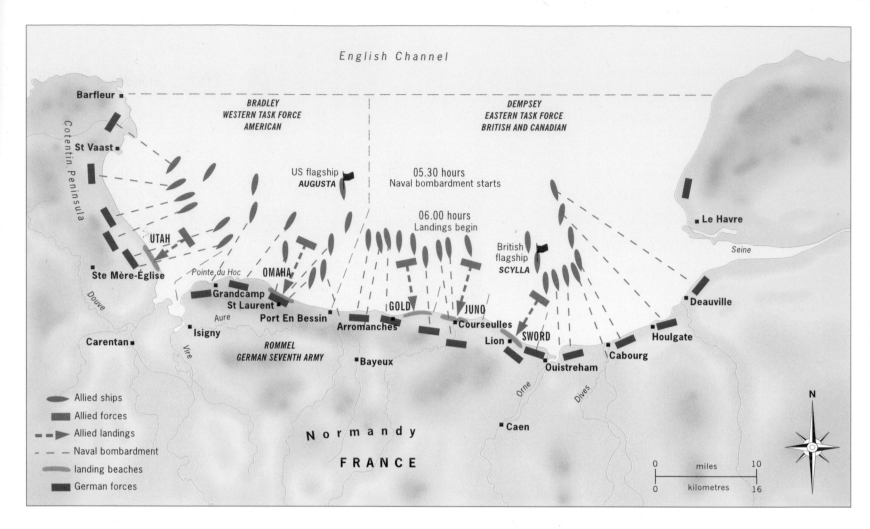

BRADLEY
WESTERN TASK FORCE
AMERICAN

DEMPSEY
EASTERN TASK FORCE
BRITISH AND CANADIAN

Barfleur

Cotentin Peninsula

St Vaast

Le Havre

Seine

US flagship
AUGUSTA

05.30 hours
Naval bombardment starts

06.00 hours
Landings begin

UTAH

British
flagship
SCYLLA

Ste Mère-Église

Pointe du Hoc   OMAHA

Deauville

Grandcamp
St Laurent

Douve

Port En Bessin

GOLD   JUNO

Isigny

Aure

Arromanches

Courseulles

Houlgate

Carentan

Vire

*ROMMEL
GERMAN SEVENTH ARMY*

Lion   SWORD

Cabourg

Bayeux

Ouistreham

Orne   Dives

N o r m a n d y

Caen

F R A N C E

N

Allied ships

Allied forces

Allied landings

Naval bombardment

landing beaches

German forces

0   miles   10

0   kilometres   16

Above: The Allied landings of 6 June 1944 on the five code-named Normandy beaches.

of the beaches east of the Cotentin Peninsula in Normandy: five landing points were given the code-names of Utah, Omaha, Gold, Juno, and Sword. The American, British and Commonwealth troops were opposed by the German Seventh Army, a mixture of veteran German soldiers and less effective Axis allies. US General Eisenhower was the Allied Supreme Commander, while Britain's General Montgomery was in command of ground forces. The US First Army under General Bradley was to land at Utah and Omaha, while the British Second Army under General Dempsey, with a Canadian corps, was to land at Gold, Juno and Sword. If the first day went well, there was a total of a million Allied soldiers waiting to exploit any success.

HITTING THE BEACHES

The amphibious landings were preceded by a paratroop drop behind enemy lines and a massive bombardment delivered by Allied aircraft and ships. Much of the preliminary bombardment, however, fell behind the German beach defences, and this failure was felt most strongly at Omaha. As the American ships approached the beaches there, rough seas swamped many of the amphibious tanks and dragged them to the bottom, with their crews still trapped inside. Only six of the thirty-three tanks were left to support the troops on shore. US soldiers drowned in the choppy waters and those who did manage to struggle

ashore were met by a storm of fire from German machine guns and artillery, which fired straight down the beach at them.

US Sergeant John Slaughter was only 19 when he 'hit the beach' at Omaha, where a terrible scene greeted him: 'There were dead men floating in the water and there were live men acting dead, letting the tide take them in. I was crouched down to chin-deep in the water when I saw mortar shells zeroing in at the water's edge. Sand began to kick up from small arms fire from the bluffs. It became apparent that it was past time to get the hell across that beach. I don't know how long we were in the water before the move was made, but I guess close to an hour.' The American landing at Omaha turned into a disaster, with more than three thousand soldiers lost by nightfall.

Another brave but chaotic incident was the daring raid by the US Rangers at Pointe du Hoc, which overlooked Omaha Beach. German gun batteries had been identified in the bunkers that guarded this stretch of the coast. The 2nd Ranger Battalion, commanded by Colonel Jim Rudder, was given the awesome task of scaling these cliffs and knocking out the gun batteries. At 04.15 hours on D-Day, the US Rangers approached the rocky shore beneath the 30-m (100-ft) cliffs in their landing craft and immediately came under heavy fire as they neared the beach. Once ashore, they fired their rocket lines cliffwards, which were supposed to attach grappling hooks to the top, but the ropes failed to extend further than 15m (50ft) because they had been soaked by water during the landing.

With only ladders and daggers to help them, the US Rangers fearlessly tackled the rocks, climbing up the cliff-face while under fire. After half an hour, one hundred men had scaled the cliffs and moved forwards to destroy their target: the 155-mm (6-in) guns in the bunkers. But there were no guns! Allied intelligence had got it wrong. Rudder sent out patrols to find the guns, which had not yet been placed in the bunkers, and then destroyed them once they had been located. German soldiers then counter-attacked, forcing the isolated US Rangers to fight a fierce battle lasting two days. When they were eventually relieved, the final cost was 135 killed or wounded out of a total of 225 men landed, a casualty rate of 60 per cent.

COSTLY SUCCESS

The British faced similar problems on Gold Beach, where rough seas and strong defences hampered their landing. Specially designed tanks came to their rescue, using flails to explode the

mines and allow the British troops to press ahead, despite having suffered a thousand casualties. The Canadians stumbled ashore at Juno Beach to be greeted by mangled bodies and equipment, but they had the motivation of revenge for the death of their fellow Canadians at Dieppe and they advanced further inland than any of the other Allied forces. They too suffered one thousand casualties.

The landing on Sword Beach claimed a further one thousand soldiers, but the troops managed to break the German defences and advance a little way inland. At Utah Beach, a landing on the wrong beach saved American soldiers from a more heavily defended section of the coast that could have cost them similar casualties to those received at Omaha.

By the end of the day, Allied troops were ashore and determined to stay there, despite fierce German counter-attacks. The Allies had learned their lessons from previous amphibious operations at Dieppe, in North Africa and Italy, and their organization proved thorough. On the days that followed, more and more men and supplies landed on the beaches and built up Allied strength. The next challenge was to break out from the landing zone.

Above right: **General Eisenhower, Supreme Allied Commander at D-Day, visits the US 82nd Airborne Division before their air drop behind German lines in Normandy.**

Above: **British soldiers capture the Hindenburg gun emplacement and declare it 'under new management'.**

COLONEL PATRICK PORTEOUS

FRIGHTENING LANDING
'One of the subalterns stood up [in the landing craft] to get out and he was absolutely bowled over by machine-gun fire and he was cut to ribbons. It was very frightening. And then a flail tank on the beach just in front of us was hit by a shell or something and just blew up, and there was machine-gun fire all around, and there were bodies washing about in the engine oil at the water's edge, and men kneeling in the water trying to fire, and then they'd get hit.'
Quoted in *D-Day – Those who were there* by Juliet Gardiner (Collins & Brown, 1994)

ST LÔ, 1944

Following the D-Day landings on 6 June 1944 (see pp.144–147, Allied forces needed to break out from Normandy, and the biggest use to date of concentrated bombing was used to blast a way through at St Lô. Such destruction delivered so close to their own lines caused Allied deaths, but the Germans were devastated by the onslaught and their lines broke.

D-Day itself was a success, with five divisions ashore by nightfall. Over the next few days, tremendous quantities of men, vehicles and supplies were funnelled through a series of artificial harbours put in place along the Normandy beaches. Hitler still believed that another attack would come through the Pas de Calais, and the German counter-attack in Normandy was hampered by his insistence. The territory beyond the landing beaches proved to be an unexpected obstacle to the Allied advance, with the nature of the *bocage* landscape meaning that the Allies had to fight from hedgerow to hedgerow. The British aimed for Caen but found the city difficult to take. The Americans drove up the Cotentin Peninsula to take Cherbourg on 27 June. By the beginning of July, there were a million men and one hundred and fifty thousand vehicles ashore.

General Field Marshal Rommel was in charge of the German counter-attack and he slowly amassed the armoured divisions he needed. Montgomery and the British were held by seven panzer divisions and two infantry divisions, only finally managing to take a ruined Caen on 13 July. Seven panzer divisions opposed the advance of the US First Army, and General Bradley slowly pushed towards St Lô, suffering 11,000 casualties on the way. Rommel was wounded by an air attack on 17 July and Marshal Gunther von Kluge took over his role. A massive breakout operation was needed by the Allies and they code-named it Cobra.

AIR SUPREMACY

The American dimension to Operation Cobra was to the west of St Lô. The Allies enjoyed complete domination of the air, and Bradley decided to use this air supremacy to break the German forces opposite him. He knew from reconnaissance photographs that he possessed superior numbers of men and supplies and that the roads behind the German lines were empty of reinforcements, whereas behind his First Army was General Patton's Third Army ready to exploit any breakthrough. But Bradley could not carry on grinding away at the panzer divisions with his infantry. The road from St Lô to Periers was clearly observable to Allied aircraft, and Bradley decided to use this as his marker for a concentrated aerial bombardment of the German positions.

An argument broke out between how close American units should be to the St Lô road. Bradley wanted them within 800m (870yds) so as to take immediate advantage of the bombing, but the air force itself was not as confident as he was in its aim. It wanted a buffer zone of at least three kilometres (two miles). Reluctantly, Bradley agreed to a compromise of 1,200m (1,300 yds), which meant his infantry had to draw back and give up

Left: The US Army's capture of the German line to the west of St Lô allowed the Allies to break out of the area of the Normandy landings. Little over a month later, they had reached Paris.

Below: Once past the German defensive line on the St Lô to Periers road, the US Army made rapid progress across the Normandy countryside, despite German counter-attacks.

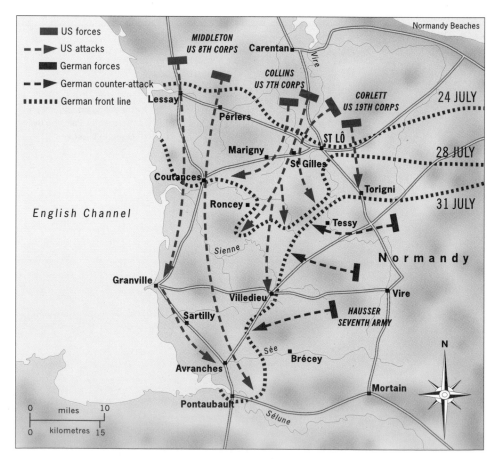

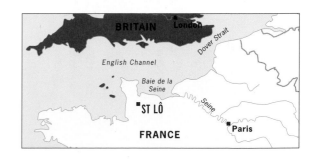

hard-won ground. By 24 July, rainy weather had passed and it was deemed a good day for the Allied bombers to take off.

As the B-17 Flying Fortresses took off, the order was cancelled, but one-third of the aircraft had already left the ground and they approached the designated target road from a perpendicular angle, not parallel as instructed by Bradley. The air force argued that this was the safest approach for aircraft because they could fly in a wider formation than the narrow funnel demanded by following the road. But some of the bombs fell short and caused casualties among the US 30th Division. Bradley was furious, but the air force insisted it was the best approach for its aircraft.

CARPET BOMBING

On 25 July the sky was clear and 550 P-47 Thunderbolt fighter-bombers approached the German lines firing rockets and dropping 227-kg (500-lb) bombs. Their aim was precise, causing explosions to ripple along a line just 300m (325yds) from the US infantry. After them came 1,800 B-17 bombers. It was an awesome sight. 'A new sound gradually droned into our ears,' recalled journalist Ernie Pyle, 'a gigantic far-away surge of doom-like sound. It was the heavies... Their march across the sky was slow and studied. I've never known anything that had about it the aura of such a ghastly relentlessness.' They dropped bombs for a full hour and the result for the Germans was catastrophic: General Bayerlein lost 70 per cent of his men.

Tragically, dropping bombs from 3,660m (12,000ft) and using the line of smoke as a marker meant that the aim of the bombers was less than accurate, and as the prevailing wind blew the smoke over the Allied positions, the bombs began to fall on American troops. Panic ensued and 111 American soldiers were killed and 490 wounded. General McNair was the most senior fatality. Artillery fire supported the bombers by targeting German anti-aircraft guns. As a final blow, the P-47s reappeared to drop napalm on the German lines. All in all,

Above: **US troops with a Sherman tank move through the devastated town of St Lô, part of the Allied breakout from Normandy. Painting by Ogden Pleissner.**

16,250 tonnes (16,000 tons) of bombs had been dropped in what was the most concentrated use of explosives in American military history to date.

As the barrage ceased, infantry and tanks of the US 30th Division moved forward. What they had hoped for was a complete lack of resistance, but the surviving Germans dug themselves out, righted their guns and created pockets of fierce resistance. The Americans were disappointed and by nightfall there was little to show for the saturation bombing. Field Marshal von Kluge insisted that the Germans hold the line, but General Bayerlein knew it was only a token effort, declaring, 'Not a single man is leaving his post. They are lying silent in their foxholes for they are dead.' His division was smashed, and on the second day after the aerial assault, on 27 July, its desperate resistance was finally broken and the Americans passed through the line.

Operation Cobra had succeeded, and as the Germans retreated across France, the Allies pounded them mercilessly. The US Third Army could now follow through and its completely motorized columns outstripped the horse-drawn and battered German divisions, which they then surrounded in a pincer movement. A fierce German counter-attack was fought at Avranches, but the general movement was eastwards. By 25 August the Allies had reached Paris and liberated the city.

MAJOR JOACHIM BARTH, COMMANDER, ANTI-TANK BATTALION

NO LEAVES ON THE TREES

'When the shelling finally stopped, I looked out of my bunker. The world had changed. There were no leaves on the trees. It was much harder to get around.

We had wounded, we needed medics, but no ambulances could come forward. Our big guns had been tipped over.'
Quoted in *Citizen Soldiers* by Stephen E. Ambrose (Simon & Schuster, 1997)

LEYTE GULF, 1944

The largest naval battle of the Second World War, Leyte Gulf opened the way for the American reconquest of the Philippines. It was also one of the most complicated naval battles ever fought. There were several stages of attack and counter-attack, with aircraft carriers proving once more to be the decisive element, delivering destructive air assaults on both sides.

In 1942, General Douglas MacArthur was forced to flee the Philippines, the US force surrendering behind him to its Japanese conquerors. In Australia, he declared to journalists that 'I shall return!' It took two and half years of fierce fighting, but in October 1944 he waded ashore on Leyte Island alongside the president of the Philippines.

MacArthur was committed to the liberation of the Philippines, although from a strategic point of view, Admiral Nimitz wished to proceed to Formosa and then China, from where the Americans could bomb Japan into submission. The Japanese were similarly diverted by the defence of the Philippines, hoping to fight a decisive battle against the Americans and halt their reconquest of the Pacific region. As American forces landed in Leyte Gulf, the Japanese decided to deliver a crushing naval blow.

Above: **The final moment as a kamikaze plane attacks a US battleship.**

Left: **Kamikaze pilots carrying samurai swords. Severe losses meant that the quality of Japanese pilots declined rapidly through the war.**

Surigao Strait, with the intention of crushing the US amphibious landing force in Leyte Gulf between these two fleets.

On 23 October, two US submarines, *Darter* and *Dace*, intercepted the Centre Force as it sailed past the island of Palawan towards the central Philippines and the San Bernadino Strait. Their torpedoes sank two Japanese heavy cruisers and damaged a third. The alarm was raised and the US Third Fleet alerted, as the Japanese sailed on through the Sea of Sibuyan. US aircraft took off from their carriers and subjected the Japanese fleet to two days of bombardment, resulting in the sinking of the *Musashi*, one of its major battleships. The Japanese fleet now turned round and the US Third Fleet presumed it was retreating, but Japanese land-based aircraft struck back, sinking a carrier and damaging a cruiser. At night, the Centre Force resumed its advance through the San Bernardino Strait.

FINAL BLOWS

In single line ahead, the Southern Force entered Surigao Strait on 24 October. Admiral Oldendorf met these ships with his destroyers, which sank the battleship *Fuso* and four destroyers.

Above: **American soldiers take cover on the beach during landings on Leyte Island.**

Right: **The fleet movements and battles that made up the three days of the Battle of Leyte Gulf.**

PINCER ATTACK ON LEYTE GULF

The US amphibious force assembled in Leyte Gulf was impressive, consisting of some seven hundred vessels and two hundred thousand men. It was supported by six battleship survivors from Pearl Harbor, five heavy cruisers, four light cruisers and sixty-six destroyers, all under the command of Rear Admiral Oldendorf. An air support fleet of nine destroyers, sixteen escort carriers and eleven destroyer escorts was commanded by Rear Admiral Sprague. The US Third Fleet stood nearby and four US submarines cruised beneath the waves.

The landings on Leyte Island began on 20 October following a heavy naval bombardment. The Japanese responded by enacting their *Sho*, or 'Victory Plan'. This consisted of using some of their ships to divert the interest of the US aircraft carriers, while the main Japanese fleet attacked the amphibious support ships, thus isolating the American soldiers on shore.

Such an assault, however, depended on strong air power, which the Japanese lacked. Nevertheless, the Japanese concentrated their ships into three main fleets and sailed towards the Philippines. The Northern Force, with Japan's four remaining carriers, two battleships and three cruisers, threatened Luzon and acted as a decoy for the US Third Fleet, which sailed to meet it; the Centre Force, which included five battleships, twelve cruisers and fifteen destroyers, entered the San Bernadino Strait; while the Southern Force, with two battleships, one heavy cruiser and four destroyers, sailed through the

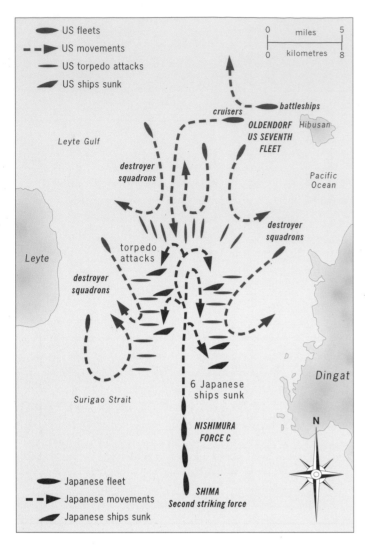

He then manoeuvred to cross the Japanese T, and American naval guns and torpedoes devastated the Japanese fleet, sinking all but one destroyer. Admiral Nishimura went down with his flagship. Joined by aircraft from Sprague's carrier force, Oldendorf now pursued the Japanese through Surigao Strait, sinking another cruiser.

Despite the southern pincer having been shattered, the Centre Force, commanded by Vice Admiral Kurita, carried on with its planned assault through San Bernardino Strait. Part of the Japanese plan even seemed to be working, because although the US Third Fleet had savaged the Centre Force, it was now diverted to the north by the Northern Force as had originally been hoped for. On 25 October, Rear Admiral Sprague was completely surprised by the appearance of the Centre Force – and outgunned too. The heavier Japanese ships pounded the American amphibious support boats. Even Sprague's aircraft were armed with fragmentation bombs meant for land attacks and not for use against armoured battleships (a weird echo of the Japanese aircraft at Midway, which had also been armed with the wrong kind of bombs). One US carrier was sunk, along with two destroyers, but Sprague's ships fought bravely and boldly and held the line until aircraft from other American carriers had swarmed to the area. Kurita's nerve now failed him and he feared the renewed attack of the US Third Fleet. News had also reached him of the defeat of the Southern Force.

The Centre Force withdrew through the San Bernardino Strait, being harassed by US aircraft all the way. The battle was not over, however, and Japanese land-based planes assaulted Oldendorf's fleet at Surigao Strait as it sailed back from the battle, sinking the USS *St Lô*. Kamikaze ('divine wind') suicide

Left: **On 24 October the Japanese Southern Force was intercepted and virtually destroyed by the US Seventh Fleet in the Suriago Strait.**

Below left: **In one of the engagements on 25 October, the Centre Force clashed with part of the US 7th Fleet.**

Below: **A Japanese heavy cruiser trying to manoeuvre away from US bombers flying from nearby carriers. The cruiser was eventually caught and sunk.**

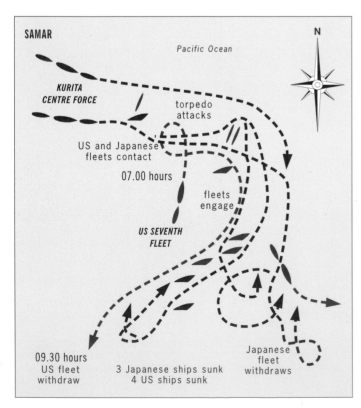

Above: USS *St Lô* explodes following a kamikaze attack off Samar on 25 October.

PETER PADFIELD, HISTORIAN

SUBMARINE ATTACK

US submarines struck the first blow at the battle of Leyte Gulf and naval historian Peter Padfield describes their first encounter with the Japanese Centre Force:

'Both submarines tracked, pulling ahead to submerge and attack just before dawn, McClintock [in Darter] taking the port column, Lt-Cdr Bladen Claggett in Dace the starboard. McClintock fired first, launching six torpedoes at the leading cruiser, in fact Kurita's flagship Atago, and then swinging to fire his stern tubes at the second in the line. Four of the first salvo hit Atago, detonating with heavy explosions as he was making his final observations for the second salvo at what proved to be the cruiser Takeo. Two of these hit. He ordered the boat deep and, swinging the periscope back to the first target, saw her settling by the bows, issuing bright flames and smoke."

Quoted from *War beneath the Sea* by Peter Padfield (John Murray, 1995)

pilots then made an appearance for the first time, plunging their aircraft into the decks of American ships. In the north, off Luzon, the US Third Fleet caught up with the Japanese decoy Northern Force and thoroughly pounded it with aircraft attacks. Most of the aircraft from the Japanese carriers had been sent ashore and there was little they could respond with. The decoy fleet paid a heavy price for its deception, having all four of its carriers sunk, plus three other ships.

Japanese tactics had worked in part, with the Centre Force almost severely damaging the amphibious support fleet at Leyte Gulf, but its weakness in air power plus the devastating defeat of its southern pincer had resulted in a decisive defeat for Japanese naval power. Virtually every ship in its combined fleets had been damaged and many of its key ships sunk; some five hundred aircraft had been lost and more than ten thousand Japanese sailors and pilots killed. Japan was now very much on the defensive.

ARDENNES, 1944

Hitler's last gamble in the war in western Europe was designed to secure a peace with the Allies so he could concentrate resources on the fight against the Soviet Union. German tanks and troops emerged out of the forest of the Ardennes under the cover of mist and snow and caught the Allies off their guard. But the Americans recovered and held their position at Bastogne.

By autumn 1944, Hitler was fighting a devastating war on two fronts. It was what German military planners had feared most since they had devised the Schlieffen Plan before the First World War. The western Allies had broken out of Normandy and were steadily advancing towards the River Rhine. In the east, the Red Army had reversed its earlier defeats and was steam-rolling across Europe towards

Berlin. Hitler had to neutralize one of the fronts in order to concentrate on the other. It was too late to strike a peace deal with Stalin, which might have been possible in 1943. Soviet forces were too successful now and their thirst for vengeance was too strong.

The western Allies were Hitler's only chance of striking a deal that might avert total defeat and preserve something of the Third Reich. To achieve this, Hitler had to prove to the Western powers that it was not worth fighting all the way to the Rhine and that the Germans still possessed enough fight to make the continued advance too costly to justify. This was the reasoning behind the German offensive in the Ardennes at the end of 1944 – Hitler's last gamble in the western arena.

Above: **German infantry advance across a road in the Ardennes littered with damaged Allied vehicles.**

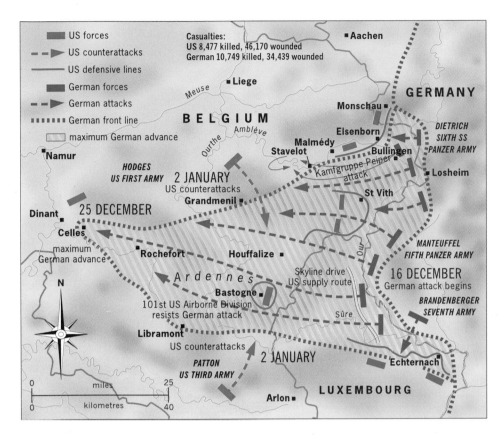

The Americans were caught out completely. The skies over the Ardennes were overcast, which severely limited Allied air support. Fog cloaked the Belgian landscape, restricting visibility to no more than 90m (100yds). Thick mud bogged down the Allied trucks, and when snow fell, it added further to the chaos of moving troops and supplies around the battlefield. Advanced units of English-speaking Germans dressed in American uniforms completed the confusion. The 106th and 28th divisions of the US Army collapsed before the onslaught. To the north of the bulge, V Corps held firm, while in the south the US 4th Division also remained solid.

So surprised were the Americans by the German assault that Peiper entered Honsfeld by joining a column of retreating US Army vehicles. His opposition-avoiding detours had cost him fuel, however, and put him behind his original schedule. With his tanks freshly filled with gasoline, Peiper

Above: The December 1944 German offensive through the Ardennes, creating the bulge in the Allied lines that gave the battle its name.

Right: US troops march along a road in the Ardennes wearing sheets as improvised snow camouflage.

A SURPRISE ATTACK

The Ardennes forest lies on the border between Belgium and Germany. The densely wooded landscape and narrow country roads are not good terrain in which to attack motorized columns, which is exactly why the Germans chose this location for their surprise assault westwards. A similar armoured thrust in this region had caught the French by surprise in 1940 (see pp.90–93) and the Germans repeated this strategy. On 16 December, three panzer armies, consisting of 24 divisions, 10 of them armoured, thrust against exhausted US Army units and created a bulge in Allied lines (hence its other name – Battle of the Bulge).

The German armoured units were equipped with the latest version of the formidable Tiger tank, which mounted a high-velocity 88-mm gun and could far outrange any tank the Allies could field. Jochen Peiper, a tank ace and commander of the élite 1st SS Panzer Division – the Führer's regimental bodyguard – spearheaded the attack. Beginning at 02.00 hours on 16 December at Blankenheim, Peiper's panzer units moved rapidly along the little forest roads. When he encountered pockets of American resistance, he went round them, leaving the smaller conflicts to be resolved later by infantry troops. Peiper's intention was to reach Antwerp and split the Allies in two.

Above: US troops watch for parachute supply drops during the defence of Bastogne.

DWIGHT D. EISENHOWER, ALLIED SUPREME COMMANDER

DESPERATE RISK

'My headquarters and 12th Army group had felt for some time that a counter-attack through the Ardennes was a possibility, since American forces were stretched very thinly there in order to provide troops for attack elsewhere and because Field Marshal von Rundstedt had gradually placed in this quiet sector six infantry divisions, a larger number than he required for reasonable security.

However, we did not consider it highly probably that von Rundstedt would, in winter, try to use that region in which to stage a counter-offensive on a large scale, feeling certain that we could deal with any effort and that the result would ultimately be disastrous to Germany... In order fully to appraise the desperate risk which the enemy undertook in making this venture it must be recognised that he aimed his blow, above all, at the will

of the Allied Command. If he could weaken our determination to maintain that flaming, relentless offensive which, regardless of his reaction, had carried us from the beaches to the Siegfried Line, his sacrifices would not altogether be futile.'

Quoted from *Report by the Supreme Commander to the Combined Chiefs of Staff on the Operations in Europe of the Allied Expeditionary Force* (HMSO, 1946)

roared towards Ligneuville, where his unit defeated an American column and captured many American troops. Being Waffen SS – among Hitler's most fanatical supporters – the German soldiers had a particularly ruthless attitude towards prisoners, and in a field near the crossroads at Baugnez, some one hundred unarmed Americans were crowded into a field and shot. Whether Peiper himself was

aware of this is uncertain, but as commander he must undoubtedly take responsibility for this war crime.

Peiper pushed on to Stavelot on the northern edge of the bulge in the Allied lines. Only 13 American soldiers defended this position, but their brave stand halted the German column and provided valuable time for more Allied reinforcements to reach the area. Peiper took Stavelot, but the Americans surrounded him and cut his supply line, drawing two thousand soldiers and two hundred vehicles into a pocket they could not escape from. Forced back into Stavelot, Peiper and his men fought desperately, but few escaped the Americans closing in. Peiper was captured and the spearhead of the German assault had been broken. Attention now shifted to Bastogne and the American defence of this position in the heart of the bulge.

AMERICAN RESISTANCE

Allied Supreme Commander General Dwight D. Eisenhower committed his reserves in order to stem the German advance. The US 101st Airborne Division arrived in the town of Bastogne to face the Fifth Panzer Army, and the 82nd Airborne Division reinforced the northern flank. In the south, Lieutenant General George Patton turned his Third Army to attack the German southern flank. Some 18,000 American soldiers filled the perimeter of Bastogne. Hitler was determined that the little Belgian town should be taken at all costs, but the Americans were equally resolute about holding on to it, despite being completely surrounded by the Germans.

On 22 December, German officers waved a flag of truce and delivered a note to Brigadier General McAuliffe, who commanded the defence at Bastogne. The note demanded that McAuliffe surrender. 'Aw, nuts!' he responded, and after

a conversation with his staff, it was agreed that the official American response should be 'Nuts!' This was met by a fierce German assault, which began on Christmas Eve with a heavy bombardment. Next came a determined tank attack on the western sector of the town. The fighting was ferocious, but the Americans held their own against the veteran German troops. 'Fog, rain, snow, freezing sleet,' recalled Private Bill Butler of the US 106th Division, 'combined with someone trying to kill you. I was in a foxhole alone. I had no one to wish me a Merry Christmas.'

To the south of Bastogne, Patton ordered the 4th Armoured Division to 'drive like hell.' In the meantime, the sky had cleared over Bastogne and Allied aircraft could bomb the German supply lines. It was a pivotal moment in the battle, when the Allies could finally make their supremacy in the air count. By 2 January, the Americans in Bastogne had weathered the storm and the battle was all but over. With British and US. forces counter-attacking in the north and Patton surging forward in the south, Hitler was forced to withdraw his exhausted panzer divisions. His final gamble had failed. American casualties in the battle included 8,477 men killed, 46,170 wounded and 20,905 taken prisoner. German losses were 10,749 killed, 34,439 wounded and 32,487 prisoners or missing. The road to Berlin was open and the Allied forces duly crossed the River Rhine.

Below: An American 105-mm howitzer is used during the Allied counter-attack during the Battle of the Bulge.

Below right: German SS troops, smoking captured American cigarettes, stand in front of a destroyed US armoured car.

OKINAWA, 1945

United States warships
United States forces
United States movements
Japanese forces
Japanese defensive lines
Japanese kamikaze attacks

Iheya

Pacific Ocean

Hedo
13 APRIL

Ie Shima

Motubu Peninsula

Aha
19 APRIL

17–21 APRIL

20 APRIL

3000 Japanese kamikaze
attack US Fifth Fleet

Okinawa

1 AND 2 APRIL
US Tenth Army lands

Hagushi

JAPANESE THIRTY-SECOND ARMY

Kerama

Naha
27 MAY

Shuri

Machinato Line broken
24 APRIL

N

26 MARCH

Final resistance
21 JUNE

Mabuni

1 AND 2 APRIL
US diversionary landings

0   miles   20
0   kilometres   30

US TENTH ARMY

The final island conquest by American forces in the Pacific War offered horrific demonstrations of Japanese suicide attacks. Kamikaze aircraft targeted American ships, and Japanese civilians killed themselves in a panic provoked by their own soldiers. The rate of casualties suffered at Okinawa on both sides encouraged the Americans to use the atomic bomb instead of assaulting mainland Japan.

Although by the beginning of 1945 it was inevitable that Japan would be defeated by the western Allies, it was feared that Japan's reluctance to admit defeat could make the war last for many more years. Despite setbacks in the Pacific theatre, Japan still held on to much of southeast Asia and in China it had executed a successful campaign in 1944. It was even considered that the Japanese leadership might evacuate their own islands and continue the war from bases in Korea, Manchuria and China.

Advancing across the Pacific Ocean from the east in their island-hopping campaign, the Americans reached Iwo Jima in March 1945. Their next target was the Ryukyu Islands, half-way

between Formosa and Kyushu, the southernmost island of Japan. The largest island in this group was Okinawa. It would make an excellent airbase from which to strike Japan with more devastating air raids, and it would provide a launching site for an invasion of Japan itself.

OPERATION ICEBERG

The Americans called it Operation Iceberg and Admiral Nimitz's Fifth Fleet was at the core of it, transporting some 180,000 troops of the US Tenth Army. The American carrier force was joined by Britain's own, with four aircraft carriers and one battleship. Despite naval supremacy, the Americans remained fearful of continued Japanese aerial assaults. Both Formosa and Kyushu were still in enemy hands and the Japanese were committed increasingly to kamikaze ('divine wind') attacks in which tremendous damage could be caused to American ships by pilots crashing their explosives-laden planes into them on suicide missions. Okinawa itself was defended by 130,000 Japanese

Above: US Marines rest during the relentless fighting to take Japanese positions buried in the rock of the island.

Above left: The course of the American advance through Okinawa and the surrounding islands from their landing points between 26 March and 21 June 1945.

soldiers, and the native population were terrified into committing desperate acts, believing it was better to commit suicide than yield to the American invasion.

The American operation began with air strikes against airbases on Kyushu and Formosa in an attempt to neutralize the aerial threat to the invasion fleet. Waves of kamikaze then responded by attacking the major US carriers, so badly damaging the USS *Franklin* that she had to be towed away. The British steel-decked carriers survived the attacks better than the wooden-decked US carriers. American air power, though, managed to halt the Japanese assaults, and the US Navy prepared to attack Okinawa. A pre-invasion barrage was initiated by the escort ships. The capture of the island of Kerama provided a secure anchorage for the invasion fleet. On the island, they discovered a chilling variant on the kamikaze: 350 suicide boats packed with explosives, all destined for use against the invasion fleet. Their capture removed a major threat to the Allied ships.

The landings began on 1 April with a decoy assault force diverting the attention of the defending Japanese to the southeast coast, while the actual invasion fleet of landing craft surged

Right: A Japanese suicide aircraft making an attack on the USS *Sangamon* during the battle for Okinawa. The aircraft missed the ship by just 7.5m (25ft).

Below: A US Marine aims his Tommy gun at a Japanese sniper at Wana Ridge outside the town of Suri on Okinawa.

towards beaches on the western coast of Hagushi with sixty thousand troops. The landing itself was unopposed, because the Japanese planned to defend their island further inland. As the Americans built up their beach-head, the Japanese sent in some 355 kamikaze aircraft. Private Townsend of the 2nd US Marines describes the impact of these attacks: 'The plane's engines ripped through the LST [landing ship] and exploded in the Amtrac compartment, killing and wounding the sleeping Marines in the Amtracs... I'll never forget that day or the kamikaze days that followed. My LST had at least two or three near misses during the attacks. I truly believe that there is nothing more terrifying than having a man, hell-bent on committing suicide, guiding his winged bomber at you. I had been through the banzai attacks but we were able to control those. We had no control over the Divine Wind.'

The US fleet lost two destroyers and a few other minor ships to the kamikaze assault, but struck back by attacking the *Yamato*, the largest battleship built thus far, eventually sinking it after four hours of aerial bombing, along with four destroyers and a cruiser. This action put an end to the Japanese Navy.

DESPERATE DEFENCES

As the Americans advanced further inland they hit the Machinato Line, an awesome series of interconnecting fortified emplacements dug into the rock. Clearing out position after position made for tough and exhausting fighting, and heavy rains did nothing to help American morale. US Marines took the brunt of the action; they fought on two fronts, by advancing to the north of the island and to the south. The Machinato Line was eventually pierced on 24 April, but then a further bloody assault had to be undertaken against Shuri Castle, which had a maze of tunnels beneath it. This was eventually taken on 28 April with flanking attacks, and on 21 June resistance in the south was finally crushed. On 27 May, the island's capital was captured. All the time, the Americans had to face almost constant kamikaze attacks, some three thousand suicide sorties in all, which exhausted Japanese air strength but also accounted for a total of 21 American ships.

Japanese losses in the battle were staggeringly high, reflecting the increasingly suicidal nature of their defences. At least 107,500 were killed, with a possible 20,000 more buried alive in caves by American soldiers who preferred to seal up the defenders rather than risk their own lives by trying to capture them. Some four thousand Japanese aircraft were destroyed. The US Tenth Army lost 7,374 men killed and 32,056 wounded, while the US Navy lost 5,000 men killed and 4,600 wounded.

Below: **US landing craft wait off Okinawa while support ships fire a devastating barrage of 1,000 13-cm (5-in) rockets per minute. Japanese forces did not contest the landings on the beach but fought stubbornly inland.**

Above: A Japanese soldier surrenders to US Marines during the desperate fighting on Okinawa.

EUGENE SMITH, 5TH US MARINES

HORROR STRICKEN

'When enemy artillery shells exploded in the area, the eruptions of soil and mud uncovered previously buried Japanese dead and scattered chunks of corpses. Like the area around our gun pits, the ridge was a stinking compost pile. If a Marine slipped and slid down the back slope of the muddy ridge, he was apt to reach the bottom vomiting. I saw more than one man lose his footing and slip and slide all the way to the bottom only to stand horror-stricken as he watched in disbelief while fat maggots tumbled out of his muddy dungaree pockets, cartridge belt, legging lacings, and the like. Then he and a buddy would shake or scrape them away with a piece of ammo box or knife blade.'
Quoted in *Marine* by Ron Field (Military Illustrated, 1999)

It had been a costly victory and the Japanese had virtually annihilated their own air force in the process. US aerial bombardment of Japan intensified, inflicting huge destruction on Japanese industry and the civilian population. Okinawa demonstrated how desperately the Japanese would defend their homeland, and the American experience of this, along with other strategic concerns, helped them to decide on the use of atomic bombs to end the war. They reasoned that the huge losses expected from a land invasion of Japan would dwarf those inflicted by atomic bombs. It would certainly come at a high cost in American lives in addition to those of Japanese soldiers and civilians. Thus it was that the dropping of two atomic bombs on Hiroshima and Nagasaki in August finally ended the war in the Pacific without the need of an Okinawa-style invasion of Japan.

BERLIN, 1945

The final battle of the Second World War in Europe, the battle for Berlin in 1945, was a massive assault on the capital of Nazism and a momentous occasion in world history. Soviet commanders raced for the prize of getting there amid fighting that was brutal and merciless. The Soviet victory was Stalin's greatest moment: the Third Reich had been decisively destroyed. But it was also the beginning of the Cold War, a new confrontation in which the communist East would face the capitalist West for almost fifty years.

As the Red Army advanced towards Berlin in April 1945, Hitler was determined that his people should go down fighting. His capital was prepared with three massive defensive lines, including anti-tank ditches and gun emplacements along a line 300km (200 miles) long from the Baltic Sea to the Czech border. The main defensive position was the Seelow Heights, directly in front of Berlin where the Soviets were expected to attack.

Eisenhower and the western Allies could have reached Berlin before the Soviet Army, but it seems likely that they feared the desperate resistance promised by Hitler would create a sacrifice too high to justify to the public back home. There was also the possibility of clashes with the Red Army itself, for the politics of the forthcoming Cold War was already evident in the pronouncements of Stalin and western Allied leaders.

ARMY OF VENGEANCE

Marshal Zhukov, commander of the Red Army, presented his plan of attack to Stalin on 8 March 1945. It was simple and direct. Zhukov's 1st Byelorussian Front would launch its assault from bridgeheads on the River Oder and attack the city from the Seelow Heights as Hitler had predicted. A separate flanking movement from the north would curve round and attack the city from the west. General Koniev's 1st Ukrainian Front would

Above: Russian Ilyushin IL-2 Sturmovik ground-attack aircraft take part in a bombardment of Berlin.

complete the encirclement of the city with a move from the south. Stalin approved the plan, not least because it encouraged rivalry between the two Soviet commanders over who would enter the city first. That way, he was assured, they would perform aggressively and give him a definitive end to the war.

Two weeks was needed to position the 29 Soviet armies for the final attack on Berlin. A ferocious last stand was anticipated because there were still two million people left in the city, all of them highly fearful of the retribution the Red Army's soldiers would wreak on them for the death and destruction they had witnessed in the Soviet Union. It was very much an army with vengeance in its heart that approached the outskirts of Berlin. A million German men were ready to sacrifice their lives to halt the Soviets. Alongside the weary front-line troops, who were armed with 1,500 tanks and 9,000 artillery pieces, there were numerous young and elderly volunteers of the citizens' militia

known as the Volkssturm. Hitler was in the city, deep in his bunker. Formidable barricades were erected everywhere. The Red Army could not risk any setbacks and gathered its own awesome force of more than two million troops, with thousands of guns, tanks and rocket-launchers.

The assault on Berlin began before dawn on 14 April, heralded by a massive barrage delivered by artillery, rockets and aircraft. The bombardment was so intense that Soviet soldiers found it difficult to move across the churned-up ground. When they arrived at the first German defensive line, it was found to be abandoned, with much of the barrage having fallen on already empty positions. Vehicles were stuck in the mud, and a dense cloud of dust and smoke hindered the advance. Tanks could do little in the soft soil of the Seelow Heights and became sitting targets for German counter-attacks. Soviet losses mounted with little to show for all the effort. It was everything Stalin had

Above: **Russian soldiers run past a dead German soldier. Many Germans, citizens and soldiers, committed suicide rather than surrender to the Russians.**

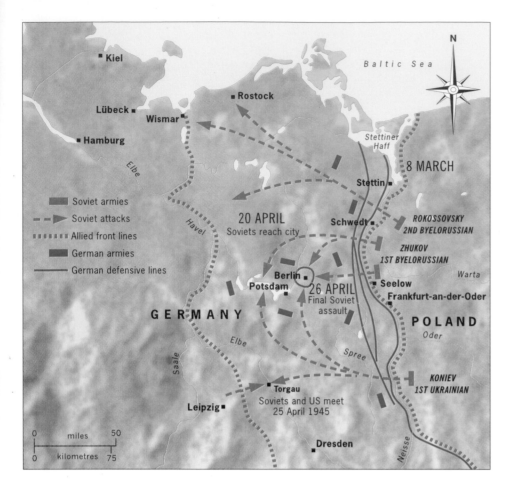

Soviet armies
Soviet attacks
Allied front lines
German armies
German defensive lines

Kiel
Baltic Sea
Rostock
Lübeck
Wismar
Hamburg
Stettiner Haff
Elbe
8 MARCH
Stettin
20 APRIL
Soviets reach city
Schwedt
ROKOSSOVSKY
2ND BYELORUSSIAN
Havel
ZHUKOV
1ST BYELORUSSIAN
Warta
Berlin
Potsdam
26 APRIL
Final Soviet
assault
Seelow
Frankfurt-an-der-Oder
GERMANY
POLAND
Elbe
Oder
Spree
KONIEV
1ST UKRAINIAN
Torgau
Soviets and US meet
25 April 1945
Leipzig
Neisse
Dresden

miles 50
kilometres 75

feared and he urged Koniev to take the city from the south. Meanwhile, Zhukov's men, slowly and painfully, had reached the northern outskirts of the city by 20 April.

FINAL BLOW

It was Hitler's birthday on 20 April and immediately after a gathering of friends for the occasion there had been plans for him to leave in order to create a Nazi redoubt in the Bavarian Alps. Himmler and Göring left Berlin, but Hitler decided to stay, in the belief that a final German counter-attack could achieve a remarkable last-minute victory. It was a grotesque delusion. Gas and electricity supplies had been cut throughout the city and there was little food left for its exhausted and frightened citizens.

The final Soviet blow came on 26 April, preceded by another massive aerial bombardment. General Chuikov's Eighth Guards Army was the first Soviet unit to break into the city and it fought block by block towards the centre. It was met by German youths and old men firing panzerfaust anti-tank rockets. The Soviets quickly improvised tank defences by attaching sandbags or thin sheets of iron set at an angle on their tanks so as to deflect the rockets. Elsewhere, Koniev's troops battled their way into the centre from the south, much to Zhukov's irritation. It looked as though Koniev might win the race to the centre of the city.

Koniev's soldiers had had an easier entry into Berlin, conducting an amphibious assault over the rivers Neisse and Spree under cover of a smokescreen. Koniev directed his tanks towards the Reichstag, but as they began firing he was told to halt, because he

Above: **The final Soviet movements encircling Berlin before they invaded the city itself.**

Below: **American and Russian troops meet at Torgau on the Elbe.**

was hitting Soviet troops. Both the leading Soviet commanders were now in the centre of Berlin, and Zhukov had the edge. Koniev had to relent and leave it to Chuikov and the Eighth Guards Army, under Zhukov's command, to take the heart of the city.

An indication of the fear and desperation felt by the Germans as the Soviets closed in on them is described by Vladimir Abyzov, a soldier in the Red Army, remembering his attack on an SS club in the centre of the city: 'Short of breath from running and excitement we rushed up the stairs to the second and third floor. Germans were firing at us from the top. But there were too many of us for them. The men running in front did not see those that fell below. In the billiard room, candles were burning. Slumped over the green cloth of the table with yellow billiard balls on it was the dead body of a general, a pistol in his hand. He had shot himself.'

Many Germans, both men and women, killed themselves rather than face retribution at the hands of the Soviets. Such suicidal thoughts also permeated Hitler's bunker, deep beneath the Reich Chancellery. The Führer blamed his own people for letting him down in this final test and had no pity for the destruction and horror now being visited on them. He could see no way out, and in a final, grotesque ceremony, he married his long-time mistress Eva Braun. Together they entered his private rooms in the bunker, where she took poison and he shot himself in the head. Not wanting their bodies to be captured by the Soviets, Hitler's servants then carried out his final orders to set fire to them in a shallow grave in the garden outside. With Hitler dead, the war was almost over and the German garrison tried to negotiate an armistice with the Soviet commanders, but they were only interested in unconditional surrender.

RAISING THE HAMMER AND SICKLE

As the fighting continued, ever more desperately, Soviet troops were informed that whoever raised the Soviet emblem, the red flag with the 'hammer and sickle' symbols,

Above: Wrecked military vehicles stand in the heart of Berlin after the city had been captured by the Red Army. The Brandenburg Gate is in the background, formerly a symbol of German militarism and now an ironic comment on where militarism had taken the German people.

CORNELIUS RYAN, AUTHOR

GUILTY FEAR

Best-selling author Cornelius Ryan interviewed many veterans of both sides for his epic description of the battle for Berlin. He reconstructed the impact of Russian bombardments:

'The merciless shelling had no pattern. It was aimless and incessant. Each day it seemed to increase in intensity. Mortars and the grinding howl of rocket-firing Katushkas soon added to the din. Most people now spent much of their time in cellars, air raid shelters, flak tower bunkers and subway stations. They lost all sense of time. The days blurred amid the fear, confusion and death that was all about them. Berliners who had kept meticulous diaries up to April 21 suddenly got their dates mixed... Their terror of the Russians was often intensified by a certain guilty knowledge...'

Quoted from *The Last Battle* by Cornelius Ryan (William Collins, 1966)

on the Reichstag would be decorated as a Hero of the Soviet Union. This honour fell to men of Zhukov's 150th Rifle Division who pressed on suicidally through withering German fire. A small group of infantry broke into the Reichstag and fought hand-to-hand to secure the building floor by floor. After eight hours of combat, the Soviet troops finally reached the roof of the building, where they emerged next to the shattered dome and waved their national flag triumphantly on 30 April.

Fighting in Berlin finally ended on 2 May. More than two hundred thousand German citizens and soldiers died in the defence of their capital, but the Soviets had lost heavily as well and they were in no mood for showing any mercy, assaulting and raping the surviving civilians. It was a bloody victory, and one the Berliners would not be allowed to forget for almost 50 years because their city was to remain divided between Soviet occupation forces and those of the western Allies until the Berlin wall came down in 1989.

INCHON, 1950

The Korean War was the first major conflict of the Cold War era. Nuclear-armed superpowers fought one another in a third country by supporting the opposing sides in that land's civil war. The brilliance of the US landing at Inchon completely broke the advance of the North Koreans and placed the Americans at the heart of the conflict. An unwelcome side effect was that it provoked the Chinese into direct intervention.

When the Soviet Union accepted the surrender of the Japanese in the northern half of Korea in 1945, the 38th Parallel was established as the dividing line in the country. This became a Cold War frontier: north of it, communism was the dominant influence; south of it, the Americans. By 1950, after a long and bitter civil war, the communists had triumphed in China, creating a communist superpower to rival the Soviet Union. Emboldened by this development, the North Korean communist regime, trained and supplied by the Soviet Union, invaded South Korea in June 1950 in an attempt to reunite the country under communist rule.

The newly formed United Nations (UN) called for an end to communist aggression, and a UN force, with the United States taking the lead role, was dispatched to help the army of the southern Republic of Korea resist the invasion. General Douglas MacArthur was appointed commander in chief of the UN force, but initially it was not strong enough to resist the invaders and was pushed back to the southern tip of Korea at Pusan. The UN needed to strike back with a decisive blow – and that blow would be delivered at Inchon.

Left: **The UN amphibious landings at Inchon in September 1950 were designed to cut off the supplies of the North Korean forces positioned around the UN forces at Pusan.**

Below left: **General Douglas MacArthur, commander in chief of the United Nations army in Korea and chief architect of the Inchon landings, visits the US 1st Marines near the front line.**

AMPHIBIOUS ASSAULT

With Lieutenant General Walker's US Eighth Army hanging on desperately in defiance of the North Koreans at Pusan in August 1950, the clock was ticking as MacArthur pondered his next move. The UN mission was facing total defeat and the US Army faced humiliation; the whole of Korea was close to falling to the communists. In just one month, MacArthur and his command team planned an ingenious assault aimed at the centre of Korea. An amphibious attack would be sent ashore at Inchon, to the west of Seoul and not far from the 38th Parallel. He would thus appear to the rear of the main North Korean force and cut its supply routes. It was a brilliant scheme, but the UN did not have the time to plan it thoroughly. The Inchon area was deemed by some not to be a favourable site for such a landing, so it would be a tremendous gamble. Despite misgivings, the assault went ahead on 15 September 1950.

Rare high tides gave the landing craft safe passage over the treacherous Inchon mudflats, and a fleet of 260 UN ships took full advantage of the conditions to edge forward through narrow channels and past numerous little islands. Air cover was

Above: **US Marines use ladders to scramble over a sea wall on the beach at Inchon.**

provided by Vought F4-U Corsairs of the 214th and 323rd US Marine Fighter Squadrons. The 1st Marine Division was the chosen landing force and could draw upon much hard-won tactical experience gained in the island-hopping campaign of the Pacific War (see Tarawa, pp.132–35). It was the first major amphibious assault by US troops since Okinawa in 1945.

Despite the risks of approaching an enemy-held coast, the US Marines caught the North Koreans completely by surprise. The first island to be taken was Wolmi-do, which guarded the harbour. The American flag was raised just after 07.00 hours when the neighbouring island of Sowolmi-do was also captured by US Marines, who used tanks to cross a causeway. Over 200

North Koreans were either killed or captured, but 100 others refused to surrender and were sealed by US Marine bulldozers in the caves into which they had fled.

The main attack could now hit the beaches, and the first wave of US Marines landed at Red Beach, only to be confronted by a sea wall that needed to be scaled by ladders. Beyond that there were trenches and bunkers full of enemy soldiers. In a fierce firefight the US Marines suffered their first casualties. Troops making a landing at Blue Beach also had to tackle a sea wall and then found some of their objectives obscured by smoke from the battlefield. Overall, however, the US Marines suffered light casualties and pressed on inland towards the Inchon–Seoul highway. By the early hours of the 16th, the Americans had secured their landing zone. It was a remarkable success for MacArthur – all the more so because of the speed with which it had been planned – and with it the situation of the UN forces in Korea was transformed.

ON TO SEOUL

Over the next five days, the US Marines closed in on Seoul, capturing Kimpo airfield in the process. US Marine Corsairs continued to provide air cover, destroying North Korean T-34 tanks with napalm and forcing Korean soldiers to flee. The capture of Kimpo denied air support to the Koreans and allowed the US Army to expand its air strikes. By 26 September, Seoul was surrounded and UN forces liberated it. Meanwhile, in coordination with the assault at Inchon, the US Eighth Army had broken out from the perimeter around Pusan. As envisaged, the North Korean army surrounding the Americans had had its supply lines cut by the landing at Inchon and had come under threat from the rear. It collapsed in the wake of the US breakout from Pusan, and US forces soon joined their comrades in Seoul; some 125,000 North Korean soldiers were taken prisoner.

UN forces moved quickly to take advantage of the North Korean defeat. Crossing the 38th Parallel and taking control of most of the country, they pushed deep into northern Korea and reached the border with Manchuria on the River Yalu. The capital of North Korea was captured on 20 October. The speed and

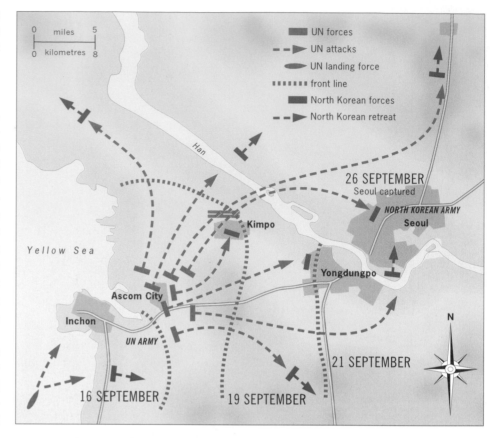

Above: After their successful landing at Inchon, it took only ten days for the US-led UN forces to capture Seoul.

Left: Chinese communist troops on their way to confront UN forces in 1950, in reaction to UN intervention at Inchon.

Above: **Chinese Red Army soldiers surrender to US 1st Marine Division soldiers during the three years of war that followed the UN landing at Inchon.**

CORPORAL CHEEK, US MARINE

MONEGAN THE TANK-KILLER

After the landing at Inchon, US Marines faced some tough fighting on the road to Seoul. Corporal Cheek recalls the action of a 19-year-old private called Walter C. Monegan Jr:

'We went down the hill, huddled behind a water tank for a moment until we got the rocket launcher loaded, and Monegan scored a direct hit on the first try. We were about 100 yards [90m] from the tanks, but they didn't know where we were... About that time, Pfc Robert Perkins showed up with additional ammo and loaded the rocket launcher, and Monegan got a second hit. Then, at the third attempt, we had apparently been spotted, because there was a blast of machine gun fire from somewhere, and Monegan was hit... It was later estimated that altogether we probably killed 400 enemy that morning because we had good tactical positions on both sides of the road and the road cut made it a kind of shooting gallery. Perkins and the corpsman received the Silver Star; myself the Bronze Star, and Monegan the Medal of Honor posthumously for this action. The captain told me later that he believed that the destruction of the tanks saved the battalion position.'

Quoted in *All Hell Broke Loose* by Ron Field (Military Illustrated, 2000)

completeness of this military success put the communist world into a panic. China in particular was placed on the alert; it had threatened intervention if the 38th Parallel was crossed and it responded by massing troops in Manchuria.

As General MacArthur tested the strength of the Chinese opposition in Manchuria, his army was struck a massive counter-blow by the Chinese on 26 November 1950. Two Chinese armies, totalling more than three hundred thousand troops, threw back the UN forces, initiating some of the hardest fighting of the war. It completely negated the spectacular achievements springing from Inchon and the war was to continue until 1953.

DIEN BIEN PHU, 1954

Dien Bien Phu offers a classic example of military overconfidence. Hoping to draw the Viet Minh into a decisive battle in which Western arms would triumph, the French found themselves surrounded by a superior force. French paratroopers fought a desperate battle for survival against wave after wave of Vietnamese attacks.

The town of Dien Bien Phu in northwest Vietnam is surrounded by jungle. It is not easy to reach, but any visitor who makes the effort will be rewarded by the sight of a well-preserved battlefield with bunkers and tanks and artillery pieces scattered across it to remind visitors of the epic encounter fought there. For the Vietnamese, it is the site of one of their greatest victories in the struggle for national liberation; for the West, the Battle of Dien Bien Phu marked the most spectacular defeat during the decline of empire in Asia in the wake of the Second World War.

When the Japanese defeated the British, Americans, French and Dutch in southeast Asia in the Second World War, their victory encouraged native nationalist movements to challenge their colonial rulers once the war was over. These same Western powers hoped to resume their empires after 1945, but their authority had been profoundly damaged. In 1947, Britain removed itself rapidly from India, and from 1948 Britain also fought a long, but ultimately successful war against communist guerrillas in Malaysia, although the country eventually gained its independence. The Dutch ended their control of Indonesia in 1949. In French Indochina, Ho Chi Minh of the Viet Nam Doc Lap Dong Ming Hoi, meaning League for the Independence of Vietnam and usually shortened to Viet Minh, had proclaimed a republic on 2 September 1945. This initiated a series of wars that would become one of the longest and most bitter military struggles of the second half of the 20th century.

Above: **Communist Viet Minh troops, wearing camouflage for jungle fighting, assemble with their unit flag. Initially dismissed as opportunist guerrilla fighters, these soldiers proved their ability to fight a set-piece confrontational battle at Dien Bien Phu.**

Left: Ho Chi Minh, Communist president of North Vietnam from 1954 to 1969, led the fight against the French and the Americans.

Right: The unrelenting advance of the Viet Minh forces on French positions in and around Dien Bien Phu between March and May 1954.

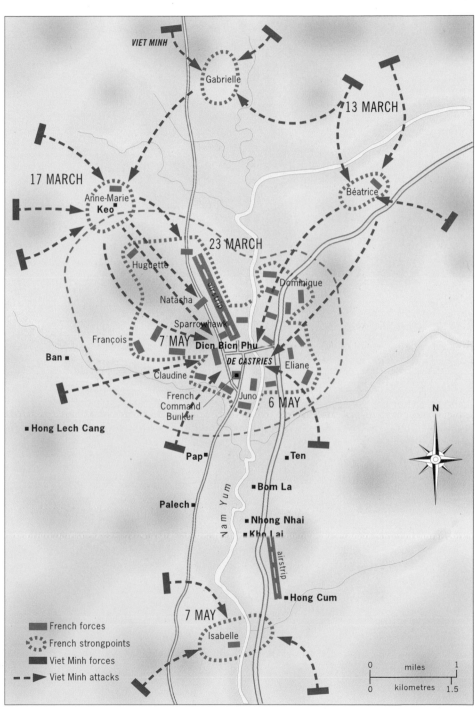

The French did not wish to lose their colonies in the region and in 1946 they moved against the independence movement by bombarding Haiphong, controlled by the Vietnamese communists. The event marked the beginning of the First Indochina War.

Encouraged from 1950 onwards by both the Chinese and Russian communists, the Viet Minh were to inflict several defeats on the French when the war moved on from its low-intensity beginnings. In December 1950, Marshal Jean de Lattre de Tassigny took command of French forces in Indochina and restored French control, but the Viet Minh continued their rebellion. In January 1953, French ships destroyed a number of Viet Minh bases, and the French, now led by General Henri Navarre, decided to launch a knock-out blow at Dien Bien Phu.

JUNGLE CONFRONTATION

Dien Bien Phu was the chosen point of confrontation, a village near the Laos border. The French wanted to lure the Viet Minh guerrillas, commanded by Vo Nguyen Giap, into a conventional battle where the French felt confident that their weaponry and logistics would exhaust an enemy better suited to hit-and-run tactics. An airstrip at the centre of Dien Bien Phu was crucial to this strategy as it would keep the French well supplied during the fighting. Similar tactics had worked in Vietnam 70 years previously when a French garrison had resisted an assault of native guerrillas, and this outdated model gave the French the confidence to take up their positions in November 1953.

The French force, commanded by Brigadier General Christian de la Croix de Castries, numbered just over ten thousand men. Among them were the French Foreign Legionnaires, élite soldiers used to fighting in trouble spots around the world. Some 28 howitzers and 10 M-24 light tanks were placed around the

Left: **French and allied Vietnamese troops receiving supplies by parachute. The central airstrip at Dien Bien Phu was supposed to provide constant reinforcements and resupply by air, but was swiftly captured, leaving the French isolated and vulnerable.**

Below: **The devastation that Dien Bien Phu suffered is apparent in this photograph taken during the first wave of attacks in the middle of March 1954.**

perimeter in strongpoints. Far from being intimidated by these defences, the Viet Minh were ready for a decisive battle and assembled a vastly greater force of more than 37,000 troops and 200 pieces of artillery. The French had badly miscalculated their opponents' will to face them.

After several months of preparation, the Viet Minh began their main assault on 13 March with a fierce bombardment of the French strongpoint named Beatrice. The artillery overwhelmed its defences, but the Foreign Legionnaires bravely held out for over eight hours until De Castries ordered them to withdraw.

Next, the Viet Minh attacked the strongpoint Gabrielle, held by Algerian soldiers and a Foreign Legion mortar unit. De Castries ordered a counter-attack by paratroopers, Indochinese soldiers and M-24 tanks. It reached the River Nam Yum but came under heavy artillery fire, and the Indochinese retreated. The Legionnaires fought on, determined to rescue their comrades at Gabrielle, but they were too few and the strongpoint had to be abandoned. The Viet Minh now commanded the high ground above Dien Bien Phu and directed their guns at all the French strongpoints around the airstrip.

THE RING TIGHTENS

Another strongpoint fell on 17 March, when the defenders of Anne-Marie deserted en masse. The lifeline of the French

position was the airstrip, but when this was captured on 23 March it marked the beginning of the end. Most of the air-dropped supplies fell into the hands of the enemy, although French air support tried to supply their comrades – an effort for which they paid dearly, with 62 aircraft shot down. Paratrooper reinforcements dropped at night were killed in the air.

With the airstrip abandoned, the French withdrew to their few remaining strongholds. In April, a fierce battle centred on Isabelle as Legionnaires fought for a month against the waves of Viet Minh assaults. Their North African comrades deserted, but the Legionnaires hung on until courage and ammunition were exhausted. Eliane had been under attack since March, but held out until 6 May. Huguette and Claudine were also under heavy attack. Giap's superior numbers and fire power could not be resisted and De Castries finally emerged out of his command bunker on 7 May to surrender. Isabelle fell that evening.

It was a resounding victory for Giap and one that dramatically ended French rule in Vietnam. Giap had out-prepared his enemy and turned the confrontation on its head, by using Dien Bien Phu as an anvil on which to crush the French, not the other way round. But victory had come at a heavy cost, with at least eight thousand Vietnamese dead and fifteen thousand wounded. The French lost four thousand dead in the battle, and many more died as prisoners in Viet Minh captivity.

Above: An aerial view of the air strip at Dien Bien Phu, which was meant to keep the French forces well supplied but was quickly captured by the Viet Minh.

ROBERT BARR SMITH, US ARMY OFFICER

FATAL ERROR

As the Viet Minh closed in on the French strongpoints at Dien Bien Phu, the fighting became ever more desperate. Former US Army officer Robert Barr Smith describes the situation at Gabrielle:

'*Some of the French survivors shot their way out to meet the Vietnamese paras about eight-thirty. The handful who could not or would not leave the hill fought to the last cartridge in the ruins of their positions. Gabrielle was gone for good, and the battalion meat grinder had begun. On this day, too, one-armed Colonel Piroth realised that he could not fend off the Viet artillery. Weeping, he visited infantry command posts, trying pitifully to apologise for the failure of the guns. Then, in despair, he hugged a grenade to his chest, pulled the pin, and paid for his error in the only way he knew how.*'
Quoted from *To The Last Cartridge* by Robert Barr Smith (Avon Books, 1994)

SIX DAY WAR, 1967

Although called a war, this conflict between Israel and the Arabs was a battle fought over several days. It is a classic example of the pre-emptive strike, demonstrating the importance of both air power and tank attacks and it influenced tactics in both NATO and the Soviet Union.

With the decline of British imperial power in the Middle East after the Second World War, the creation of the independent Jewish state of Israel in 1948 was met with hostility by its Arab neighbours. The Arab inhabitants of the former Palestine considered the newcomers to be invaders of their land. As the Cold War intensified, the Soviet Union tended to favour and supply arms to Arab states, while Western nations, especially the United States, came to the aid of Israel. This raised the military capabilities of both the Israelis and the Arabs, creating a tension that persists today despite several decisive wars and moves towards peace.

In 1966, President Nasser of Egypt concluded an alliance with Syria. The next year, he moved several divisions closer to the Israeli border in eastern Sinai. In May 1967, he blockaded the Strait of Tiran, which closed the Israeli port of Eilat. Later that month, Nasser signed a mutual security treaty with Jordan. Israel was now surrounded by aggressive Arab states and it mobilized its army, the Israel Defence Force (IDF). With some 230,000 personnel, the IDF was well trained and possessed high-quality aircraft. Facing it, however, was a combined Arab force numbering four hundred thousand, also equipped with modern aircraft and tanks.

FIRST BLOW

On 5 June 1967, Israel launched a pre-emptive attack by air and land against the Egyptian forces in the Sinai. Under the command of the chief of staff, Lieutenant General Itzhak Rabin, it was a spectacular success. Israel's air force flew over the Mediterranean, then plunged southwards to strike at virtually all the Egyptian airfields, wiping out Egypt's air capabilities in one blow. Similar raids later in the day did substantial damage to the air forces of Jordan, Syria and Iraq. Ground forces drove north against Syria in the Golan Heights, and poured into the West Bank and the Gaza Strip, while in the south Israeli tanks roared across Sinai and pushed the Egyptian forces back towards the Suez Canal.

By the second day, Egypt had surrendered in the Gaza Strip. IDF divisions pressed on against an Egyptian force badly demoralized by its own commander having ordered it to withdraw behind the Suez Canal. The withdrawal turned into a rout. The rapid Israeli advance outstripped all expectations and some vehicles ran out of fuel and ammunition, allowing retreating Egyptians to inflict some minor damage. By 8 June, the entire Sinai Peninsula was in Israeli hands.

Right: A truckload of Egyptian prisoners is removed from the El Arish area as the Israelis advance towards the Sinai Desert.

PARATROOPERS TAKE JERUSALEM

At the same time as the drive west, the IDF was tempted to take the West Bank area from Jordan and secure control over the holy city of Jerusalem. Following an artillery barrage by the Jordanians, the Israelis sent a parachute brigade against Jerusalem. Aircraft and tanks smashed Jordanian resistance and the city was taken by 7 June, along with Bethlehem, Hebron and Etzion. Hard fighting was also encountered in an attack on Nablus, but eventually the Jordanians retreated behind the River Jordan and a ceasefire was agreed between the two nations.

Fighting on the Golan Heights against Syria consisted of long-range artillery duels. When a UN ceasefire was violated by more fighting on 9 June, the Israelis took the initiative and scaled the Golan plateau, breaking through the first line of Syrian defences. On 10 June, the Israelis occupied more land, helped by the arrival of reinforcements from the Jordanian front.

All fighting stopped on 10 June. The Israelis had lost 679 killed and 2,440 wounded. The Egyptians lost 11,500 killed and 15,000 wounded, with Jordan suffering next most with two

PETER DARMAN, AUTHOR

ISRAELI BLUFF

'Eitan then gave the order to advance to Rafah junction. However, his tanks were in trouble. Some had only an hour's worth of fuel left in their tanks, others had no ammunition left. Undeterred, he ordered the tanks with low fuel to advance as far as they could, while the ones with no ammunition were not to shoot! The force, which had no more than five tanks, charged forward. The result was amazing: hundreds of Egyptian soldiers fled to the west.'
Quoted from *Surprise Attack* by Peter Darman (Brown Books, 1993)

thousand killed and five thousand wounded. It was a humiliating defeat for the Arabs and it redrew the map of the Middle East. It encouraged a sense of overconfidence in the Israelis, which would be shaken by the improved performance of the Egyptians in 1973's Yom Kippur War. Overall, it reminded the world of how devastatingly effective pre-emptive warfare can be when executed by well-trained professional troops.

Right: The Israeli attacks of June 1967 against Arab forces in Palestine, Syria and Egypt were carefully planned and coordinated, then efficiently executed.

Above: Israeli soldiers advance during fighting in the Six Day War. Israel's well-trained troops and excellent equipment enabled it to overwhelm its neighbours' forces.

SIX DAY WAR

Mediterranean Sea

LEBANON

Golan Heights

SYRIA

Haifa

Irbid

Al-Mafraq

Nablus

Tel Aviv-Yafo

PALESTINE
West Bank

ISRAEL

Amman

Jerusalem

Gaza
Gaza Strip

Hebron

Dead Sea

JORDAN

Port Said   10 JUNE

El Mansûra

El Qantara   Romani   El'Arish

Be'er Sheva

ISRAELI DEFENCE FORCE

Nile Delta

Suez Canal

Zagazig   Ismâ'ilîya

7 JUNE

Benha

Jebel Libni

El Quseima

5 JUNE 1967

Cairo

ALLIED ARAB ARMY

Mitla Pass

Negev Desert

El Minya

Suez

8 JUNE

Nakhl

Nile

EGYPT

El Thamad

Eilat

Sinai Peninsula

Gulf of Suez

Gulf of Aqaba

SAUDI ARABIA

8 JUNE

Strait of Tiran

El Tur

Sharm-el-Sheikh

Red Sea

Israeli forces
Israeli invasion
Israeli air attacks
Israeli parachute attacks
front lines
Israeli gains
Arab allied forces

0   miles   50
0   kilometres   80

SIX DAY WAR

Mediterranean Sea

Damascus   SYRIA   Baghdad
ISRAEL   IRAQ
Tel Aviv   JORDAN
Cairo   Sinai

AFRICA

EGYPT

ARABIA

Red Sea

Nile

TET OFFENSIVE, 1968

The Tet Offensive was North Vietnam's attempt to win a decisive battle in the war with the United States. Several cities and strongholds were assaulted but the North Vietnamese miscalculated the military strength of their enemy and suffered catastrophic losses. And yet, the US media managed to portray it as a North Vietnamese victory.

Never had the Western media aided an enemy nation more effectively than during the Tet Offensive in Vietnam. It has been claimed by one military historian that the North Vietnamese had a different approach to warfare than the United States. 'For the North Vietnamese,' writes Ronnie E. Ford, 'a decisive victory occurs when a superior force can be defeated not by military means but through external political or diplomatic developments that decide the outcome.' This sounds more like a realistic approach to an already accepted failure, but the fact was that the North Vietnamese understood that new US presidential elections were approaching in 1968 and that world opinion was generally in North Vietnam's favour. A major offensive would reassure the world that they had a lot of fight still left in them and this would discourage American public opinion from supporting the war. To this end, the US media were very obliging in their defeatist reporting.

NEW YEAR ASSAULT

Tet is the Vietnamese New Year holiday, but on 30 January 1968 the North Vietnamese broke the traditional truce and launched a massive assault on South Vietnam. Some eighty thousand soldiers of the North Vietnamese Army (NVA) and the Viet Cong (VC, or Vietnamese communists) attacked 36 out of 44 provincial capitals. Saigon and Hue were the main targets. The Americans and the South Vietnamese were surprised but not devastated by the major offensive and fought back effectively. Politically, however, the most impact was gained from the communist assault on the South Vietnamese capital of Saigon.

The sight of armed Viet Cong attacking the US Embassy in Saigon had an enormous effect on the Western journalists

Far right: In the Tet Offensive, the North Vietnamese Army and Viet Cong guerillas assaulted many South Vietnamese cities and military positions at the end of January 1968.

Below right: US soldiers fought street to street in Hue during the Tet Offensive. Besieged Americans were finally relieved in bitter fighting, but many thousands of Vietnamese civilians were slaughtered by communist guerillas.

Above: A US soldier with a machine-gun in Vietnam. Superior fire power helped the Americans to defend their positions during the Tet Offensive.

Left: General William Westmoreland (second from left), commander of US ground forces in Vietnam 1964–68.

based only a few streets away in their hotels. That the Viet Cong could make such a daring attack surely implied they were masters of the battlefield and that US generals were lying when they claimed they had the offensive under control. This fed the anti-establishment prejudices of most journalists and was communicated around the world, furthering the idea that the US Army was performing badly and could not win the war. In reality, only a handful of Viet Cong had infiltrated the embassy and within six hours they were all dead.

It was a classic guerrilla attack, intended to panic defending forces into thinking their efforts were failing. At Hue, the Western media claimed that the Imperial Palace had been destroyed when in fact it was only lightly damaged. The same assault tactics were repeated in many places, to varying degrees of success. After the initial shock, the communists were soundly defeated. It had been a costly strategy: between 32,000 and 45,000 North Vietnamese soldiers had been killed in just a few weeks' fighting.

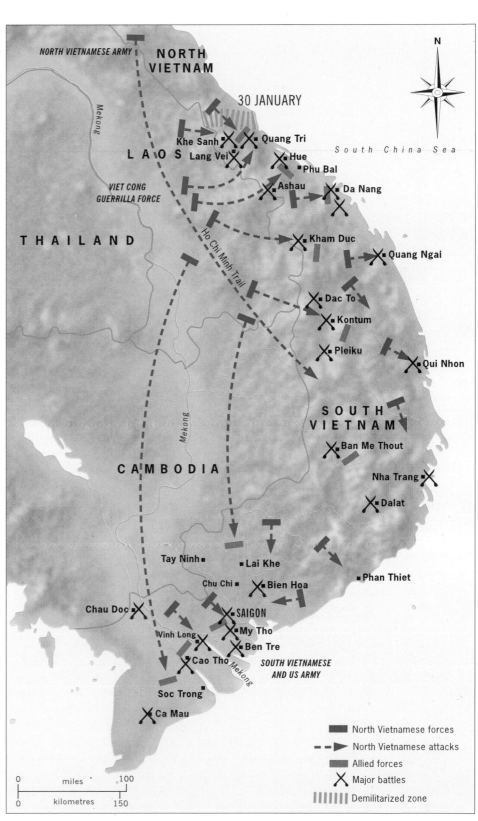

SELECTIVE REPORTING

During the initial North Vietnamese attack on the ancient city of Hue, the US soldiers situated there were hugely outnumbered and they fought a heroic battle of resistance. Vo Nguyen Giap, the veteran North Vietnamese commander and victor at Dien Bien Phu, committed nine battalions to the capture of the city. US Marine reinforcements rushed north to rescue their comrades in Hue, but there were only eighty of them, plus some South Vietnamese soldiers and a small column of four US Marine M-48 tanks. The little rescue group was ambushed by the NVA, but continued to press forward under heavy fire trying to reach the American compound. More US Marines joined them and eventually the battered column broke through to the besieged Americans. Such stubborn bravery would have been cause for national celebration in the 19th century, but because this was the Vietnam War in 1968, it was not intellectually fashionable to take pride in such heroism.

Elsewhere in Hue, the Viet Cong were exacting a terrible price on the South Vietnamese civilians. 'On the fifth day of the Communist occupation,' records Mark W. Woodruff, 'the Viet Cong came to Phu Cam Cathedral and gathered together four hundred men and boys. Some were identified by name from their lists, others because they were of military age, and still others simply because they looked wealthy. They were last seen being marched away to the south. Two years later,

three Viet Cong defectors led troops of the 101st Airborne Division to a creek bed in the dense jungle ten miles from Hue. Spread out for a hundred meters [110yds] were the bones of the men and boys of Phu Cam. The number murdered was later confirmed as 428... A total of 2,810 bodies were eventually found in shallow mass graves; 1,946 people remained unaccounted for.'

The Western media failed to make a big story out of this communist massacre, and yet My Lai, just over a month after the Tet Offensive, where US soldiers killed 200 Vietnamese civilians, became a worldwide story that, quite rightly, shocked and sickened many in the West. Such occurrences were, however, rare, and the record of the communists in Vietnam was much worse. Throughout the Vietnam War, the Western media and the intellectual forces that supported them with anti-war literature and demonstrations seem to have adopted a form of tunnel vision in which Western soldiers were vilified and the atrocities of communist guerrillas were largely ignored. By the 1970s, some journalists had begun to realize that they might have been failing to give a true picture of the war, having been led too much by their own, narrow, view of the war and their own prejudices. 'Rarely,' admitted a *Washington Post* reporter some nine years after Tet, 'has contemporary crisis-journalism turned out, in retrospect, to have veered so widely from reality.'

Above left: US Infantry carry a wounded Viet Cong prisoner to a UH1-D helicopter during operations in 1968. Helicopters created a new flexibility for US ground forces in Vietnam.

Above: Soldiers from the US 1st Cavalry Division prepare their 105mm howitzer for action.

Above right: **Vietnamese civilians flee from the fighting across the Perfume River at Hue, but many would be massacred by Viet Cong communists, who later destroyed the bridge.**

That was to come too late for the US Army in February 1968. Although Giap's offensive had been decisively defeated, the US media continued to portray Tet as a victory for North Vietnam. Such political pressure pushed the United States to attend peace talks in Paris in May 1968, and by 1969 the newly elected president, Richard Nixon, was announcing plans for a US withdrawal from Vietnam. The Tet Offensive also helped to switch North Vietnamese attention away from attacking South Vietnamese positions and instead to inflicting casualties on the American forces, knowing that this would encourage defeatist tendencies among the media. Such a strategy eventually achieved success. It was a sound lesson for future Western governments, which have since tried to maintain a tighter control over media reporting of wars.

COLONEL GENERAL TRAN VAN TRA

WEATHERING THE STORM

Since the Vietnam War ended, North Vietnamese commanders have been quite open about their failures during the Tet Offensive. Colonel General Tran Van Tra concluded:

'During Tet of 1968 we did not correctly evaluate the specific balance of forces between ourselves and the enemy, did not fully realise that the enemy still had considerable capabilities and that our capabilities were limited, and set requirements that were beyond our actual strength... For that reason, although that decision was wise, ingenious, and timely, and although its implementation was well organised and bold... everyone acted very bravely, sacrificed their lives, and there was created a significant strategic turning point in Vietnam and Indochina, we suffered large sacrifices and losses with regard to manpower and material, especially cadres at the local echelons, which clearly weakened us. Afterwards, we were not only unable to retain the gains we had made but had to overcome a myriad difficulties in 1969 and 1970 so that the revolution could stand firm in the storm.'

Quoted in *Tet 1968: Understanding the Surprise* by Ronnie E. Ford (Frank Cass, 1995)

PORT STANLEY, 1982

In the Falklands War, Britain showed it was possible to fight a 19th-century-style colonial campaign during an age of modern warfare. The efficient recapture of Port Stanley by British forces gave encouragement to other Western powers to intervene in foreign crises. Sweeping away post-Vietnam pessimism, the British taskforce operated effectively, without a land base, over a 13,000-km (8,000-mile) sea supply line.

The war for the Falkland Islands began on 2 April 1982 when Argentinian troops captured its capital, Port Stanley, and claimed the islands for Argentina. A day later, Argentinian troops also captured South Georgia. The Falkland Islands had been British possessions since 1833, providing a strategically important naval staging post in the South Atlantic.

In the wake of the Vietnam War, with many Western powers doubting their ability to intervene abroad, it would have been easy for Britain to have accepted the situation, and avoid a costly and risky war. But most of the population of the Falklands considered themselves British and Prime Minister Margaret Thatcher had a strong dislike of tyrannical states, believing this was a wrong that Britain could right. However, the islands were 13,000km (8,000 miles) away on the other side of the globe. Argentina was very close by. It would be a tremendous gamble.

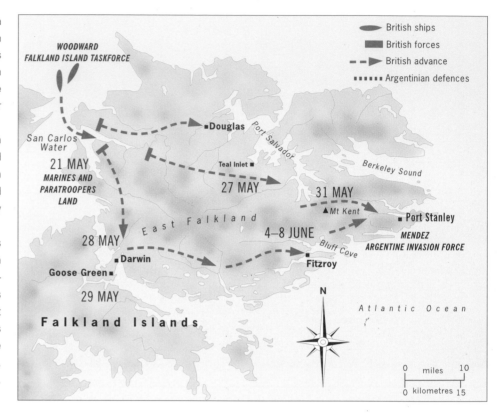

FALKLANDS ASSAULT

With Argentina having been declared the aggressor by the United Nations, Britain assembled a taskforce, and it set sail on 5 April 1982. Commanded by Rear Admiral Sir John Woodward, it consisted of two light aircraft carriers, HMS *Hermes* and HMS *Invincible*, and 28 other ships. An amphibious force of four thousand Royal Marine Commandos and the Parachute Regiment was later reinforced by a further one thousand troops, including the Scots Guards, Welsh Guards and Gurkhas. Detachments of the Special Air Service (SAS) and Special Boat Service (SBS)

were also active. Air support was provided by 22 Sea Harrier jump-jets flying from the carriers. Ascension Island, in the middle of the Atlantic Ocean, provided a vital post that enabled the taskforce to be resupplied by aircraft flying from Britain. Opposing this force were fifteen thousand Argentinian troops on the islands led by General Mario Menendez. The Argentinian Air Force, operating from the mainland and supplied with modern guided missiles, was strong and its battleships were nearby.

Reconnaissance of the islands' defences was carried out by the SAS and SBS from 18 April, and on 25 April South Georgia was recaptured, giving the Royal Navy a nearby land base. A 320-km (200-mile) exclusion zone was declared around the islands and Britain reinforced this when a submarine sank the Argentinian battleship *General Belgrano*. British forces then began preparations for a land assault by bombing airfields on the islands, putting them out of action. Argentinian air power was undiminished, however, and fighter planes armed with Excocet missiles managed to sink seven British ships and badly damage six more. It was a major blow for the British, although a night raid by the SAS on Pebble Island severely damaged the airfield and destroyed 11 aircraft.

The major British landing began on 21 May at San Carlos with Royal Marine Commandos and Paratroopers establishing a beach-head. In the fight for air supremacy above them, Harriers

Above: **The British amphibious landing at San Carlos and advance on foot across East Falkland towards Port Stanley between 21 May and 8 June.**

Left: **Royal Marine Commandos manning a trench at San Carlos during the British landings on the Falkland Islands.**

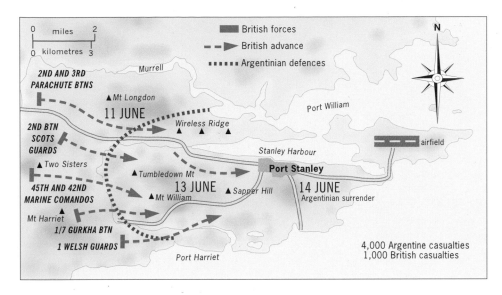

British forces
British advance
Argentinian defences

2ND AND 3RD PARACHUTE BTNS

Murrell

Mt Longdon

11 JUNE

Wireless Ridge

Port William

2ND BTN SCOTS GUARDS

Two Sisters

Tumbledown Mt

Stanley Harbour

airfield

Port Stanley

13 JUNE

45TH AND 42ND MARINE COMANDOS

Mt William

Sapper Hill

14 JUNE
Argentinian surrender

Mt Harriet

1/7 GURKHA BTN

1 WELSH GUARDS

Port Harriet

4,000 Argentine casualties
1,000 British casualties

0 miles 2
0 kilometres 3

N

downed 15 Argentinian planes for only one loss. Over the next few days, some five thousand troops were put ashore and they began to move inland. A fierce firefight took place at Goose Green in which the British stormed the Argentinian positions, and their commander on the ground, Colonel 'H' Jones, won the VC posthumously. With their southern flanks secure, the British could now advance towards their main target of Port Stanley.

BATTLE FOR STANLEY

Major General Jeremy Moore was in charge of the land operations against Port Stanley. While units of Royal Marine Commandos and Paratroopers had the difficult task of marching across the boggy land, the SAS and Royal Marine Commandos were dropped by helicopter on Mount Kent, 16km (10 miles) west of Stanley, where they could observe the Argentinian defenders in the capital. Further advances by British troops followed, but an

amphibious landing at Bluff Cove to the south of Stanley was bombed by Argentinian aircraft and many troops were lost.

The final fights in the battle for Port Stanley took place on the hills overlooking the town. On the night of 11 June, Royal Marine Commandos took three key Argentinian positions on Mount Longdon, Two Sisters and Mount Harriet. Resistance was strong on Mount Longdon, but eventually each position fell. A day later, the 2nd Parachute Battalion, victors at Darwin and Goose Green, took Wireless Ridge in a night attack on 13 June. To the south of them, the Scots Guards fought Argentinian Marines to capture Tumbledown Mountain. Gurkhas advanced on Mount William, only 6km (3 miles) west of Stanley. The high ground had been taken and the Argentinian commander in Port Stanley could see his situation was perilous. On 14 June, General Menendez surrendered and the Union Jack flag was run up in Stanley. The Falkland Islands were British once more.

Although successful, the Falklands operation was not perfect and aspects of it have been criticized. The Royal Navy underestimated the abilities of the Argentinian Air Force and lost several ships to its missiles. Communications between commanders in Britain and those on the ground were faulty and the SAS tended to act too independently. Some 255 British soldiers were killed and 777 wounded. The Argentinians lost a thousand killed and three thousand wounded, with 11,400 taken prisoner.

Overall, considering that Britain had not organized such an all-arms assault since Suez in 1956 and that the distances involved were so great, the recapture of Port Stanley was a remarkable demonstration of military prowess. The victory had its political dividend in that it reasserted confidence among Western leaders in their ability to intervene abroad. If the Falklands had not been a success, then it is unlikely that Margaret Thatcher would have been so confident in advocating that President Bush stand up to the Iraqi invasion of Kuwait in 1990 (see pp.186–89).

Top: **The final British assault on Port Stanley following their capture of the high ground around the town.**

Above: **Royal Marine Commandos await transport by Sea King helicopter from the deck of HMS *Hermes* onto the Falkland Islands.**

FIRST LIEUTENANT CEREZO, ARGENTINIAN ARTILLERY

TEARS OF DEFEAT

'The British advanced quickly and the threat against our position increased. We did not worry about counter-battery fire but continued firing. It seemed the situation became irreversible every minute. The last elevations passed to me by the Fire Control Centre showed we were firing between 1,500 and 2,000 metres [1,600–2,100yds] until we received orders to fire over open sights. A small number of men formed local defence... At 9am the CO ordered me to cease fire. Everything seemed to have calmed down but it was cold and snow was falling. At about 11.30am I saw the enemy advancing and was ordered by the CO to open fire but a shell was rammed up the breech and the block fell out. The CO ordered us to leave the guns and withdraw into Stanley. At 4pm he told us we had surrendered. This made us cry with the pain of impotence in the face of defeat.'

Quoted in *Nine Battles to Stanley* by Nicholas van der Bijl (Pen & Sword, 1999)

KABUL, 1988

Right: The Soviet invasion of Afghanistan took the form of a two-pronged attack on the major capitals, but much of the countryside would remain beyond their control.

Far right: Afghan *mujahideen* warriors are traditionally clothed but were increasingly supplied with sophisticated Western weapons during their war against the Soviet Union.

Above: A *mujahideen* tank points its barrel over Kabul, re-captured from Soviet forces.

The Russian withdrawal from Kabul in 1988 was the final act in a decisive defeat for the Soviet Union. It was not brought about by any set-piece battle but was the result of years of guerrilla warfare which had drained away the will of the Russians to stay. Western-armed *mujahideen* had proved more than a match for high-tech Soviet forces. Within two years of their retreat from Afghanistan, the Soviet Union collapsed.

The Russians had long considered the Muslim states to the south as legitimate areas of military interest. In the 19th century, they had conquered the Turkic states of Central Asia (see Geok Tepe, pp.44–47), and this process continued in the 20th century under the Soviet Union. In 1979, when Soviet forces invaded Afghanistan, the process became complicated because the Cold War meant that the United States and other Western-oriented powers supported those rebels who rejected the Soviet regime. It became the last major Cold War struggle.

The Soviet approach to the invasion of Afghanistan did not derive from Russia's earlier, 19th-century experiences, nor from those of Britain's colonial forces in Afghanistan; instead, it was based on its Cold War successes in eastern Europe. 'Using the same techniques as they employed during the invasion of Czechoslovakia,' writes Soviet analyst Lester Grau, 'the Soviets rapidly seized the major cities, radio stations and centres of power. They executed Amin and put an Afghan communist exile, Babrak Karmal, in power. They crushed the resistance by the Afghan Army and began consolidating their power. The Soviets soon discovered that Afghanistan was not going to be a repeat of their Czechoslovakian experience.' Many would call it a Soviet 'Vietnam'.

CHRISTMAS INVASION

Soviet tanks rolled into Afghanistan on Christmas Day 1979. Three airborne divisions flew into the country, joined by four motorized rifle divisions invading from the north. An airborne division met strong resistance in Kabul, the capital, but managed to defeat elements of the Afghan Army and surround and

the Soviets had committed over one hundred thousand troops to the war but still no overall victory was within sight. As they grew increasingly desperate, it is alleged the Soviets began to use chemical and biological weapons against their adversaries.

SOVIET COLLAPSE

Although they were able to deny the Soviets control of their country, the Afghan rebels were not in great shape. There was no one unified command structure, and the various factions frequently fought one another as well. By the mid-1980s, however, the *mujahideen* were receiving sophisticated weapons channelled through Pakistan and mainly supplied by the United States; hand-held, anti-aircraft missiles proved devastatingly effective. In 1987 and 1988, it is claimed the missiles downed an average of one Soviet aircraft a day. Such losses could not be sustained indefinitely, but already more profound changes within the Soviet Union were affecting its ability to continue the war.

In the 1980s, President Reagan led an aggressive arms build-up within the United States and a plan was mooted for an anti-missile defence – popularly called Star Wars – to shield the United States from nuclear attack. This upset the Cold War balance of power in which Mutually Assured Destruction, as it was known, had maintained a respectful peace between the two nuclear-armed superpowers. The Soviet Union had to respond to Reagan's challenge with greater expenditure of its own on new military technology,

kill President Amin in his palace. With their own choice of president in power, the Soviets now sought to pacify the country, but popular opinion was against them.

Earlier that decade, when the Soviets had first shown a strong interest in Afghanistan and backed a modernization programme of education and greater rights for women, this had been opposed by Muslim traditionalists. These same rebels now formed the *mujahideen*, a guerrilla army that would fight against Soviet dominance for the next ten years. An uprising in Kabul in February 1980 was crushed by Soviet troops, and five hundred Afghans were killed.

At first, the Soviet Union used its advantage in modern weapons to great effect, bringing in devastating air power in the form of air strikes and helicopter gunships to crush guerrilla bases and relieve besieged troops. The Soviets managed to clear the settled valleys, forcing the rebels up into the hills, but the supplies to Soviet positions and towns were constantly hampered by guerrilla ambushes. By 1984

Left: A *mujahideen* rocket explodes as it hits a suburb of Kabul. Hand-held anti-aircraft missiles proved deadly to Soviet airpower in the Afghanistan war.

but the Soviet economy was bankrupt. Communism had failed to provide a dynamic and wealthy economy for its people and it could not support such a development. The leader of the Soviet Union, Mikhail Gorbachev, realized there was a need for economic and political reform if the Soviet Union was going to survive. But events were moving faster than he could control.

In 1986, Reagan increased the pressure by calling for a record defence budget of US$320 billion. In the following year, some US$630 million was being spent in Afghanistan, the largest secret military action funded by the United States since the Second World War. Saudi Arabia and other wealthy Muslim states also contributed money and weapons to the rebels. In the meantime, Gorbachev's more open political regime meant that the Soviet media were covering the war in Afghanistan more truthfully, reporting the death and destruction experienced by ordinary soldiers, and even daring to voice public demands for withdrawal. Gorbachev could see that the war was draining his economic and political resources, and he hoped to include withdrawal as a bargaining chip in his negotiations with Reagan, but the Americans were not interested in trading for withdrawal, happy to see the Soviet Army being kept so busy.

Following the Geneva Agreement of 14 April 1988, the Soviet Union committed itself to withdrawing its troops from Afghanistan. The retreat began in phases and took several months, with Soviet forces first moving back from their southern frontier positions at Jalalabad and Kandahar. Then they

Above: Soviet armoured vehicles withdrawing from Afghanistan. Just two years later, the Soviet Union would collapse.

Left: The Soviet retreat from Kandahar and Kabul in 1988 was a virtual mirror image of their invasion nine years earlier.

moved from central Afghanistan between autumn 1988 and February 1989. In Kabul the Soviets left behind a regime dubbed the Democratic Republic of Afghanistan under the presidency of Muhammad Najibullah. Of the six hundred and forty thousand Soviets who served during the war, some fifteen thousand were recorded as either dead or missing, a further 415,932 becoming casualties of diseases such as hepatitis and typhoid. Over one million Afghans are thought to have lost their lives during the war.

The Najibullah regime failed to survive in the wake of a civil war between Afghan nationalists and Muslim fundamentalists.

Najibullah went into hiding in 1991 and a fundamentalist regime took charge. Western military support had flooded the country with weapons, militarizing it and contributing to the deaths of countless more Afghans in internecine warfare. By the end of 1991, the Soviet Union had collapsed. Gorbachev, the last Soviet leader, had been replaced by Boris Yeltsin, and independent nations arose in place of the old Soviet Union. The lessons learned by the Soviet military in Afghanistan helped the Russian Army to fight successful wars against Chechen separatists in central Asia. The Cold War was over and a new era of warfare had begun.

A.N. SHISKOV, SENIOR ASSISTANT TO SOVIET CHIEF OF AIR OPERATIONS

DUMMY TROOPS

Although Afghan guerrillas generally proved elusive, sometimes they could be pinned down. In 1987, A.N. Shiskov was senior assistant to a Soviet chief of air operations and describes a major assault on a *mujahideen* stronghold at Satukandav Pass:

'On 28 November, following unsuccessful negotiations, the 40th Army divisions and regiments plus the Afghan regiments began the attack. General Gromov had decided to determine the location of enemy weapons systems (particularly air defence, provided by the West) and so he faked an airborne landing using 20 dummy paratroopers in parachutes. The enemy fired its weapons on these "paratroopers" which enabled artillery reconnaissance to pinpoint enemy strong points and firing positions. Army and frontal aviation then hit these positions. The airstrikes were followed with a four-hour artillery barrage.'
Quoted from The *Bear Went Over the Mountain* edited by Lester W. Grau (Frank Cass, 1998)

DESERT STORM, 1991

Operation Desert Storm was a major offensive undertaken by a coalition of Western and Arab countries intended to right an international wrong. Considered an enormous gamble at the time, it demonstrated the awesome military power of modern high-technology weapons. Cruise missiles, precision bombing, helicopter gunships and tanks equipped with night sights combined to overwhelm the Iraqi land forces.

With the end of the Cold War and the disintegration of Soviet power (see Kabul, pp.182–85), the United States was left as the only superpower in the world. The United States's military capabilities were far ahead of those of any other nation and ensured that it could now take on the role of the 'world's policeman' if it chose to. However, there has always been a wariness in this great democracy towards becoming involved in any overseas wars not strictly related to 'national defence' and which might be interpreted as being imperialist.

Supporters of such sentiments, known as 'isolationists', do not like to see Americans dying abroad for what they feel is little good reason. Because of this, the United States had been reluctant to enter both world wars, and by the late 20th century this caution had grown markedly as a result of a perceived military failure in the Vietnam War (see Tet Offensive, pp.176–79). Events in Vietnam had also dented the United States's confidence in its ability to fight a decisive war against a foe who might possess inferior weapons, but could rely on motivation and an inhospitable landscape to sustain and protect it. This cautious view was challenged in 1990 when Iraq invaded Kuwait.

DESERT SHIELD

On 2 August 1990, Iraqi forces crossed the border dividing Iraq from Kuwait and proceeded to occupy the tiny oil state. Iraq's leader, Saddam Hussein, claimed the rights to the oilfield on the

Below: **Egyptian artillery shells Iraqi forces during the land battle phase of the Gulf War known as Desert Storm.**

0 miles 100
0 kilometres 150

N

24 FEBRUARY

Allied forces
Allied attacks
Allied air strikes
Kuwaiti oilfields
Iraqi forces
Iraqi front line

the Iraqi dictator. As she recalled it, 'This was no time to go wobbly.' Britain had already shown that a Western power could fight a war a long distance away against a foreign aggressor and win (see Port Stanley, pp.180–81). With the support of other Western allies, including Britain and France, and a number of Arab states, Bush committed a major US force to Saudi Arabia, where it formed the greatest part of a coalition force assembling along the Saudi Arabian border with Iraq. In total, 18 nations provided some 600,000 troops for the coalition army, of which the United States provided 532,000. Iraq could call upon 550,000 troops and 4,200 tanks. With the coalition forces in place along the border, preventing any further aggression by Saddam, the first phase of the operation, called Desert Shield, against Iraq was completed.

THE AIR WAR

The second phase was to remove Saddam's forces from Kuwait – Operation Desert Storm. Overall command of the allied forces was in the hands of US lieutenant general Norman Schwarzkopf. Faced with such a large Iraqi army, the West was nervous and many commentators predicted a catastrophe that would combine the worst elements of Vietnam and Afghanistan. It did not look hopeful. Mindful of the risks involved in a ground invasion, and feeling the need to avoid high casualties to maintain political and media support for the operation, the United States decided to open Desert Storm with an air war. American investment in new military technology during the 1980s was given the opportunity to prove its effectiveness. On 16 January 1991, Cruise missiles and Stealth bombers opened the air assault on Iraq and proved to be remarkably successful, striking at the heart of Saddam's regime and destroying vital communications and air

Above: The Allied swinging advance during Operation Desert Storm completely outflanked the Iraqi forces.

Right: Saddam Hussein, leader of Iraq during the Gulf War, is portrayed a defender of his people on a fresco in Basra.

border, but the United Nations condemned the invasion and urged Iraq's withdrawal. Saudi Arabia feared the move might lead to an attempt by Iraq to control all the oil production in the region. This possible ambition alerted the Western nations, which depended on Arab oil and could not afford to have such a valuable resource fall into the hands of a hostile dictator. Iraq's army was formidable, and had become well armed and experienced as a result of its 1980–88 war with Iran. It had even received covert Western support because the revolutionary Iranians were perceived as a destabilizing power in the region. But now Saddam was openly challenging the West and all eyes turned to the United States.

During the crisis weeks of decision-making in 1990, Britain's prime minister, Margaret Thatcher, visited President George Bush in Washington, D.C., and encouraged him to stand up to

defence centres. Rather than face this onslaught, the majority of Iraq's air force pilots flew to Iran, where they took no further part in the war. Conventional bombing raids followed these first strikes in ceaseless 24-hour warfare that destroyed Iraq's ability to contest the coalition's air supremacy.

The main fear of the West was that Saddam would attempt to broaden the conflict by attacking Israel with Scud missiles. If Israel retaliated, then the Arab elements of the coalition might feel compelled to withdraw, causing the coalition to collapse and making it more difficult to defeat Saddam. To help Israel defy this missile threat, the United States provided Israel with Patriot anti-missile missiles. In the event, these did not prove as effective as promised, but by keeping Israel out of the war their political impact was useful. In the meantime, Special Forces units, including Britain's Special Air Service (SAS), were sent behind Iraqi lines to find and destroy these missiles. In the event, Saddam's limited missile attacks failed to provoke Israel.

GROUND ATTACK

Complete air supremacy over Iraq having been established, the next stage of Operation Desert Storm was to eject the Iraqi occupation force from Kuwait. To achieve this, Schwarzkopf planned a massive encircling movement. Diversionary attacks were made on Kuwait City, but the main assault came across the Saudi border moving north and then east. On 24 February

1991 the ground assault began with a massive aerial and artillery bombardment of the Iraqi front lines. Then the US XVII Corps, 101st Division and French 6th Daguet Division plunged deep into Iraq. Next to them was the US VII Corps, including the British 1st Armoured Division, which swung eastwards towards Kuwait. Finally, the US Marines· and Arab ground forces advanced directly over the Kuwaiti frontier towards the capital.

The initial allied bombardment was so intense that many Iraqi troops were buried alive in their bunkers, while others were so shaken that they immediately surrendered, some even giving themselves up to unmanned reconnaissance craft. Night vision capability and depleted-uranium-tipped shells gave Western armour an advantage over the older Soviet tanks operated by the Iraqis, and what little resistance was encountered was swiftly overcome. The much-feared Republican Guard – the élite core of Saddam's army – was quickly surrounded and bombed into submission. The ground war was over by 28 February and Kuwait was liberated.

The Western media began to portray the decisive victory as a 'turkey shoot', and this, plus the United States's intention to stick to its limited aim of Kuwaiti liberation (bearing in mind the drifting, damaging objectives of Vietnam), meant that the war was not carried on into Iraq. A war to topple Saddam and free his people might well have backfired on the West, which would then be perceived as being the aggressor. This risked losing

Above: **US crewmen on duty near a Patriot missile system launcher in Saudi Arabia. Patriot missiles were intended to defeat Iraqi missile attacks and helped to keep Israel out of the fighting.**

Above: **A group of British Challenger tanks in the desert during Operation Desert Storm.**

world and Arab support for very little gain. The US view was that it was up to the Iraqi people to liberate themselves from Saddam, and although there were short-lived rebellions, these were not sufficient to overthrow the tyrannical regime. A cold analytical view of the situation might be that Western powers were happy to see the Iraqi regime remain as a strong but isolated power in order to counter the regional ambitions of Iran and Syria, and the relative peace and the balance of power evident in this region over the course of the next decade would make this appear a wise decision.

In total, just over four hundred coalition soldiers were killed and a thousand wounded in the Gulf War. The Iraqis lost an estimated one hundred thousand dead and three hundred thousand wounded. The disparity in losses made the Gulf War a decisive demonstration of the superiority of Western military technology, the likes of which had not been seen since the Battle of Omdurman a hundred years earlier. The war hastened the demise of the Soviet Union as a military rival and left the United States as the uncontested master of the battlefield.

COLONEL BARRY HORNE, US ARMY

BAT CASUALTIES

Stealth F-117A aircraft were key weapons in the initial air strike on Iraq in Operation Desert Storm. US colonel Barry Horne describes the moment he first knew that their radar-defying technology would work:
'Bats were the first visual proof I had that stealth really worked. We had deployed thirty-seven F-117As to the King Khalid Air Base, in a remote corner of Saudi Arabia... The Saudis provided us with a first-class fighter base with reinforced hangars, and at night the bats would come out and feed off insects. In the mornings we'd find bat corpses littered around our airplanes inside the open hangars. Bats use a form of sonar to "see" at night, and they were crashing blindly into our low-radar-cross-section tails.'
Quoted in *Skunk Works* by Ben R. Rich and Leo Janos (Little, Brown, 1994)

MOGADISHU, 1993

For a superpower, it seemed to be a simple operation for the United States to help to quell a tribal war in Somalia, east Africa. US Special Forces stormed into the centre of the city of Mogadishu in search of rebel leaders, but their helicopters crashed and suddenly they were surrounded by hostile citizens. The resulting loss of lives shocked the American public and quickly ended the United States's role as 'world policeman'.

Civil war had been raging in Somalia, on the tip of the Horn of Africa, since 1974 when Major General Siyad Barre seized power and began a long war with Ethiopia. When the fighting with Ethiopia ceased in 1988, tribal warfare broke out in Somalia as various clans tried to dominate the country. No one side could decisively defeat the others, but by January 1991 the fighting had

reached a climax, with tribal rebels leading major assaults and the government replying with powerful military sweeps across the country during which some fifty thousand people died. By 27 January, General Barre had fled the capital, Mogadishu, and Somalia had been reduced to a state of chaos. The breakdown of its food supplies meant that ordinary citizens were starving. The humanitarian crisis prompted the United Nations (UN) to become involved and in December 1992 the United States landed troops.

To many people – who did not know the history of incessant tribal warfare that had preceded this intervention – this seemed like a perfect example of using military power for good ends. Television images of starving women and children added to the sense of urgency. The United States, working hand in hand

Above: **US troops practise fighting from Somalian buildings, skills that became vital during a later firefight in the heart of Mogadishu.**

ARABIA

Red Sea

AFRICA

Nile

Gulf of Aden

SOMALIA

Indian Ocean

MOGADISHU

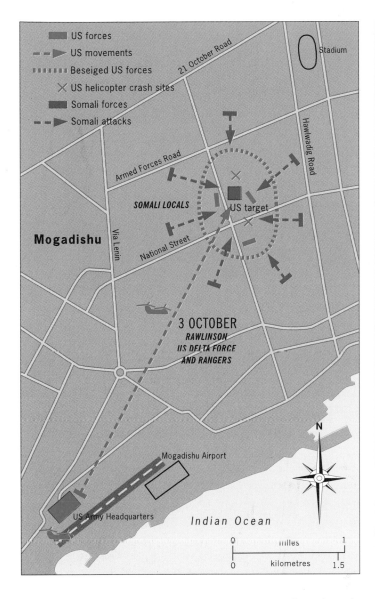

US forces

- - -► US movements

▪▪▪▪▪▪▪ Beseiged US forces

✕ US helicopter crash sites

Somali forces

- - -► Somali attacks

Stadium

21 October Road

Hawlwadig Road

Armed Forces Road

SOMALI LOCALS

US target

Mogadishu

Via Lenin

National Street

3 OCTOBER
RAWLINSON
US DELTA FORCE
AND RANGERS

N

Mogadishu Airport

US Army Headquarters

Indian Ocean

miles 0 — 1

kilometres 0 — 1.5

Far left: The US helicopter-borne operation in October 1993 to capture rebel leaders in the centre of Mogadishu.

Left: US troops in desert camouflage call up air support during a military exercise in Somalia in 1993.

Below: A US helicopter fires missiles during an exercise. US helicopters proved vulnerable when struck by hand-held missiles and several were downed in the centre of Mogadishu.

with the United Nations, had just won a tremendous victory in the Gulf War and there was a new president in the White House. Bill Clinton was keen to prove that American military force could have a moral dimension to it, by helping to bring peace and food to the helpless.

However, UN Secretary-General Boutros Boutros-Ghali, who initiated the intervention, had previously been an Egyptian diplomat who had worked against one of the leading clans, that commanded by General Muhammad Aidid. Those Somalis who supported Aidid considered Boutros-Ghali to be an enemy who was continuing the war against them by using the United Nations and the US Army. This bit of history compromised the whole operation and should have raised questions beforehand.

When the US Army and its UN allies, which included Pakistan, Australia and Nigeria, landed in Somalia, they were viewed not as saviours but as another force to be fought.

BLACK HAWK DOWN

Most journalists thrive on the reporting of crises around the world and do not question the long-term effects of international intervention. US journalist P.J. O'Rourke travelled to Somalia and wondered at the effects of having so much food aid provided by international charities. 'But to do some good briefly is better than doing no good ever,' he later wrote in *All the Troubles in the World*. 'Or is it always? Somalia was being flooded with food aid. The only way to overcome the problem of theft was to make food too cheap to be worth stealing. Rice was selling for ten cents a pound in Somalia, the cheapest rice in the world. But what, we thought, did that mean to the people with the fields of corn and sorghum and the herds of goats and cattle? Are those now worth nothing, too? Had we come

Above: **Somali militiamen sit on a 'technical', the armed jeeps they used to fight each other and terrorize the local population.**

MARK BOWDEN, JOURNALIST

SWEATING AND TERRIFIED
'They were still pointed north. Some of the men were at the breaking point. In the same Humvee with Burns, Private Jason Moore saw some of his Ranger buddies just burying their heads behind the sandbags. Some of the unit's most boisterous chest-beaters were among them. A burly kid from Princeton, New Jersey, Moore had a dip of snuff under his lower lip and brown spittle on his unshaved chin. He was sweating and terrified. One RPG [Rocket Propelled Grenade] hadpassed over the vehicle and exploded with an ear-smarting crack against a wall alongside. Bullets were snapping around him. He fought the urge to lie down... He would go down fighting.'
Quoted from *Black Hawk Down* by Mark Bowden (Bantam Press, 1999)

to a Somalia where some people sometimes starved only to leave a Somalia where everybody always would?'

Such questions were not the concern of troops working to support the UN in Mogadishu. Their role was to reduce the anarchy created by the warring clans. In furtherance of this aim, on 3 October 1993 some 140 élite US Delta Force and Ranger soldiers made a heliborne raid into the heart of Mogadishu to seize two key figures from General Aidid's clan. It should have been a straightforward operation, achieved quickly and effectively by the same well-armed US troops who had proved so overwhelming against the Iraqis.

Instead, the Americans failed to capture their targets and were surrounded in the heart of the city by angry Somalis, some of them armed with automatic rifles and grenades, others just hurling sticks and stones. For an entire night, the US troops fought a running battle with the local citizens. Eventually, the next day, the US troops managed to break out to safety, but 18 of them had been killed and 70 wounded. American fire power had proved deadly – accounting for more than five hundred Somalis killed and a thousand wounded – but the benefits of high technology had seemed less than overwhelming when. in close-up, street-to-street fighting helicopters. could easily be brought down by hand-held rockets.

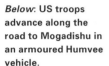

Below: **US troops advance along the road to Mogadishu in an armoured Humvee vehicle.**

'THIS THING SUCKS'

A small defeat was bad enough, but what was far worse for Americans to stomach was that one of the downed helicopter pilots was dragged through the streets by the jubilant mob. The image of his dead body, mutilated and insulted by the Somali crowd, was beamed around the world. It made Americans wonder why their troops, supposedly on a humanitarian operation to help starving Somalis, should be treated with such hatred and derision by the very people they had come to help. As one American lieutenant, quoted by O'Rourke, succinctly commented, 'This thing sucks – helping people who don't give a shit.'

The result of this and similarly futile military operations, which failed to capture Aidid or quell the fighting, led to a rapid rethink of the entire operation in Somalia. In Operation Quickdraw on 31 March 1994, US forces were hastily withdrawn. The United States had learned its lesson, and the immediate effect of its abandonment of military power for humanitarian ends was felt in Rwanda in 1994. In a genocidal civil war, over one million Rwandans were murdered. Journalists and other opinion-makers again asked the West to intervene, but this time the United States and the United Nations declined to send in military forces. The experiences in Mogadishu had decisively eroded their goodwill.

KRAJINA, 1995

the Soviet bloc. At the end of the Cold War, with the collapse of the Soviet Union and its satellite regimes in eastern Europe, ethnic pressures for self-rule led to the break-up of Yugoslavia.

Slovenia was the first to secede in 1990, then Croatia and Bosnia-Herzegovina followed. Serbia increasingly saw these moves towards independence as declarations of aggression against itself. Fighting broke out as the Yugoslavian Army, which was under Serb control, clashed with Croatians and Bosnians. Centuries-old ethnic animosity between Catholic Croats, Muslim Bosnians and Orthodox Serbs fuelled many of the atrocities committed against civilians throughout the region. From 1992 onwards, peace-keepers working on behalf of the United Nations became involved in an effort to pacify the region, but the lack of any decisive military intervention from outside allowed the fighting to continue, and by the end of 1994 it was estimated that some four hundred thousand lives had been lost. In 1995, Croatia decided to put a decisive end to its war with Serbia by launching a major offensive in the Krajina region.

OPERATION STORM

Krajina, a finger of land that poked from Bosnia in the east towards the Dalmatian coast of Croatia, had been controlled by the local Serbs since 1991. Croatia wanted to assert its own dominance in this region, and forged a temporary alliance with Bosnian forces to confront the Serbs. The offensive began at Bosanko Grahovo on 25 July 1995 in western Bosnia when the Croats built a road to the summit of a hill and then sent their tanks through the Serb front line, followed by assault troops. Krajina now looked vulnerable and the Croats concentrated an impressive force of more than one hundred thousand soldiers, hundreds of tanks and artillery pieces, and dozens of helicopters and fighter aircraft. Opposing them were less than fifty thousand Krajina Serbs. The Croats

Below: **Croat soldiers and police holding a captured Serbian flag. Croatian paramilitary forces fought alongside its army.**

Operation Storm was the largest military offensive in Europe since the Second World War. In five days, Croatia shattered the illusion of Serbian military supremacy and secured freedom for its people. But the military effectiveness of Croat forces was not matched by professional behaviour, and terrible persecution of the Serbs followed.

The nation-state of Yugoslavia was invented in 1918 by peace-makers as part of the settlement of the First World War. It was a federal entity composed of states including Slovenia, Croatia, Serbia and Bosnia-Herzegovina. After 1945, under the leadership of Tito, Yugoslavia became a communist country, independent of

---

TIM RIPLEY, JOURNALIST

LOOTING

'The 5th Corps went on looting sprees into Krajina, with columns of cars returning to Bihac loaded down with household goods and agricultural equipment. Abandoned ARSK [Serbian] military equipment was also fair game for General Atif Dudakovic's troops, who acquired more than 20 M-84 and T-55 tanks along with dozens of heavy artillery pieces, trucks and thousands of shells... The supposedly well-disciplined Guards Brigades were not adverse to looting, with the commander of the 7th Guards Brigade, Major General Ivan Korade, reputedly using his unit's engineering equipment and transport to remove the entire contents of a fertiliser factory from Bosanko Grahovo for sale on Split's black-market.'
Quoted from *Operation Deliberate Force* **by Tim Ripley (Lancaster University, 1999)**

they ordered their troops to fall back on Bosnia, and the defences around Knin fell swiftly. By 5 August, Croat tanks were inside the city and United Nations peace-keepers could do nothing to stop the ill-disciplined Croats from hunting down Serbs and killing them. In the countryside, Serb houses were also looted and civilians murdered. The Croats showed they could ethnically cleanse an area as effectively and ruthlessly as the Serbs, who had first practised the policy in the war.

With Knin captured, resistance crumbled elsewhere in Krajina along the northern frontier, although Serbian defenders fought harder than in Knin. One Croat Guards Brigade had 40 per cent of its tanks destroyed in a frontal attack on Serb positions. By 6 August, some 180,000 Serb refugees were streaming out of the region, but heavy fighting around the fleeing columns meant that many civilians were killed by Croat artillery and air strikes. On 7 August the United Nations managed to broker a ceasefire and the refugees were allowed to escape.

Operation Storm was a decisive victory for Croatia. It cleared Krajina of Serb resistance and changed the balance of power in the region, pushing the hitherto dominant Serbs onto the defensive. Croatia lost only 409 soldiers dead and 2,460 wounded, but the triumph was marred by extensive atrocities committed by its army, acts which have largely gone unreported because the world's media focused its attention on Serbian war crimes.

Above: UN soldiers observe military activity in Bosnia but could do little to stop the major Croatian offensive.

Right: War damage during fighting in Bosnia. Civilians on both sides suffered terribly from mistreatment by soldiers who let their desire for vengeance override their professional duty.

called their next move Operation Storm.

Operation Storm began on the morning of 4 August with a massive artillery and rocket bombardment of the Serbian lines. The Krajinan capital of Knin was a principal target and some three hundred shells rained down there in the first half-hour. The aim of the Croat bombardment was to spread fear among the civilian population and make them move away from what was now deemed to be the front line. Because many of the Serb soldiers were militiamen with families to look after, this frequently encouraged them to desert the front line as well. Artillery fire continued throughout the day, killing numerous civilians and soldiers. US fighter planes flew over the region to observe the attack, but were targeted by Serb air defences and were compelled to fire back, but it was not, as has been claimed by the Serbs, part of any covert Western support for the Croats.

THE FALL OF KNIN

The Croats pressed forward in three separate attacks. Colonel General Ante Gotovina, a former French Foreign Legionnaire, led the attack on Knin. His assault was spearheaded by Croatian Guards Brigades armed with Soviet-built T-55 tanks. Croat advances against the south of Knin were met with Krajinan Serb counter-attacks, and the Guards Brigades found it easier to approach from the east. Meanwhile, thousands of refugees headed north out of the city. When the Krajinan Serb commanders heard they would receive no reinforcements from Serbia,

BIBLIOGRAPHY

GENERAL HISTORIES

Black, J., *War and the World*, New Haven, 1998

Diamond, J., *Guns, Germs and Steel*, London, 1997

Dupuy, R.E., & Dupuy, T.N., *The Encyclopedia of Military History*, London, 1986

Huntingdon, S.P., *The Clash of Civilizations and the Remaking of World Order*, New York, 1996

Keegan, J., *The Face of Battle*, London, 1976

Kennedy, P., *The Rise and Fall of the Great Powers*, London, 1988

Murray, W., Knox, M. & Bernstein, A. *The Making of Strategy*, Cambridge, 1994

Newark, T., *War in Britain*, London, 2000

Parker, G., *The Military Revolution*, Cambridge, 1996

The Times History of War, London, 2000

NAPOLEONIC ERA

Blanning, T.C.W., *The French Revolutionary Wars 1787–1802*, London, 1996

Blond, G., *La Grande Armée*, London, 1995

Chandler, D., *The Campaigns of Napoleon*, London, 1966

Esposito, V.J., & Elting, J.R., *A Military History and Atlas of the Napoleonic Wars*, London, 1999

Griffith, P., *The Art of War of Revolutionary France 1789–1802*, London, 1998

Haythornthwaite, P., *Waterloo Men*, Marlborough, 1999

Hofschroer, P., *1815: The Waterloo Campaign*, London, 1998

Horne, A., *How far from Austerlitz?*, London, 1996

Howarth, D., *Trafalgar: The Nelson Touch*, London, 1969

Nosworthy, B., *Battle Tactics of Napoleon and his Enemies*, London, 1995

Weller, J., *Wellington in India*, London, 1972

IMPERIAL ERA

Grant, U.S., *Personal Memoirs of U.S. Grant*, New York, 1885–86

Griffith, P., *Battle Tactics of the Civil War*, New Haven, 1989

Guy, A.J., & Boyden, P.B. (editors), *Soldiers of the Raj*, London, 1997

Heathcote, T.A., *The Military in British India*, Manchester, 1995

Horne, A., *The Fall of Paris*, London, 1989

James, L., *The Rise and Fall of the British Empire*, London, 1994

Knight, I., *Go to your God like a Soldier*, London, 1996

Marvin, C., *The Russian Advance towards India*, London, 1882

Neillands, T., *The Dervish Wars*, London, 1996

FIRST WORLD WAR

Bond, B., & Cave, N., (editors), *Haig: A Reappraisal*, Barnsley, 1999

Brown, M., *1918 Year of Victory*, London, 1998

Chappell, M., *The Somme 1916*, London, 1995

Donovan, T., *The Hazy Red Hell*, London, 1999

Griffith, P., *Battle Tactics of the Western Front*, New Haven, 1994

Holmes, R., *The Western Front*, London, 1999

Lee, J., *A Soldier's Life*, London, 2000

Livesey, A., *Atlas of World War I*, London, 1994

Macdonald, L., *They Called It Passchendaele*, London, 1978

Macksey, K., *Why the Germans Lose at War*, London, 1996

Prior, R., & Wilson, T., *Command on the Western Front*, Oxford, 1992

Sheffield, G., *Forgotten Victory: Myths and Realities of the First World War*, London, 2001

Steel, N., & Hart, P., *Defeat at Gallipoli*, London, 1994

Tucker, S.C., *The Great War 1914–18*, London, 1998

SECOND WORLD WAR

Ambrose, S., *D-Day*, New York, 1994

Ambrose, S., *Citizens Soldiers*, New York, 1997

Barnett, C., *The Lost Victory*, London, 1995

Bourne, J., Liddle, P., Whitehead, I. (editors), *The Great World War 1914–45* London, 2000

Bungay, S., *The Most Dangerous Enemy*, London, 2000

Chang, I., *The Rape of Nanking*, New York, 1997

Elphick, P., *Singapore: the Pregnable Fortress*, London, 1995

Gannon, M., *Black May*, London, 1998

Glantz, D.M., & House, J.M., *The Battle of Kursk*, Kansas, 1999

Goldhagen, D.J., *Hitler's Willing Executioners*, London, 1996

Middlebrook, M., *Arnhem 1944*, London, 1994

Overy, R., *Why the Allies Won*, London, 1995

Overy, R., *Russia's War*, London, 1998

Ryan, C., *The Last Battle*, London, 1966

Weinberg, G.L., *A World at Arms*, Cambridge, 1994

WARFARE AFTER 1945

van der Bijl, N., *Nine Battles to Stanley*, Barnsley, 1999

Bowden, M., *Black Hawk Down*, London, 1999

Clancy, T., & Franks, F., *Into the Storm*, New York, 1997

Fehrenbach, T.R., *This Kind of War*, New York, 1963

Grau, L.W., *The Bear Went Over the Mountain*, Washington, 1996

Issacs, J., & Downing, T., *Cold War*, London, 1998

Judah, T., *Kosovo*, New Haven, 2000

Mackay, D., *The Malayan Emergency*, London, 1997

Mockaitis, T.R., *British Counterinsurgency in the Post-Imperial Era*, Manchester, 1995

Odon, W.E., *The Collapse of the Soviet Military*, Yale, 1998

Pryce-Jones, D., *The War That Never Was*, London, 1995

Ripley, T., *Operation Deliberate Force*, Lancaster, 1999

Smith, T. (editor), *The End of the European Empire*, Lexington, 1975

Woodruff, M.W., *Unheralded Victory*, Arlington, 1999

INDEX

ACKNOWLEDGEMENTS

PICTURE ACKNOWLEDGEMENTS IN SOURCE ORDER:

AKG, LONDON half title, 94, 96, 103 bottom, 128, 130 bottom, 142, 172 bottom, 173, /Archiv fur Kunst und Geschichte, Berlin 161, /Musee Historique, Palais de Versailles. Copy by J.B. Mauzaisse after a painting by Horace Vernet (1883) 11 /painting by von Louis-Francois Lejeune. Musee de Chateau, Versailles 21 Bottom

CORBIS 60, 152, 159 top right, 169, 179 right, /Robin Adshead 189, /Bettmann 59 left, 61, 86, 87, 88, 89, 106 bottom, 109, 143, 151 centre, 159 bottom, 174 centre right, /Howard Davies 184, /Yves Debay 186, /Stephen Dupont 183, /Hulton-Getty 58, 108 top, 110-111, 181, /Vittoriano Rastelli 174 top right, /Peter Turnley 192

MARY EVANS PICTURE LIBRARY 13

HULTON GETTY PICTURE COLLECTION 39 top, 127 top

IMPACT PHOTOS/Alex MacNaughton 182

MAGNUM PHOTOS/S. Franklin 185

TOPHAM PICTUREPOINT 168, 188, /Associated Press 134 bottom, 135 /D. Visnjic 194

ALL OTHER PICTURES PROVIDED BY PETER NEWARK'S MILITARY PICTURES, RESEARCHED BY TIM NEWARK.
Thanks to U.S. Department of Defense for pictures on pages 190, 191 top and bottom, and 193; and Tim Ripley for pictures on page 195. 'Battle of Gettysburg' painted by Thure de Thrulstrup 33 centre, /'Charge of the Scots Greys' by Lady Butler title, 24, /'Dawn 20th November 1917' painting by W.L. Wyllie 78, /'Death of Nelson' painting by Denis Dighton 19, /'Duke of Wellington' painting by Goya, 1812 25 centre left, /'Quatre Bras' by Lady Butler 27, /'Tarawa Landing' painting by Tom Lovell 134 top, /painting by Wilhelm Camphausen 39 bottom, /Alexander Gardner 34 top, /illustration by R. Caton Woodville 43, 52, /Ivan Shagin 163 top right, /painting by Lemuel Abbott 17 left, /painting by C. Escalante 31, /painting by C.E. Fripp 40, /painting by de Mesnier 23, /painting by Delaroche 20 right, /painting by Ellis Silas 64 bottom

THE PUBLISHER IS GRATEFUL FOR PERMISSION TO REPRODUCE THE FOLLOWING COPYRIGHT MATERIAL:

p.11 *The French Revolutionary Wars 1787–1802*, T.C.W. Blanning, Arnold, London, reproduced by permission of Edward Arnold (Publishers) Limited; p.15 *Wellington: A Personal History*, Christopher Hibbert, HarperCollins Publishers, London; p.19 *The Oxford Illustrated History of the Royal Navy*, edited by J.R. Hill, Oxford University Press, Oxford; p.23 *The Narrative of Captain Coignet*, translated by M. Carey, Chatto & Windus, London; p.27 *The Recollections of Sergeant Morris*, edited by John Selby, Longman & Green, London; p.31 *The Mexican-American War*, Ron Field, Brassey's, London, reproduced by permission of Chrysalis Books Plc; p.35 *Pickett's Men*, Walter Harrison, New York; p.39 *William Russell: Special Correspondent of the Times*, edited by Roger Hudson, The Folio Society, London; p.43 *Anatomy of the Zulu Army*, Ian Knight, Greenhill Books, London, reproduced by permission of Greenhill Books; p.47 *The Russian Advance to India*, Charles Marvin, London; p.49 *The Rough Riders*, Theodore Roosevelt, New York; p.53 *The Last Charge*, Terry Brighton, The Crowood Press, Wiltshire, reproduced by permission of The Crowood Press; p.57 *The Undefeated*, Robert Harvey, Macmillan, London; p.61 *Christmas Truce*, M. Brown and S. Seaton, Macmillan, London; p.64 *Defeat at Gallipoli*, N. Steel and P. Hart, Macmillan, London; p.69 *The Eastern Front 1914–18*, Alan Clark, BPC, London; p.73 *A Sergeant Major's War*, edited by Bruce Rossor, The Crowood Press, Wiltshire, reproduced by permission of The Crowood Press; p.75 *They Called It Passchendael*, Lyn Macdonald, Michael Joseph, London; p.81 *Everyman at War*, edited by C.B. Purdom, London; p.85 *1918 Year of Victory*, Malcolm Brown, Sidgwick & Jackson, London; p.89 *The Rape of Nanking*, Iris Chang, Basic Books, London; p.93 *The Other Side of the Hill*, B.H. Liddell Hart, Cassell & Co., London; p.97 *The Most Dangerous Enemy*, Stephen Bungay, Aurum Press, London, reproduced by permission of Arurum Press; p.99 *Hitler's Green Devils*, I.M. Baxter, reproduced by permission of Military Illustrated; p.103 *The Volga Rises*, Curzio Malapate, Brown Books, London; p.107 *Churchill – The End of Glory*, John Charmley, Hodder and Stoughton, London, reproduced by permission of Hodder and Stoughton Limited; p.111 *The Pregnable Forest*, Peter Elphick, Hodder and Stoughton, London, reproduced by permission of Hodder and Stoughton Limited; p.115 *200,000 Miles*, C. Snelling Robinson, Kent State University Press, Kent, reproduced by permission of Kent State University Press; p.119 *The Forgotten Soldier*, Guy Sajer, The Orion Publishing Group Ltd, London, reproduced by permission of the Orion Publishing Group Ltd; p.123 *With Rommel in the Desert*, Heinz Walter Schmidt, Eric Dobby Publishing Ltd, Kent; p.127 *Black May*, Michael Gammon, Aurum Press, London, reproduced by permission of Aurum Press; p.131 *Panzer Leader*, Heinz Guderian, Michael Joseph, London; p.135 *Marine*, Ron Field, reproduced by permission of Military Illustrated; p.138 The Other Side of the Hill, Basil Liddell Hart, Cassel & Co., London; p.143 *The Unforgettable Army*, Michael Hickey, Spellmount Publishers, Kent, reproduced by permission of Spellmount Publishers; p.147 *D-Day – Those Who Were There*, Juliet Gardiner, Collins & Brown, London, reproduced by permission of Collins & Brown; p.149 Citizen Soldiers, Stephen E. Ambrose, Simon & Schuster, London; p.153 *The War Beneath the Sea*, Peter Padfield, John Murray, London, reproduced by permission of John Murray; p.156 *Report by the Supreme Commander to the Combined Chiefs of Staff on the Operations in Europe of the Allied Expeditionary Force*, Her Majesty's Stationary Office, Norwich, reproduced by permission of Her Majesty's Stationary Office; p.161 *Marine*, Ron Field, reproduced by permission of Military Illustrated; p.165 *The Last Battle*, Cornelius Ryan, HarperCollins, London, reproduced by permission of HarperCollins Publishers; p.169 *All Hell Broke Loose*, Ron Field, reproduced by permission of Military Illustrated; p.173 *The Last Cartridge*, Robert Barr Smith, Avon Books, London; p.174 *Surprise Attack*, Peter Darman, Brown Books, London; p.179 *Tet 1968: Understanding the Surprise*, Ronnie E. Ford, Frank Cass Publishers, London, reproduced by permission of Frank Cass Publishers; p.181 *Nine Battles to Stanley*, Nicholas van der Bijl, Pen & Sword Books Limited, Yorkshire, reproduced by permission of Pen & Sword Books Limited; p.185 *The Bear Went Over the Mountain*, edited by Lester W. Grau, Frank Cass Publishers, London, reproduced by permission of Frank Cass Publishers; p.189 *Skunk Works*, B.R. Rich and L. Janos, Little & Brown, London, reproduced by permission of Little, Brown and Company (UK); p.192 ©Mark Bowden. Extracted from *BLACK HAWK DOWN* by Mark Bowden, published by Corgi, an imprint of Transworld Publishers, a division of the Random House Group Ltd. All rights reserved; p.194 *Operation Deliberate Force*, Tim Ripley, Lancaster University Press, Lancaster.

Despite every effort to trace and contact copyright holders prior to publication, this has not always been possible. If notified, the publisher will be pleased to rectify any errors or omissions at the earliest opportunity.